I'LL BRING THE
CAKE

I'LL BRING THE
CAKE

RECIPES FOR *Every Season* AND *Every Occasion*

MANDY MERRIMAN

HARVEST
An Imprint of WILLIAM MORROW

HarperCollins books may be purchased for educational, business, or sales promotional use. For information, please email the Special Markets Department at SPsales@harpercollins.com.

FIRST EDITION

Designed by Tai Blanche

Contents page background image © Ploipiroon/Shutterstock

Library of Congress Cataloging-in-Publication Data has been applied for.

ISBN 978-0-358-69724-4

23 24 25 26 27   TC   10 9 8 7 6 5 4 3 2 1

For my husband, Ryan, and our blondie boys, Jake and Liam. Thank you for believing in me and for being okay with living with a kitchen covered in sprinkles forevermore.

And for my dad, who was taken far too soon. I miss you every single day.

This one's for you, with an extra slice of your favorite carrot cake.

Del Hillary 1954–2020

CONTENTS

Chapter 1: SPRINGTIME BAKES   1

Chapter 4: WHIMSICAL WINTER BAKES   183

Chapter 5: BIRTHDAY HITS *and* EVERYDAY CAKES 249

INTRODUCTION

We celebrate some of life's most special moments with a beautifully decorated slice of cake. Whether we're blowing out the candles to commemorate another year older and wiser, watching a couple slice into a beautiful wedding cake surrounded by loved ones, celebrating the milestones in our lives (big or small), having a simple family gathering on a Sunday afternoon, or merely baking for the pure love of it, cake is something that will always be there to make any and every day extra special.

I believe that anyone should be able to make a cake worthy of any celebration. Whether you are baking your very first cake or are a more seasoned baker, baking, stacking, and decorating a cake should be accessible to all. For years, I've featured game-changing easy recipes, tips, and methods—unlocking the secrets of creating a cake that is not only beautiful on the outside but mouthwatering on the inside—on my blog, Baking with Blondie; Instagram; and previous book, *Cake Confidence*.

Mastering a cake recipe shouldn't be intimidating. While there's so much that can go wrong (dry cakes, sinking cakes, overbaked cakes, underbaked cakes, crumbling cakes, flavorless cakes, anyone?), my recipes get great results because I've taken all the margin for error out of the experience. I don't just tell you what to do but why you should do it and what will happen if you don't. Bakers around the globe know that Baking with Blondie cakes are moist, flavorful, and rich. My doctored-up cake mix recipes taste the same as, if not better than, from-scratch cake recipes, and they are always reliable. I take all the guesswork out of baking, which leaves more time to explore the creative process behind flavor building and decorating. No more worrying about whether the taste or texture is going to be perfect every time—you're all set! My recipes have been tested, tried, and proven to be a hit in hundreds of thousands of kitchens. Building that spark of cake confidence in the heart of every baker is my passion and mission.

A common method of testing a cake for doneness is to insert a toothpick in the center, and if the toothpick comes out clean (a.k.a. with no crumbs), then the cake should be done. But I've found that this method actually leads to overbaking (and makes for drier cakes). I take my cakes out once the center of the cake springs back when I touch it.

Let's rewind—I said "cake mix" and want to make sure we're all on the same page. I use a box cake mix but add five to seven ingredients in addition to the premeasured dry ingredients. This means I don't just "use a cake mix" and add in the usual water, oil, and eggs listed on the package. There's a special way to make a cake mix taste like it's from scratch, and my recipes are the best way to make that possible.

There are many different types of cake mixes at the grocery store (some countries have more available than others). So which one do I use? Is there one that's better than the others? One to avoid? I've tested my recipes with a handful of different brands of cake mixes. The main differences between them have been taste, height, and texture. Although I prefer using Duncan Hines and Betty Crocker, Pillsbury and other grocery store brands will yield similar results. As long as they are near 15.25 ounces per box (you'll see that right on the package in the bottom corner), they'll be the right measurements for my recipes. I have also tried my vanilla cake recipe with a gluten-free Pillsbury cake mix and it worked really well.

When close friends and family gather to watch the bride and groom slice into a beautifully decorated cake, I'm sure not a single person is wondering whether that cake is made from scratch. Not at all. All eyes are on the mouthwatering memory in the making.

The same is true for any occasion with a cake on the table to celebrate. The cake was made with love, and it was made for a memory-enriching moment. It's not a party without a cake, and whoever brings the cake is always welcome! With my easy recipes, inspiring decorating ideas, and tips and tricks, you'll be able to confidently say, "I'll bring the cake!" to any gathering or celebration.

With some classic and some unique cake flavors that fit every occasion and event for the young and young at heart, beautifully bold cakes dressed up for the holidays, cakes for those with an extra-sweet tooth, and stunning seasonal cakes made with ingredients at the peak of their flavor, I'll Bring the Cake will arm you with a cake for every occasion. Although each cake in this book has its own special design and embellishment that complement the flavor or occasion, you're more than welcome to make it in your own style. If it looks too simple for the celebration, add some flair with extra sprinkles, different decorative piping tips, more swirls, extra cookies or candy, or custom-themed cake toppers to make it something special for your gathering. If the design looks a little intimidating, feel free to simplify it to your comfort level. A simple, classic cake will be just as beautiful, and the cake will taste exactly the same!

Throughout the recipes, you'll see I give instructions to chill the cakes before frosting. A cake that is chilled or nearly frozen is infinitely easier to frost than a squishy cake that moves around or crumbles. Make sure you chill the cakes for at least an hour, or up to overnight if you want to space out your baking.

The chapters cover all four seasons, holidays, birthdays, and even everyday baking—because we all know that sometimes there's no need for a special occasion to enjoy a slice of cake!

Have your cake any way you want! All my recipes can be converted into cupcakes, Bundt cake, 9 × 13-inch cake, sheet cake, or any other size of cake. The ingredients and mixing methods are always the same. You only need to change one factor: baking time! Since each recipe is different, there isn't a blanket baking time for each cake in this book. However, below are some suggested baking times. Begin with the lowest baking time, check for doneness (see page xii), then add 2 minutes or so from there until the cake is finished.

Cupcakes: 12 to 17 minutes

Bundt: 25 to 35 minutes (this will depend on your Bundt shape)

9 × 13-inch: 27 to 30 minutes

Full-size cookie sheet or jelly roll pan: 17 to 20 minutes

Three 6-inch cake pans: keep baking times as written

Two 8-inch/9-inch cake pans: keep baking times as written

One 10-inch cake pan: 15 to 17 minutes

CAKE TOOLS FOR DECORATING SUCCESS

*T*he proper tools can make or break your cake-decorating experience. Here are my top five cake-decorating tools I couldn't work without, plus a few others I love using, too.

Cake Turntable: I use the cast-iron Ateco turntable with a nonslip mat for all my cakes. With a quick spin of the turntable, you can access any part of the cake you're decorating, and it makes it much easier to get clean edges and sides on your cake.

Straight Icing Spatula: Useful for anything vertical on your cake, like the sides.

Angled Icing Spatula: Perfect for anything horizontal on your cake, like your fillings and the top of the cake.

Cake Scraper: This tool is essential for getting clean, smooth sides on your cake. It comes in different materials and heights. I love using a metal cake scraper because I can control the temperature of it, for example, when I want to heat it up for a smoother finish.

Cardboard Cake Rounds: Cake rounds come in many sizes. I usually use two: one the size of the cake I'm making taped to one the next size up. So, for instance, I'll tape a 6-inch cake round to an 8-inch one. This enables me to easily transfer the cake to the freezer without destroying it because I can hold on to the larger board. When I'm ready to transfer the cake for serving, I carefully slide a cake lifter between the two cardboard rounds, lift to gently break the tape seal, and move the cake safely onto a cake stand.

OTHER HELPFUL CAKE TOOLS

Cake Pans, Multiples of Each Size: Use three or four cake pans at once, if you can, so you don't have to wait for each cake pan to bake before adding in the next.

Drip Bottles: Some people use spoons or cups for their ganache drips, but I love using a drip bottle for the best, most controlled results.

Piping Tips: The variety is endless, and new designs are created every single day. I usually aim for the larger tips for easier and quicker designs, and smaller tips for more intricate decorative designs. You can also use couplers for switching out your piping tips with ease.

Piping Bags: I always use the 12-inch size, and I use the disposable ones for easy cleanup. It makes using multiple colors and batches easier, too.

Cake Leveler: While most of my cakes bake flat, this handy tool can help in case a dome forms during the baking process. Tip: If your cakes dome up above the rim of the pan, level them off while they're still in the cake pan (either with a cake leveler or a serrated knife); that way each layer is perfectly straight and the same size.

Stand Mixer: My KitchenAid mixers are the stars of the show in my kitchen. I use them almost every single day, and they sure work hard making batch after batch of buttercream. I use the paddle attachment for buttercream to create a thick texture.

Cookie Sheet: If you've swept up a sprinkle mess before, you know you'll never cake again without putting a cookie sheet under your cake when adding sprinkles! It catches all loose sprinkles and makes for easy cleanup.

Gel Colors: Good-quality gel colors will make your caking experience so much easier, tinting your buttercream and cake rounds vibrant colors to match your celebration! Start with one or two drops and go from there. The color of the buttercream will intensify within the day, so always aim for a shade lighter than what your ultimate color destination will be.

Multiple Small Bowls: Tinting buttercream can be a process. Have multiple bowls around so you can easily tint small batches into various shades.

Tweezers: I usually place decorations on my cake by hand, but sometimes tweezers are useful for more intricate designs.

24-Cupcake Pan: Bake the whole batch at once!

Ice Cream or Cookie Scoop with Trigger Release: A scoop will help you fill each cupcake cup with the same amount of batter to get the correct number of cupcakes and make sure they all finish baking at the same time.

Apron: Even though I've baked thousands of cakes, baking is still a messy job, and powdered sugar will most definitely end up everywhere. Have a few aprons in the kitchen to keep your clothes clean and look the part. 😊

BUTTERCREAM ESSENTIALS

VANILLA BUTTERCREAM

Makes 5 to 6 cups

- 3 sticks (1½ cups) unsalted butter
- Pinch of salt
- 1 tablespoon pure vanilla extract
- ¼ cup heavy cream (plus more if needed)
- 7 to 8 cups powdered sugar

In the bowl of a stand mixer fitted with a paddle attachment, beat the butter on medium speed until it's light and fluffy.

Add the salt, vanilla, and heavy cream and beat again until thoroughly combined. Scrape down the sides of the bowl.

With the mixer on low speed, add the powdered sugar about ½ cup at a time. Add a little more heavy cream if needed, then flip the mixer to high speed and beat until the buttercream is lighter in color and texture, about 2 minutes.

SMALL-BATCH VANILLA BUTTERCREAM

Makes 2 to 3 cups

- 2 sticks (1 cup) unsalted butter
- Pinch of salt
- 2 teaspoons pure vanilla extract
- 2 tablespoons heavy cream (plus more if needed)
- 4 to 5 cups powdered sugar

In the bowl of a stand mixer fitted with a paddle attachment, beat the butter on medium speed until it's light and fluffy.

Add the salt, vanilla, and heavy cream and beat again until thoroughly combined. Scrape down the sides of the bowl.

With the mixer on low speed, add the powdered sugar about ½ cup at a time. Add a little more heavy cream if needed, then flip the mixer to high speed and beat until the buttercream is lighter in color and texture, about 2 minutes.

BUTTERCREAM TIPS

Taste, texture, and consistency are just as important in your buttercream as they are in your baked cake layers. I love using American buttercream because it can be made into just about any flavor, and it really enhances the overall experience of decorating—and eating—the cake. Here are a few tips and tricks to make sure you are nailing not only the perfect flavor but also the best consistency every time.

Use unsalted butter, and then add in salt later. This will help you control the amount of salt that's in your buttercream. I always list a "pinch" of salt in my recipes, but truth be told, I sometimes go a little heavier on that pinch when I'm making my deeper and richer buttercream flavors like chocolate, caramel, Biscoff, and others.

Your butter should be cold but not too cold. You should be able to squeeze the butter slightly with your hands and leave an indent. Having the correct butter temperature will help the butter whip up faster in the stand mixer.

Beat your butter until it's light and fluffy. This will ensure that the rest of the ingredients melt in perfectly with the butter and that you won't have any butter clumps in the buttercream on your cake.

Extracts vs. emulsions . . . which one do I use? I often use either extracts or emulsions to flavor my buttercream recipes: with a tablespoon or even a teaspoon, you can have almost any flavor you'll ever need. Extracts are made with alcohol and tend to be a bit more potent, so you won't need as much to get your flavor across. Emulsions are water-based and aren't diluted in alcohol like extracts. I find both of these at my local grocery stores, baking/craft stores, or online.

When adding in cookies or crumbles, make sure they're ground to a fine powder. A lot of my buttercream recipes include powdered ingredients for even more flavor. When adding in graham crackers, cookies, freeze-dried strawberries, or even nuts, make sure they're ground to a fine powder (unless the recipe says differently!). They will mix into the buttercream more evenly and will make it a lot easier to spread an even layer on the side of the cake, and the buttercream will come through the piping tips much easier, too!

The heavy cream matters. It needs to be heavy cream. I've tried using almond milk, oat milk, whole milk, skim milk, and even other varieties of milk, and the buttercream never gets quite the perfect consistency as it does with heavy cream. Look for heavy cream or heavy whipping cream and you'll be all set.

Sift the powdered sugar? Not anymore. I used to always sift the powdered sugar. However, after years and years of teaching, frosting, baking, and decorating, I've concluded that the amount of work it takes to sift each and every cup of powdered sugar I use does not justify the result. Does sifting make the buttercream silkier? Nope! I haven't noticed it being less silky, so I skip that step and have never looked back!

Heavy cream and powdered sugar control the consistency. With the exception of the butter temperature, the buttercream's consistency is controlled mainly by these two ingredients. If your buttercream is too thick, add in a touch more heavy cream. If it's too thin, you need a bit more powdered sugar.

For the best buttercream texture, you need to let your mixer stay on high speed for at least 2 minutes. When all the ingredients have been added to the buttercream, simply beating the mixture on high speed for about 2 minutes can be a game changer. It whips up the texture and activates the heavy cream so that it can be as light and fluffy as possible—perfect for your cake!

Let's fix those air bubbles. While the last step whips up the buttercream texture in a great way, we also need to make sure we don't end up with too many air bubbles. So after we whip up the buttercream, we beat it down with a wooden spoon to create the perfect silky consistency. Simply remove your bowl from the stand mixer, then stir the buttercream with a wooden spoon to get rid of the air pockets.

Color your buttercream a shade lighter. Buttercream tends to soak up gel coloring really well, almost too well sometimes. I've learned that when you are aiming for a specific color of buttercream, you should tint the buttercream a shade lighter than you want. The color will intensify and darken overnight.

Flavor buttercream with fresh or freeze-dried fruit. I often use freeze-dried fruit or emulsions to get the best fruit flavor in my buttercreams, but there are a couple in which I use fresh fruit. Fresh fruit in buttercream is a gamble but worth it if you can nail it. It has a lot of extra moisture that may change the consistency of your buttercream. However, if you make sure to use either a reduction of the fresh or frozen fruit, or enough powdered sugar to counter the added moisture, you should be all set.

Storing your buttercream is simple. If you need to make your buttercream in advance, or have enough left over for a cake, cupcake, or macaron filling, simply cover it with plastic wrap and place it in the fridge. When you need it, set it on the counter for about an hour to soften (the time will depend on how much buttercream you have stored), then place it back into the stand mixer to whip it up to the best consistency.

BAKING TIPS *and* TROUBLESHOOTING

*B*aking beautifully even cake layers with the perfect texture and flavor can sometimes be a daunting task, especially when there's so much that can go wrong. After baking thousands of cakes and making just about every mistake one can make, I know how to sidestep all the ways your cake can end up dry, underbaked, overbaked, bland, sunken in the center, or even too crumbly. We want moist, tall, flavorful cakes that could stand alone (even without buttercream) because they're so tasty! With my doctored cake-mix recipes, there's already less of a margin for error, but here are a few tips and tricks that will help you bake perfect cakes every single time.

Convection vs. conventional oven settings: Some ovens have both conventional and convection settings; a convection oven circulates air for even baking. I prefer convection because it bakes my cakes more evenly. Convection ovens also bake slightly faster; if you're using a conventional oven, your cakes may need a tiny bit more time in the oven, which is why I always include a range of time in my recipes.

Oven temperature accuracy: Not all ovens bake at the temperature you set them at. If your cakes are coming out a bit overdone or underdone, your oven temperature may be off. To test, simply place an oven thermometer in your oven about 15 minutes after it's preheated to see if it matches the setting.

Ingredients at room temperature: All my recipes include eggs, sour cream, and buttermilk. These ingredients, and any ingredients from the fridge, need to be at room temperature before you add them to the cake batter, so that they react the way they're supposed to in the oven and also add height to your cake.

All about the prep: The way you prep your cake pans can set you up for success or . . . pieces of cake sticking in your pans. I wipe shortening on the inside of the pans (usually with a plastic baggie over my hand to keep it clean), then add a layer of flour, tapping out the excess.

Good-quality ingredients: I never use fat-free or reduced-sugar ingredients in my cakes. The full-fat options taste best, and after all, it's cake we're making!

Break it up with a sifter: You'll want to sift any dry ingredients (cake mix, cocoa, flour) before adding them to the batter to avoid either overmixing or pockets of dry ingredients. I use a hand-crank sifter.

Let cool, then freeze: We want maximum moisture and freshness from our cakes. The easiest way to do this is by letting your cake layers cool completely on a wire rack (out of the pan), then wrapping them twice in plastic wrap. Freeze the cakes on a flat surface, or stack them with cardboard cake rounds in between, until you're ready to assemble your cake.

Enlist the help of a kitchen scale: Each of your cake layers should use roughly the same amount of batter so that the cakes rise to the same height and finish baking at the same time. You can use a digital kitchen scale, if you have one, to weigh each cake round individually before baking.

Overmixed cakes = dry or sunken cakes: When stirring in the dry ingredients, mix only until everything is barely combined. If you keep stirring, the batter will be overmixed and your cake will come out dry or will sink in the oven.

How to avoid a dry cake: Cake tends to dry out if it's in the oven too long, the batter has been way overmixed, too much of a dry ingredient was added, or the oven temperature was far too hot.

Avoid substitutions: With the exception of those avoiding ingredients for allergies, I don't recommend changing a recipe the first time you make it. I've tried and tested these recipes to perfection. If you change an ingredient (for example, substituting applesauce, Greek yogurt, or something else), that's fine, but know that you may end up with a different result.

ASSEMBLING *and* FROSTING BASICS

*T*eaching cake classes is one of my favorite ways to connect with other bakers and fans. I love seeing that "light bulb" moment when everything makes sense and locks into place! I've had people attend my classes who have never frosted a cake before, and many who already own their own bakeries. There is still something to learn from every cake we make, and whether this is your first cake or you're a more seasoned baker, this primer will boost your own cake confidence!

The process of stacking, filling, crumb coating, final frosting, and getting those crisp, clean edges is the backbone of every cake in this book (and beyond).

STACKING *and* FILLING

1. Start by fitting your cake turntable with a nonslip baking mat. This keeps the cake in place while decorating. Tape a 6-inch cardboard cake round onto an 8-inch cardboard cake round (for a 6-inch cake). Make sure to use a strong piece of tape so that the tape doesn't break free while decorating. These cardboard cake rounds will make it easier to transfer your cake to the freezer during the decorating process and to a cake stand afterward.

2. Add your buttercream to a piping bag without a piping tip, then dot a bit of buttercream in the center of the cardboard round.

3. With an angled icing spatula, spread the buttercream in an even layer. This will act as "glue" to adhere the cake to the cardboard round.

4. Place your first cake layer, top side down, in the center of the cardboard round.

5. **If you are filling the cake with buttercream only:** Pipe an even layer of buttercream onto the first cake round. (If you are using a softer filling, see step 9.)

6. Spread the buttercream evenly with an angled icing spatula.

7. Place the next cake layer right on top, making sure to line up the layers as evenly as possible.

8. Get eye level with the cake to make sure it's straight, too.

9. If you're adding a soft filling to the cake, Dot a little bit of buttercream in the center of the cake layer.

10. Spread the buttercream in a thin layer to create a barrier between the cake and the filling.

11. Pipe a buttercream dam around the outside rim of the cake layer. This needs to be thick enough to keep the filling inside the cake without leaking.

12. Spoon in the filling. A little filling goes a long way, so I usually don't use more than about ½ cup between each cake layer.

13. Place the next cake layer on top, lining it up with the cake layers underneath it.

14. Get eye level again to make sure the sides and top are all even and straight.

CRUMB COATING

15. A thin first coating of frosting, called a crumb coat, will seal in stray crumbs so they don't appear on the finished frosted cake. With your straight icing spatula, begin spreading the buttercream at the bottom of the cake. Pull the buttercream toward yourself while spinning the turntable away from you.

16. Continue to frost the sides of the cake. As mentioned, this should be a thin layer (you should see the cake underneath). If your cake layers are cold/frozen (like I prefer), frost quickly so that the buttercream doesn't harden. This step should take less than 5 minutes. No one will see the crumb coat, so don't pamper it to look perfect.

17. With an angled icing spatula, add a thin layer of buttercream to the top.

18. Using a cake scraper placed at a 45-degree angle from the cake, gently smooth out the crumb coat. Fan out your fingers and use a gentle touch to create even pressure on the outside of the cake while doing so.

19. Pull the unfinished edges on the top of the cake inward with an angled icing spatula. Make sure to wipe off the spatula after each stroke, so that leftover buttercream won't mess up the clean edges you're trying to create.

20. Finish pulling in the edges around the entire top of the cake, then place the crumb-coated cake in the freezer for 2 to 3 minutes.

FINISH FROSTING

21. Stir the remaining buttercream with a wooden spoon or spatula to remove as many air pockets as possible, then begin to spread the final coat of buttercream on the sides with a straight icing spatula.

22. Then, using an angled icing spatula, spread some buttercream on the top.

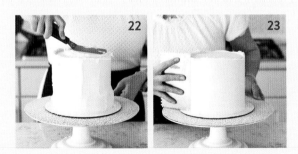

23. Holding a cake scraper straight up and down, and at a 45-degree angle from the cake, smooth out the final coat of buttercream on the sides, spinning the turntable as you work.

24. Surprise! It's not going to be perfect after smoothing out the sides with the cake scraper the first time. No worries—simply add on a bit of buttercream in any spots that need attention.

25. Smooth it out again with the cake scraper and repeat. If the buttercream isn't behaving, at this point you can always heat up your metal cake scraper in hot water, wipe it off, then go around *one* more time for a smooth finish. Buttercream will have inched over the top a bit, and that's perfectly fine. Leave it for our next step.

26. Place the cake into the freezer for 10 minutes to let the buttercream firm completely. Using a very sharp knife perpendicular to the cake top, gently slice off the excess buttercream on top in a straight line. You should be able to easily carve the buttercream off the top. If not, place the cake back into the freezer for a minute or heat up your knife with hot water for easier slicing.

27. Use an angled icing spatula to tidy up the edges if needed.

Chapter 1

SPRINGTIME BAKES

In my family, spring is a magical time when we visit the tulip festival, admire trees bursting like popcorn with white blossoms around the Capitol building, fawn over the new baby animals at the local farms, and watch the lightning storms roll into our neighborhood while the sweet smell of our lilac bush fills the air around us. We snack on fresh berries and shred carrots into my favorite carrot cake for Easter dinner after our annual egg hunt in the yard.

LEMON BLACKBERRY POPPY SEED CAKE

In one corner of our backyard, we have a berry patch in a small garden box. We excitedly picked out a couple of strawberry plants, a raspberry plant, and a blackberry plant (I love blackberries!). A few months in, I noticed my blackberry and raspberry bushes looked oddly similar. They grew the same, the leaves looked the same, and the berries looked similar as well. Eventually one plant was covered in ruby-red raspberries, and the neighboring one was studded with . . . *black raspberries*. I had planted one raspberry and one black raspberry plant, thinking it was a blackberry. Whoops!

Lemon and berries are basically meant for each other. The bright citrus complements the tart berries, which in turn cut through the sweetness of the buttercream; a handful of poppy seeds added to the batter really makes this cake something extra special. The blackberries (or black raspberries, if you make the same mistake I did) pack a triple punch—in a jam-like filling, in the soft-pink buttercream, and on top of the cake as whole berries.

Lemon Poppy Seed Cake

- Zest and juice of 1 large lemon
- ¾ cup buttermilk (room temperature)
- ⅔ cup sour cream (room temperature)
- 3 large eggs plus 1 egg white (room temperature)
- ⅓ cup vegetable oil
- 1 tablespoon pure vanilla extract
- 1 tablespoon poppy seeds
- ¼ cup flour
- 1 box lemon cake mix

Blackberry Filling

- 1 cup fresh blackberries
- ½ cup sugar
- 2 tablespoons lemon juice
- 2 teaspoons cornstarch

Lemon Blackberry Buttercream

- 1 batch Vanilla Buttercream (page xvii)
- Zest from 1 lemon (about 1 teaspoon)
- ½ cup fresh blackberries

For Assembly

- Fresh blackberries

For the Lemon Poppy Seed Cake

Preheat the oven to 325°F, then prep three 6-inch round cake pans with a swipe of shortening and dusting of flour to prevent sticking.

In a large bowl, whisk together the lemon zest and juice, buttermilk, sour cream, eggs, oil, vanilla, and poppy seeds until thoroughly combined. Sift in the flour and cake mix and whisk until just combined. Do not overmix. Split the batter evenly among the prepared pans.

Bake for 30 to 32 minutes, until the center is baked through and the center of the cake springs back when you touch it. Let the cakes cool in the pan for a minute before flipping them out onto a wire rack to cool completely. Wrap and freeze the cakes before assembly.

For the Blackberry Filling

In a small saucepan over medium heat, stir together the blackberries, sugar, and lemon juice, and cook until thick and bubbly, about 5 minutes. Sift in the cornstarch and stir until thickened, about 2 minutes. Strain the seeds if desired. Place the filling in a bowl, cover, and refrigerate until thickened and cooled completely.

For the Lemon Blackberry Buttercream

In the bowl of a stand mixer fitted with a paddle attachment, beat the buttercream and lemon zest until combined, then scrape down the sides with a spatula. Toss in the blackberries. As you beat the blackberries in, the color will change to a light purple, and the buttercream texture will change slightly, depending on how much moisture is in the blackberries (see Tip).

To Assemble

Place a cardboard cake round on a cake turntable. Dot a little bit of buttercream in the center of the round and spread it out with an angled icing spatula. Place the first chilled cake layer in the center. Add a thin layer of buttercream. Pipe a buttercream dam around the outside rim of the frosted cake layer, and then fill with about ½ cup of the blackberry filling. Place the next cake layer on top, then repeat, making sure to line the layers up evenly. After adding the top cake layer, crumb coat the cake by spreading a thin layer of white buttercream around the entire cake. Freeze for 2 minutes to set the buttercream.

Using a wooden spoon, beat out any air bubbles in the remaining buttercream. Spread an even layer of buttercream over the entire cake, using a cake scraper to create clean edges and sides.

Finish with a layer of fresh blackberries on top.

TIP: Buttercream tends to be temperamental if too much liquid is added; the excess moisture can cause it to separate. You can avoid this by using barely ripe berries or by precooking them down into a compote before adding them to your buttercream. Also, if you don't want any blackberry seeds in your buttercream, press your berries through a fine-mesh sieve before adding them to your whipped-butter mixture.

LAVENDER CAKE *with Honey Lavender Buttercream*

When my boys were little, my mother-in-law, Ruth, showed them how touching the stems of her lavender plant would release its sweet scent. Now whenever I pass a lavender plant, I often find myself reaching out as I go by, just as they did. Paired with honey and steeped into my soft white cake, the floral overtones of lavender in this recipe are subtle but so lovely. To achieve the lavender flavor, I soak dry organic lavender flowers in the buttermilk for the cake batter and in the cream for the buttercream. The soft-purple buttercream petals remind me of springtime flowers, but you could also go for a simpler rustic decoration by swirling the buttercream back and forth with the back of a spoon.

Lavender Cake

- ¾ cup buttermilk (room temperature)
- 1½ tablespoons dried lavender flowers
- ⅔ cup sour cream (room temperature)
- 4 egg whites (room temperature)
- ⅓ cup vegetable oil
- 1 tablespoon pure vanilla extract
- 1 box white cake mix

Honey Lavender Buttercream

- ⅓ cup plus ¼ cup heavy cream
- 3 teaspoons dried lavender flowers
- 1½ cups (3 sticks) unsalted butter
- ¼ cup honey
- 1 tablespoon pure vanilla extract
- Pinch of salt
- 7 to 8 cups powdered sugar

For Decorating

- Violet gel coloring
- Dried lavender flowers, for garnish
- Piping bag
- Wilton 127 piping tip

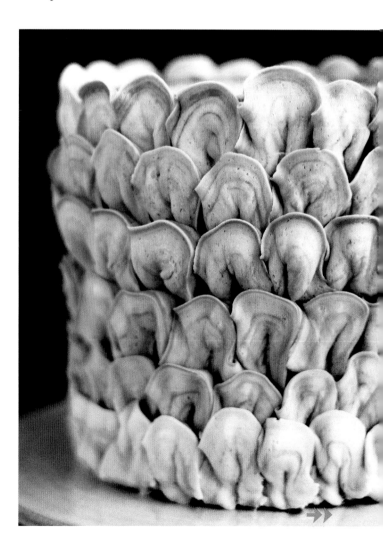

For the Lavender Cake

Preheat the oven to 325°F, then prep three 6-inch cake rounds with a swipe of shortening and dusting of flour to prevent sticking.

In a small microwave-safe bowl, whisk together the buttermilk and lavender, then microwave for 30 seconds. Stir again, then let soak for 15 minutes.

In a large bowl, whisk together the lavender buttermilk (do not strain), sour cream, egg whites, oil, and vanilla until thoroughly combined. Sift in the cake mix and whisk until just combined. Do not overmix. Split the batter evenly among the prepared pans.

Bake for 27 to 30 minutes, until the center is baked through. Let the cakes cool in the pan for a minute before flipping them out onto a wire rack to cool completely. Wrap and freeze the cakes before assembly.

For the Honey Lavender Buttercream

In a small microwave-safe bowl, whisk together the ⅓ cup heavy cream and the lavender, then microwave for 30 seconds. Stir again, then let soak for 15 minutes. Strain the lavender from the heavy cream.

In the bowl of a stand mixer fitted with a paddle attachment, beat the butter on medium speed until it's light and fluffy, then add in the lavender heavy cream, honey, vanilla, and salt. Beat again to combine and scrape down the sides with a spatula.

With the mixer on low speed, add the powdered sugar about ½ cup at a time. The buttercream will be thick. Add the last ¼ cup heavy cream to thin it out if needed, and then flip the mixer to high speed and beat until the buttercream is lighter in color and texture, about 2 minutes.

To Assemble

Place a cardboard cake round on a cake turntable. Dot a little bit of buttercream in the center of the round and spread it out with an angled icing spatula. Place the first chilled cake layer in the center. Add a layer of buttercream. Place the next cake layer on top, then repeat, making sure to line the layers up evenly. After adding the top cake layer, crumb coat the cake by spreading a thin layer of buttercream around the entire cake. Freeze for 2 minutes to set the buttercream.

Spread a final layer of buttercream on the top of the cake (not the sides). Using a wooden spoon, beat out any air bubbles in the remaining buttercream. Finish frosting the cake as desired or follow the decorating instructions below.

To Decorate the Cake

To make the buttercream ruffles, fit a piping bag with the Wilton 127 tip. Then, using a straight icing spatula, smear a streak of violet gel coloring (about a drop or two) onto the side of the piping bag. Fill the bag with buttercream and squeeze it a little until a purple streak is visible on the buttercream. Hold the bag with the thin edge of the piping tip on the outside. Moving in an upside-down "U" shape, pipe a row of petals along the top rim of the cake, then repeat right underneath it row by row until you reach the bottom of the cake.

Sprinkle a few dried lavender blossoms around the top of the cake.

TIP: For the lavender buttercream ruffles, don't thoroughly mix the violet gel coloring into the buttercream. The swirls of white and purple add a little something extra to the ruffles. When piping the ruffles, think of piping an upside-down "U," and hold the thicker part of the petal piping tip against the cake. The thin edge of the other end of the piping tip creates a more delicate texture to the ruffle exterior.

DARK CHOCOLATE HUCKLEBERRY SHAKE CAKE

Have you ever had a big salad and then wanted to balance it out with a giant milkshake? (Asking for a friend.) My family loves a local restaurant called Cubby's. Whenever we go, I order their tri-tip steak salad—but then I can't help but get their Hucklelala shake on my way out. It's flavored with huckleberry syrup and mixed with tiny bits of dark chocolate. With every sip, you get that creamy huckleberry flavor and a few dark chocolate pieces that linger afterward on your tongue. The first time I tried it, I knew right away it needed to be a cake.

This shake-to-cake has rich dark chocolate cake layers flavored with a little bit of that same huckleberry syrup and huckleberry buttercream flecked with little bits of dark chocolate.

Dark Chocolate Huckleberry Cake

- ¾ cup buttermilk (room temperature)
- ⅔ cup sour cream (room temperature)
- 3 large eggs plus 1 egg white (room temperature)
- ⅓ cup vegetable oil
- 1 tablespoon pure vanilla extract
- ¼ cup cocoa powder
- 1 box dark chocolate cake mix
- ½ cup huckleberry syrup

Huckleberry Buttercream with Dark Chocolate Bits

- 1 cup chocolate chips
- 1½ cups (3 sticks) unsalted butter
- ¼ cup huckleberry syrup
- ¼ cup heavy cream (plus more if needed)
- 1 tablespoon pure vanilla extract
- Pinch of salt
- 8½ cups powdered sugar

For Decorating

- Dark chocolate bits
- Dark chocolate chunks

For the Dark Chocolate Huckleberry Cake

Preheat the oven to 325°F, then prep three 6-inch round cake pans with a swipe of shortening and dusting of flour to prevent sticking.

In a large bowl, whisk together the buttermilk, sour cream, eggs, oil, and vanilla until thoroughly combined. Sift in the cocoa powder and cake mix and whisk until just combined. Do not overmix. Split the batter evenly among the prepared pans.

Bake for 30 to 32 minutes, until the center is baked through. Let the cakes cool in the pan for a minute before flipping out onto a wire rack

to cool completely. Poke holes in the bottom of each cake round with a toothpick, then brush on the huckleberry syrup to soak. Wrap and freeze the cakes before assembly.

For the Huckleberry Buttercream

In a food processor, pulse the chocolate chips until they're chopped into small bits. You should have about ½ cup.

In the bowl of a stand mixer fitted with a paddle attachment, beat the butter on medium speed until it's light and fluffy. Add the huckleberry syrup, heavy cream, vanilla, and salt and beat again until combined, then scrape down the sides with a spatula.

With the mixer on low speed, add the powdered sugar about ½ cup at a time. The buttercream will be thick. Add a little more heavy cream, 1 tablespoon at a time, to thin it out if needed, and then flip the mixer to high speed and beat until the buttercream is lighter in color and texture, about 2 minutes. Toss in the dark chocolate bits and mix on low speed until just combined.

To Assemble

Place a cardboard cake round on a cake turntable. Dot a little bit of buttercream in the center of the round and spread it out with an angled icing spatula. Place the first chilled cake layer in the center. Add a layer of buttercream. Place the next cake layer on top, then repeat, making sure to line the layers up evenly. After adding the top cake layer, crumb coat the cake by spreading a thin layer of buttercream around the entire cake. Freeze for 2 minutes to set the buttercream.

Using a wooden spoon, beat out any air bubbles in the remaining buttercream. Finish frosting the cake as desired or follow the decorating instructions below.

To Decorate the Cake

Spread the remaining buttercream on the top and sides, using a cake scraper for smooth sides. Leave the top edge uneven for a more rustic finish.

To finish, press on some dark chocolate bits along the bottom rim of the cake, and sprinkle some dark chocolate bits and chocolate chunks on top.

TIP: For the dark chocolate bits, just pulse dark chocolate chips in a food processor until little pieces form. The smaller, the better.

Since fresh or frozen huckleberries are hard to find, I use huckleberry syrup, which you can find with the other soda flavorings at your local grocery store.

ROSE WATER CAKE *with Raspberry Rose Water Buttercream and Raspberry Filling*

If you've followed me on Instagram for more than two seconds, you know I love sharing photos of my roses during the late spring and summer months as they bloom in soft yellow, pink, and white. I didn't realize this when I first planted them, but I quickly learned that beyond their unique petal designs, each rose has its own scent, too. My rose garden inspired both the design and the flavor of this cake. Rose water (which you can find at most baking stores) gives the cake a floral undertone that pairs beautifully with a delicious raspberry filling; the top is decorated like an actual rose.

Rose Water Cake

- ¾ cup buttermilk (room temperature)
- ⅔ cup sour cream (room temperature)
- 4 egg whites (room temperature)
- ⅓ cup vegetable oil
- 1 tablespoon pure vanilla extract
- 1 teaspoon rose water
- 1 box white cake mix

Raspberry Filling

- 1 cup fresh raspberries
- ½ cup sugar
- 2 tablespoons lemon juice
- 1 teaspoon cornstarch

Raspberry Rose Water Buttercream

- 1 batch Vanilla Buttercream (page xvii)
- 1 teaspoon raspberry emulsion (see page xviii)
- ½ teaspoon rose water
- 1 drop soft-pink gel coloring

For Decorating

- White sphere sprinkles and nonpareils
- Piping bag
- Wilton 125 piping tip

For the Rose Water Cake

Preheat the oven to 325°F, then prep three 6-inch round cake pans with a swipe of shortening and dusting of flour to prevent sticking.

In a large bowl, whisk together the buttermilk, sour cream, egg whites, oil, vanilla, and rose water until thoroughly combined. Sift in the cake mix and whisk until just combined. Do not overmix. Split the batter evenly among the prepared pans.

Bake for 25 to 27 minutes, until the center is baked through. Let the cakes cool in the pan for a minute before flipping them out onto a wire rack to cool completely. Wrap and freeze the cakes before assembly.

For the Raspberry Filling

In a small saucepan over medium heat, stir together the raspberries, sugar, and lemon juice and cook until thick and bubbly, about 5 minutes. Sift in the cornstarch and stir until thickened, about 2 minutes. Strain to remove the seeds if desired. Place the filling in a bowl, cover, and refrigerate until thickened and cooled completely.

For the Raspberry Rose Water Buttercream

In the bowl of a stand mixer fitted with a paddle attachment, beat together the buttercream, raspberry emulsion, rose water, and gel color until evenly combined, then scrape down the sides with a spatula.

To Assemble

Place a cardboard cake round on a cake turntable. Dot a little bit of buttercream in the center of the round and spread it out with an angled icing spatula. Place the first chilled cake layer in the center. Add a thin layer of buttercream. Pipe a buttercream dam around the outside rim of the frosted cake layer, and

then fill with about ½ cup of the raspberry filling. Place the next cake layer on top, then repeat, making sure to line the layers up evenly. After adding the top cake layer, crumb coat the cake by spreading a thin layer of buttercream around the entire cake. Freeze for 2 minutes to set the buttercream.

Using a wooden spoon, beat out any air bubbles in the remaining buttercream. Finish frosting the cake as desired or follow the decorating instructions below.

To Decorate the Cake

Spread a final layer of buttercream around the entire cake, using a cake scraper for smooth sides and clean edges.

To make the rose design on top of the cake, fit a piping bag with a Wilton 125 tip. Fill the bag with the remaining buttercream. Pipe a series of wide "rainbow curve" shapes around the outside rim, holding the bag with the thick end of the piping tip against the cake. Repeat this pattern, staggering the curve shapes with the curves underneath, until you reach the center of the cake. Place a few white sprinkles and nonpareils in the middle of the rose and on the sides of the cake near the bottom.

TIP: Using white nonpareils on the outside of the cake and the inside of the buttercream flower creates a "dew-kissed" look, much like my roses after a rainstorm comes through. I added in a few small circle sprinkle spheres (say that ten times fast) as the center of the rose, too.

CRÈME BRÛLÉE CAKE *with Vanilla Bean Caramel Buttercream and Custard Filling*

Crème brûlée is one of those fancy desserts that finds its way onto every baker's must-learn-how-to-make list. The sweet custard filling is cold and creamy, and the signature caramelized sugar on top is to die for. But truthfully, I just like any and every excuse to use a kitchen blowtorch! Who's with me?

For this cake, I split each layer in half to make six thinner ones—the more layers, the more filling! And you're going to want to spread my custard filling on everything. To make that roasted sugar top, you'll definitely need a blowtorch.

Vanilla Bean Caramel Cake
- ¾ cup buttermilk (room temperature)
- ⅔ cup sour cream (room temperature)
- 4 egg whites (room temperature)
- ⅓ cup vegetable oil
- 2 teaspoons pure vanilla extract
- 2 teaspoons vanilla bean paste
- 1 teaspoon caramel extract
- 1 box white cake mix

Vanilla Bean Custard Filling
- 1 cup whole milk
- ½ cup sugar
- 1½ tablespoons cornstarch
- 2 egg yolks, whisked
- 1 teaspoon vanilla bean paste

Vanilla Bean Caramel Buttercream
- 1 batch Vanilla Buttercream (page xvii)
- 2 teaspoons vanilla bean paste
- 1 teaspoon pure vanilla extract
- 1 teaspoon caramel extract

For Decorating
- Granulated sugar
- 1 strawberry, sliced
- Scalloped cake scraper
- Kitchen blowtorch

For the Vanilla Bean Caramel Cake
Preheat the oven to 325°F, then prep three 6-inch round cake pans with a swipe of shortening and dusting of flour to prevent sticking.

In a large bowl, whisk together the buttermilk, sour cream, egg whites, oil, vanilla, vanilla bean paste, and caramel extract until thoroughly combined. Sift in the cake mix and whisk until just combined. Do not overmix. Split the batter evenly among the prepared pans.

Bake for 27 to 30 minutes, until the center is baked through. Let the cakes cool in the pan for a minute before flipping them out onto a wire rack to cool completely. Slice each cake round in half horizontally to create 6 layers. Wrap and freeze the cakes before assembly.

For the Vanilla Bean Custard Filling
In a small saucepan over medium heat, whisk together the milk, sugar, and cornstarch and cook, whisking constantly, until thickened, 3 to 5 minutes. While whisking, add in the egg yolks very slowly (a little at a time) so they don't scramble. Remove from the heat and whisk in the vanilla bean paste. Place the filling in a bowl, cover, and refrigerate until thickened and cooled completely.

For the Vanilla Bean Caramel Buttercream
In the bowl of a stand mixer fitted with a paddle attachment, beat together the buttercream, vanilla bean paste, vanilla extract, and caramel extract until evenly combined, then scrape down the sides with a spatula.

To Assemble
Place a cardboard cake round on a cake turntable. Dot a little bit of buttercream in the center of the round and spread it out with

an angled icing spatula. Place the first chilled cake layer in the center. Add a thin layer of buttercream. Pipe a buttercream dam around the outside rim of the frosted cake layer, and then fill with about ¼ cup of the custard filling. Place the next cake layer on top, then repeat, making sure to line the layers up evenly. After adding on the top cake layer, crumb coat the cake by spreading a thin layer of buttercream around the entire cake. Freeze for 2 minutes to set the buttercream.

Using a wooden spoon, beat out any air bubbles in the remaining buttercream. Finish frosting the cake as desired or follow the decorating instructions below.

To Decorate the Cake

Spread a final layer of buttercream around the entire cake, using a scalloped cake scraper for clean decorative edges on the sides. Leave the top edge uneven for a more rustic finish.

Sprinkle a thin layer of granulated sugar on top, then freeze for 5 minutes to set the buttercream.

When ready to serve, carefully use a kitchen blowtorch to caramelize the granulated sugar top to a light golden brown (see Tip). Place the sliced strawberry on top.

 TIP: To prevent the buttercream from melting when you use the blowtorch, freeze your decorated cake until it's firm, then sprinkle a layer of granulated sugar on top. While the cake is still frozen, point the kitchen torch directly at the sugar (and only the sugar) until it caramelizes and starts to bubble. This will create the traditional caramelized shell on top of the cake.

STRAWBERRY SHORTCAKE ICE CREAM BAR CAKE *with Strawberry Crumble*

When I got to middle school, I thought I was so cool because every day I got to choose what I'd like to have for lunch from multiple options. I quickly fell hard for a strawberry shortcake ice cream bar—strawberry and vanilla ice cream coated in shortbread and strawberry crumbles. Each bite was a bit crunchy and creamy and made any middle school drama during my brace-faced band-geek days fade right away.

Strawberry Swirl Cake

- ¾ cup buttermilk (room temperature)
- ⅔ cup sour cream (room temperature)
- 4 egg whites (room temperature)
- ⅓ cup vegetable oil
- 1 tablespoon pure vanilla extract
- 1 box white cake mix
- 1 tablespoon strawberry emulsion

Strawberry Crumble

- 12 shortbread cookies (7 ounces; such as Sandies)
- 2 tablespoons unsalted butter
- ¼ cup flour
- 1 ounce freeze-dried strawberries, pulsed into a fine powder

Strawberry Vanilla Bean Buttercream

- 1½ cups (3 sticks) unsalted butter
- ⅓ cup heavy cream
- 1 ounce freeze-dried strawberries, pulsed into a fine powder
- 1 tablespoon strawberry emulsion
- 2 teaspoons vanilla bean paste
- 1 teaspoon pure vanilla extract
- Pinch of salt
- 7 to 8 cups powdered sugar

For Decorating

- 8 to 10 small fresh strawberries, stemmed
- Piping bag
- Wilton 6B piping tip

For the Strawberry Swirl Cake

Preheat the oven to 325°F, then prep three 6-inch round cake pans with a swipe of shortening and dusting of flour to prevent sticking.

In a large bowl, whisk together the buttermilk, sour cream, egg whites, oil, and vanilla until thoroughly combined. Sift in the cake mix and whisk until just combined. Do not overmix. Transfer half the batter to another bowl, and then gently fold the strawberry emulsion into one of the bowls. Alternating between the strawberry batter and white cake batter, add a little bit of each batter to each of the cake pans until the batter has been evenly split among them.

Bake for 27 to 30 minutes, until the center is baked through. (Keep the oven on for the strawberry crumble.) Let the cakes cool in the pan for a minute before flipping them out onto a wire rack to cool completely. Wrap and freeze the cakes before assembly.

For the Strawberry Crumble

Preheat the oven to 325°F, if needed. Line a cookie sheet with parchment paper.

In a food processor, pulse together the shortbread cookies, butter, and flour until a crumbly mixture forms. Spread the crumble out onto the prepared cookie sheet and bake for 5 minutes, stirring after 2 minutes. The mixture should be slightly toasted. Sprinkle the freeze-dried strawberry powder on half the cookie sheet over the shortbread crumbles. Let cool completely. Mix the crumble together. Set aside.

For the Strawberry Vanilla Bean Buttercream

In the bowl of a stand mixer fitted with a paddle attachment, beat the butter on medium speed until it's light and fluffy. Add ¼ cup of the heavy cream, the freeze-dried strawberry powder, strawberry emulsion, vanilla bean paste, vanilla extract, and salt and beat again until combined, then scrape down the sides with a spatula.

With the mixer on low speed, add the powdered sugar about ½ cup at a time. The buttercream will be thick. Add the remaining heavy cream to thin it out if needed, and then flip the mixer to high speed and beat until the buttercream is lighter in color and texture, about 2 minutes.

To Assemble and Decorate

Place a cardboard cake round on a cake turntable. Dot a little bit of buttercream in the center of the round and spread it out with an angled icing spatula. Place the first chilled cake layer in the center. Add a layer of buttercream. Place the next cake layer on top, then repeat, making sure to line the layers up evenly. After adding on the top cake layer, crumb coat the cake by spreading a thin layer of buttercream around the entire cake. Freeze for 2 minutes to set the buttercream.

Using a wooden spoon, beat out any air bubbles in the remaining buttercream.

Spread an even layer of buttercream on the top and sides of the cake, reserving about 1 cup to pipe a few decorative swirls on top later. Place the cake on a cookie sheet on top of the turntable. Gently press the strawberry crumble all around the entire cake, letting the cookie sheet catch any crumbs.

Fit a piping bag with a Wilton 6B tip, fill it with the reserved buttercream, and pipe on 8 to 10 spots of buttercream around the outside rim of the top of the cake. Gently place the strawberries on top of the piped buttercream.

TIP: For this cake, I created a crumble using shortbread cookies and freeze-dried strawberries. The key is to toast the shortbread crumbles in the oven without burning them. Just like browned butter, these crumbles can go from beautifully roasted to dark brown pretty quickly if you're not watching them carefully.

LEMON ALMOND CAKE *with White Chocolate Almond Buttercream*

Sometimes I keep my cakes pretty simple, and sometimes I feel like I want to use every possible piping tip on a single cake! For this cake, I went full piping-tip crazy with every rosette, swirl, dollop, and ruffle I could think of in bright white and yellow hues, plus a few fresh lemon slices. With its cheery disposition and flavors to match, this cake is sure to brighten anyone's day.

Lemon slices have a lot of moisture (and we love them that way, just not when we want to attach them to a cake!). So before adding them to the sides or top of your cake, make sure to let them sit on a paper towel to soak up some of the moisture first. Or better yet, use candied lemon slices.

Lemon Almond Cake

- ¾ cup buttermilk (room temperature)
- ⅔ cup sour cream (room temperature)
- 3 large eggs plus 1 egg white (room temperature)
- ⅓ cup vegetable oil
- 1 tablespoon pure vanilla extract
- ½ teaspoon almond extract
- Zest and juice of 1 large lemon
- ¼ cup flour
- 1 box lemon cake mix

White Chocolate Almond Buttercream

- ½ cup white chocolate chips
- 2 tablespoons heavy cream
- 1 batch Vanilla Buttercream (page xvii)
- ½ teaspoon almond extract (see Tip)

For Decorating

- Lemon-yellow gel coloring
- Lemon slices, patted dry with a paper towel to remove most of the moisture
- White sprinkles (sixlets, spheres, and jimmies)
- Piping bags
- Piping tips, such as Wilton 1M, 125, 6B, 32, and optional coupler

For the Lemon Almond Cake

Preheat the oven to 325°F, then prep three 6-inch round cake pans with a swipe of shortening and dusting of flour to prevent sticking.

In a large bowl, whisk together the buttermilk, sour cream, eggs, oil, vanilla, almond extract, and lemon zest and juice until thoroughly combined. Sift in the flour and cake mix and whisk until just combined. Do not overmix. Split the batter evenly among the prepared pans.

Bake for 30 to 32 minutes, until the center is baked through. Let the cakes cool in the pan for a minute before flipping them out onto a wire rack to cool completely. Wrap and freeze the cakes before assembly.

For the White Chocolate Almond Buttercream

In a small microwave-safe bowl, microwave the chocolate chips and heavy cream for 30 seconds, then stir until smooth. Let cool slightly.

In the bowl of a stand mixer fitted with a paddle attachment, beat together the buttercream, white chocolate ganache mixture, and almond extract until evenly combined, then scrape down the sides with a spatula.

Split the buttercream evenly between two bowls. Tint half the buttercream yellow with 1 drop of the lemon-yellow gel coloring. Add about 1 cup of each buttercream to piping bags without a tip.

To Assemble

Place a cardboard cake round on a cake turntable. Dot a little bit of buttercream in the center of the round and spread it out with an angled icing spatula. Place the first

chilled cake layer in the center. To make the striped buttercream pattern on the inside, make a "target" by piping the yellow and white buttercreams in alternating rings. Place the next cake layer on top, then repeat, making sure to line the layers up evenly. After adding the top cake layer, crumb coat the cake by spreading a thin layer of white buttercream around the entire cake. Freeze for 2 minutes to set the buttercream.

Using a wooden spoon, beat out any air bubbles in the remaining buttercream. Spread an even layer of white buttercream around the entire cake, using a cake scraper for clean edges and sides.

To Decorate the Cake

Add the remaining yellow and white buttercreams to piping bags fitted with the decorative piping tips.

Place the lemon slices on the sides and top of the cake, then pipe a variety of designs with the piping tips. For the rosettes, use the Wilton 1M tip. For the ruffles, use the #125. For the large stars, use the #6B. For the smaller star dollops, use the #32 tip. Press on sprinkles throughout the design.

 TIP: Almond extract tends to be a bit stronger than the other flavorings I love to use. A little goes a long way. Start with ½ teaspoon, then taste the buttercream. If you'd like a stronger flavor, use another ½ teaspoon until you've reached your sweet spot.

STRAWBERRY MALT SWIRL CAKE

This cake flavor is 100 percent inspired by my husband, who loves a good strawberry malted milkshake. Saturday is "burger Saturday" for our family, and a sweet and cold strawberry malt is a frequent addition when we hit up one of our local burger places. A malt is like a milkshake but with the addition of malted milk powder. It enhances the flavors in the milkshake and gives it a really sweet, rich taste. Adding malted milk powder to buttercream will not change the color, but it will make your cake taste just like a malt shake. (Malted milk powder can be found next to the evaporated and condensed milk at the grocery store.)

For this particular cake, I use strawberry emulsion for a candy-like taste that complements the vanilla bean flavor. Strawberry emulsion also has a naturally pink tint to it, so there's no food coloring needed for the cake swirl or buttercream. Everything will have a soft, sweet pink shade just from the emulsion.

Strawberry Malt Swirl Cake

- ¾ cup buttermilk (room temperature)
- ⅔ cup sour cream (room temperature)
- ½ cup vegetable oil
- 3 egg whites (room temperature)
- 1 tablespoon vanilla bean paste
- 1 box white cake mix
- ¼ cup malted milk powder
- 1 tablespoon strawberry emulsion

Strawberry Malt Buttercream

- 1½ cups (3 sticks) unsalted butter
- ¼ cup heavy cream (plus more if needed)
- 3 tablespoons malted milk powder, sifted
- 2 tablespoons strawberry emulsion
- 1 tablespoon pure vanilla extract
- Pinch of salt
- 7 to 8 cups powdered sugar

White Chocolate Ganache Drip

- 1 cup bright-white white chocolate candy melts
- 3 tablespoons heavy cream

For Decorating

- Sprinkles
- 8 to 10 white gumballs
- Drip bottle

For the Strawberry Malt Swirl Cake

Preheat the oven to 325°F, then prep three 6-inch round cake pans with a swipe of shortening and dusting of flour to prevent sticking.

In a large bowl, whisk together the buttermilk, sour cream, oil, egg whites, and vanilla bean paste until thoroughly combined. Sift in the cake mix and malted milk powder and whisk until just combined. Do not overmix. Split the batter in half into two bowls and gently fold the strawberry emulsion into one half of the batter. Alternating between the strawberry and white cake batters, split the batter evenly among the prepared pans. With a toothpick or knife, gently swirl the batter in a figure-eight pattern to create a marbled effect.

Bake for 27 to 30 minutes, until the center is baked through. Let the cakes cool in the pan for about a minute before flipping them out onto a wire rack to cool completely. Wrap and freeze the cakes before assembly.

For the Strawberry Malt Buttercream
In the bowl of a stand mixer fitted with a paddle attachment, beat the butter on medium speed until it's light and fluffy. Add the heavy cream, malted milk powder, strawberry emulsion, vanilla, and salt and beat again until combined, then scrape down the sides with a spatula.

With the mixer on low speed, add the powdered sugar about ½ cup at a time. The buttercream will be thick. Add a touch more heavy cream to thin it out if needed, and then flip the mixer to high speed and beat until the buttercream is lighter in color and texture, about 2 minutes.

To Assemble
Place a cardboard cake round on a cake turntable. Dot a little bit of buttercream in the center of the round and spread it out with an angled icing spatula. Place the first chilled cake layer in the center. Add a layer of buttercream. Place the next cake layer on top, then repeat, making sure to line the layers up evenly. After adding the top cake layer, crumb coat the cake by spreading a thin layer of buttercream around the entire cake. Freeze for 2 minutes to set the buttercream.

Using a wooden spoon, beat out any air bubbles in the remaining buttercream. Finish frosting the cake as desired or follow the decorating instructions below.

To Decorate the Cake
Spread a final layer of buttercream around the entire cake, using a cake scraper for smooth sides and clean edges. Freeze the cake for 2 minutes to set the buttercream once again.

For the White Chocolate Ganache Drip
In a small microwave-safe bowl, stir together the candy melts and heavy cream, then heat for 30 seconds. Stir until the melts have completely dissolved into a ganache. Transfer to a drip bottle.

Squeeze the ganache drip onto the top edge of the cake, letting it drip a little more than halfway down the side of the cake. Add more ganache to the top and use an angled icing spatula to spread it evenly to the edges. Swirl the top with your spatula as you spin the turntable. Add the sprinkles and place the gumballs around the outer edge of the top of the cake.

TIP: I love using a cookie scoop to portion this batter, alternating scoops of white and pink in the cake pans. To get the swirled look, use a toothpick or a knife in a figure-eight motion while turning the pan.

PISTACHIO CAKE *with Pistachio Buttercream and Marshmallow Filling*

Big family dinners at my grandma June's home in Mendon, Utah, were a treat for me as a kid, and I always looked forward to her "green salad"—which wasn't what you'd usually picture when you hear those words. It was a fluffy Watergate salad made with pistachio pudding, marshmallows, whipped cream, and pineapple. Although my cake version doesn't include pineapple, the pistachio pudding in the mix, the marshmallow filling, and pistachio buttercream still remind me of one of her signature dishes.

Rather than make a homemade marshmallow filling, I use marshmallow fluff from the grocery store, mixed with a little bit of buttercream so that it's easier to work with.

Pistachio Cake

- 1 cup buttermilk (room temperature)
- 3 large eggs (room temperature)
- ½ cup vegetable oil
- 1 tablespoon pure vanilla extract
- 1 (3.4-ounce) package pistachio pudding mix
- 1 box white cake mix

Pistachio Buttercream

- 1 (3.4-ounce) package pistachio pudding mix (sifted, pistachio pieces reserved)
- ½ cup heavy cream (plus more if needed)
- 1½ cups (3 sticks) unsalted butter
- ½ cup salted shelled pistachios, pulsed to a fine powder
- 1 teaspoon pure vanilla extract
- 7 to 8 cups powdered sugar

Marshmallow Filling

- 2 cups marshmallow fluff
- ⅔ cup Pistachio Buttercream (recipe above)

For Decorating

- Whole pistachios
- Finely chopped pistachios
- Piping bag

For the Pistachio Cake

Preheat the oven to 325°F, then prep three 6-inch round cake pans with a swipe of shortening and dusting of flour to prevent sticking.

In a large bowl, whisk together the buttermilk, eggs, oil, vanilla, and pudding mix until thoroughly combined. Let sit for 5 minutes. Sift in the cake mix and whisk until just combined.

Do not overmix. Split the batter among the prepared pans.

Bake for 27 to 30 minutes, until the center is baked through. Let the cakes cool in the pan for a minute before flipping them out onto a wire rack to cool completely. Wrap and freeze the cakes before assembly.

For the Pistachio Buttercream

In a small bowl, stir together the pudding mix and heavy cream. Let sit for 5 minutes.

In the bowl of a stand mixer fitted with a paddle attachment, beat the butter on medium speed until it's light and fluffy. Add the pistachio and cream mixture, pistachio powder, and vanilla and beat again until combined, then scrape down the sides with a spatula.

With the mixer on low speed, add the powdered sugar about ½ cup at a time. The buttercream will be thick. Add a touch more heavy cream to thin it out if needed, and then flip the mixer to high speed and beat until the buttercream is lighter in color and texture, about 2 minutes.

For the Marshmallow Filling

In a small bowl, stir together the marshmallow fluff and ⅔ cup of the prepared pistachio buttercream. Place into a piping bag with the end snipped off and set aside.

To Assemble and Decorate

Place a cardboard cake round on a cake turntable. Dot a little bit of buttercream in the center of the round and spread it out with an angled icing spatula. Place the first chilled cake layer in the center. Add a thin layer of buttercream. Pipe a buttercream dam around the outside rim of the frosted cake layer. Pipe the marshmallow filling into the center. Place the next cake layer on top, then repeat, making sure to line the layers up evenly. After adding the top cake layer, crumb coat the cake by spreading a thin layer of buttercream around the entire cake. Freeze for 2 minutes to set the buttercream.

Using a wooden spoon, beat out any air bubbles in the remaining buttercream. Spread a final layer of buttercream on the top and sides of the chilled cake, using a cake scraper for smooth sides and clean edges.

Press whole pistachios on top around the outside rim of the cake, and then sprinkle on a bit of crumbled pistachios.

 TIP: The pudding works better the longer it's left in liquid, so let the pudding mix for both the cake and frosting sit a bit in their respective liquids. This will ensure the pudding mix has time to work its magic and become a creamy— rather than grainy—base.

ALMOND CAKE *with Raspberry Buttercream*

My grandma June and grandpa Fred had a massive garden, and when I went to visit them when I was young, I would often find one or both of them either working in the garden or in the kitchen canning what they harvested. Grandma would tie an empty ice cream bucket to her apron strings for picking ruby-red raspberries. Her raspberries were the most delicious I've ever tasted, and she would make the most mouthwatering jam. I can still smell the sweet scent of boiling raspberries filling their home. Picking my own small patch of raspberries takes me right back to those magical summers.

This cake has soft almond cake layers and my most favorite raspberry buttercream. Freeze-dried raspberries and raspberry emulsion give the buttercream a gorgeous raspberry taste without too much effort. I often find the freeze-dried fruits I use in my buttercream in the grocery store with the snacks, nuts, or toppings for salads.

Almond Cake

- ¾ cup buttermilk (room temperature)
- ⅔ cup sour cream (room temperature)
- ⅓ cup vegetable oil
- 4 egg whites (room temperature)
- 1 tablespoon pure vanilla extract
- 2 teaspoons almond extract
- 1 box white cake mix

Raspberry Buttercream

- 1½ cups (3 sticks) unsalted butter
- ¼ cup heavy cream (plus more if needed)
- 1 ounce freeze-dried raspberries, pulsed to a fine powder
- 1 tablespoon pure vanilla extract
- 1 tablespoon raspberry emulsion (optional)
- Pinch of salt
- 7 to 8 cups powdered sugar

For Decorating

- Slivered almonds
- Fresh raspberries
- Scalloped cake scraper

For the Almond Cake

Preheat the oven to 325°F, then prep three 6-inch round cake pans with a swipe of shortening and dusting of flour to prevent sticking.

In a large bowl, whisk together the buttermilk, sour cream, oil, eggs, vanilla, and almond extract until thoroughly combined. Sift in the cake mix and whisk until just combined. Do not overmix. Split the batter evenly among the prepared pans.

Bake for 25 to 27 minutes, until the center is baked through. Let the cakes cool in the pan for about a minute before flipping out onto a wire rack to cool completely. Wrap and freeze the cakes before assembly.

For the Raspberry Buttercream

In the bowl of a stand mixer fitted with a paddle attachment, beat the butter on medium speed until it's light and fluffy. Add the heavy cream, raspberry powder, vanilla, raspberry emulsion (if using), and salt and beat again until combined, then scrape down the sides with a spatula.

With the mixer on low speed, add the powdered sugar about ½ cup at a time. The buttercream will be thick. Add a touch more heavy cream to thin it out if needed, and then flip the mixer to high speed and beat until the buttercream is lighter in color and texture, about 2 minutes.

To Assemble and Decorate

Place a cardboard cake round on a cake turntable. Dot a little bit of buttercream in the center of the round and spread it out with an angled icing spatula. Place the first chilled cake layer in the center. Add a layer of buttercream. Place the next cake layer on top, then repeat, making sure to line the layers up evenly. After adding on the top cake layer, crumb coat the cake by spreading a thin layer of buttercream around the entire cake. Freeze for 2 minutes to set the buttercream.

Using a wooden spoon, beat out any air bubbles in the remaining buttercream. Spread a final layer of buttercream around the entire cake. Use a scalloped cake scraper to create a bubbled pattern on the side of the cake, leaving the top edge uneven and rustic.

Garnish with slivered almonds and fresh raspberries.

PINK VELVET HEART CAKE *with Vanilla Bean Buttercream*

Is this not the cutest pink velvet cake you've ever seen? With hearts all around and a tasty vanilla buttercream adorning each bite, this cake feels extra special even though it's so simple. And perhaps that's why I covered it with buttercream hearts—every cake, especially this one, is made with love.

Pink Velvet Cake

- ¾ cup buttermilk (room temperature)
- ⅔ cup sour cream (room temperature)
- ⅓ cup vegetable oil
- 4 egg whites (room temperature)
- 2 tablespoons raspberry emulsion
- 1 tablespoon pure vanilla extract
- 1 box white cake mix
- 1 batch Vanilla Buttercream (page xvii)

For Decorating

- Soft pink gel coloring
- Piping bag
- Wilton 1A piping tip

For the Pink Velvet Cake

Preheat the oven to 325°F, then prep three 6-inch round cake pans with a swipe of shortening and dusting of flour to prevent sticking.

In a large bowl, whisk together the buttermilk, sour cream, oil, egg whites, raspberry emulsion, and vanilla until thoroughly combined. Sift in the cake mix and whisk until just combined. Do not overmix. Split the batter evenly among the prepared pans.

Bake for 25 to 27 minutes, until the center is baked through. Let the cakes cool in the pan for about a minute before flipping them out onto a wire rack to cool completely. Wrap and freeze the cakes before assembly.

To Assemble and Decorate

Place a cardboard cake round on a cake turntable. Dot a little bit of buttercream in the center of the round and spread it out with an angled icing spatula. Place the first chilled cake layer in the center. Add a layer of buttercream. Place the next cake layer on top, then repeat, making sure to line the layers up evenly. After adding the top cake layer, crumb coat the cake by spreading a thin layer of buttercream around the entire cake. Freeze for 2 minutes to set the buttercream.

Using a wooden spoon, beat out any air bubbles in the remaining buttercream. Reserve about 1 cup buttercream for piping. Spread the remaining buttercream on the top and sides of the chilled cake, leaving the top edge uneven and rustic. Freeze the cake for 5 minutes.

To the reserved buttercream, add 1 drop of soft-pink gel coloring and stir to incorporate. Transfer to a piping bag fitted with a Wilton 1A tip. For the hearts: holding the piping tip perpendicular to the cake, start to pipe a small dot, then drag the end of the dot diagonally to one side, releasing as you pull up to create a tail. Start another buttercream dot right next to the first and drag the tail diagonally in the opposite direction until it meets the first one (creating the bottom point of the heart with both tails). Repeat to pipe hearts around the sides of the cake.

TIP: You can line up the buttercream hearts, space them out, or pipe them at random. Whichever way you do it, putting hearts around a pink velvet cake is a quick way to make anyone's day!

CHOCOLATE-DIPPED STRAWBERRY CAKE
with Chocolate Ganache Drip and Filling

Nothing is more quintessential around Valentine's Day than chocolate-dipped strawberries, but you could serve this cake for just about any romantic occasion. It's dressed to perfection with dark chocolate cake layers, a rich ganache filling, decadent strawberry buttercream, dark chocolate ganache drip, and freshly dipped strawberries right on top. Prefer white chocolate instead? No problem! Switch it up and substitute white chocolate for dark in the dripping ganache, filling, and strawberries. But hands off this strawberry buttercream. With its smooth texture and sweet flavor, it's surely something you and your significant other will be talking about long after the last bite.

Dark Chocolate Cake

- ¾ cup buttermilk (room temperature)
- ⅔ cup sour cream (room temperature)
- 3 large eggs plus 1 egg white (room temperature)
- ⅓ cup vegetable oil
- 1 tablespoon pure vanilla extract
- ½ cup mini chocolate chips
- ½ cup Dutch process cocoa powder
- ¼ cup flour
- 1 box dark chocolate cake mix

Strawberry Buttercream

- 1½ cups (3 sticks) unsalted butter
- ½ cup heavy cream (plus more if needed)
- 1 ounce freeze-dried strawberries, pulsed into a fine powder
- 1½ tablespoons strawberry emulsion
- 1 tablespoon pure vanilla extract
- Pinch of salt
- 7 to 8 cups powdered sugar

Chocolate Ganache Filling and Drip

- 2 cups chocolate melts
- 2 cups heavy cream

For Decorating

- 1 cup mini chocolate chips
- 8 to 10 chocolate-dipped strawberries
- Piping bag
- Ateco 825 piping tip (or any large open star piping tip)

For the Dark Chocolate Cake
Preheat the oven to 325°F, then prep three 6-inch round cake pans with a swipe of shortening and dusting of flour to prevent sticking.

In a large bowl, whisk together the buttermilk, sour cream, eggs, oil, and vanilla until thoroughly combined. Toss in the mini chips. Then sift in the cocoa, flour, and cake mix and whisk until just combined. Do not overmix. Split the batter evenly among the prepared pans.

Bake for 27 to 30 minutes, until the center is baked through. Let the cakes cool in the pan for a minute before flipping them out onto a wire rack to cool completely. Wrap and freeze the cakes before assembly.

For the Strawberry Buttercream
In the bowl of a stand mixer fitted with a paddle attachment, beat the butter on medium speed until it's light and fluffy. Add the heavy cream, freeze-dried strawberry powder, strawberry emulsion, vanilla, and salt and beat again until combined, then scrape down the sides with a spatula.

With the mixer on low speed, add the powdered sugar about ½ cup at a time. The buttercream will be thick. Add a little more heavy cream, 1 tablespoon at a time, to thin it out if needed, and then flip the mixer to high speed and beat until the buttercream is lighter in color and texture, about 2 minutes.

For the Chocolate Ganache Filling and Drip

In a medium microwave-safe bowl, microwave the chocolate melts and heavy cream for 30 seconds, then stir until smooth. Transfer to a drip bottle.

To Assemble

Place a cardboard cake round on a cake turntable. Dot a little bit of buttercream in the center of the round and spread it out with an angled icing spatula. Place the first chilled cake layer in the center. Add a thin layer of buttercream. Pipe a buttercream dam around the outside rim of the frosted cake layer, and then squeeze on about ½ cup of the ganache filling. Place the next cake layer on top, then repeat, making sure to line the layers up evenly. After adding on the top cake layer, crumb coat the cake by spreading a thin layer of buttercream around the entire cake. Freeze for 2 minutes to set the buttercream.

Using a wooden spoon, beat out any air bubbles in the remaining buttercream. Finish frosting the cake as desired or follow the decorating instructions below.

To Decorate the Cake

Spread a final layer of buttercream around the entire cake, using a cake scraper for smooth sides and edges. Press some mini chocolate chips along the bottom of the cake. Freeze for 5 minutes to set.

Using the drip bottle, pipe the ganache drips along the top rim, letting the drips cascade halfway down the sides of the cake. Freeze for 1 minute to set.

Transfer the remaining buttercream to a piping bag fitted with the Ateco 825 tip and pipe a shell border around the outside rim of the cake. Repeat with a second border just inside the first.

Place the chocolate-dipped strawberries on the buttercream border, then sprinkle a few more mini chips on the top of the cake.

TIP: Dip your strawberries in advance, but place them on the cake right before serving. They tend to gather moisture more than the cake and warm up at a different speed. To avoid condensation, cover them and store them separately (and try to avoid the temptation to eat them all!).

SHAMROCK SHAKE CAKE *with Vanilla Mint Buttercream*

Even if I don't bring it up, my boys always ask for Shamrock Shakes from McDonald's on Saint Patrick's Day. I don't mind. It's an easy one to pull off for this mom, who already has too many tabs open in her brain on most days and especially holidays. My cake has thick minty layers swirled just like the shake and a green ombre pattern in the buttercream. I top it off with whipped swirls and maraschino cherries.

White Mint Cake

- ¾ cup buttermilk (room temperature)
- ⅔ cup sour cream (room temperature)
- 4 egg whites (room temperature)
- ⅓ cup vegetable oil
- 1 tablespoon pure vanilla extract
- 1 teaspoon mint extract
- 1 box white cake mix
  Light green gel coloring

Vanilla Mint Buttercream

- 1½ cups (3 sticks) unsalted butter
- ½ cup heavy cream (plus more if needed)
- 1 tablespoon vanilla bean paste
- 1 teaspoon mint extract
  Pinch of salt
- 7 to 8 cups powdered sugar
  Light green gel coloring

For Decorating

- 8 stem-on maraschino cherries
  Piping bag
  Wilton 1M piping tip

For the White Mint Cake

Preheat the oven to 325°F, then prep three 6-inch round cake pans with a swipe of shortening and dusting of flour to prevent sticking.

In a large bowl, whisk together the buttermilk, sour cream, egg whites, oil, vanilla, and mint extract until thoroughly combined. Sift in the cake mix and whisk until just combined. Do not overmix. Split the batter in half into two bowls, then tint half the batter green with 1 to 2 drops of light green gel coloring. Divide the batter evenly among the prepared pans, alternating scoops of white and green batter. With a toothpick, gently swirl the batter in a figure-eight pattern to create a marbled effect.

Bake for 25 to 27 minutes, until the center is baked through. Let the cakes cool in the pan for a minute before flipping them out onto a wire rack to cool completely. Wrap and freeze the cakes before assembly.

For the Vanilla Mint Buttercream

In the bowl of a stand mixer fitted with a paddle attachment, beat the butter on medium speed until it's light and fluffy. Add the heavy cream, vanilla, mint extract, and salt and beat again until combined, then scrape down the sides with a spatula.

With the mixer on low speed, add the powdered sugar about ½ cup at a time. The buttercream will be thick. Add a little more heavy cream, 1 tablespoon at a time, to thin it out if needed, and then flip the mixer to high speed and beat until the buttercream is lighter in color and texture, about 2 minutes.

Transfer 2 cups of the buttercream to a separate bowl and add 1 drop of light green gel coloring. Stir to combine.

To Assemble and Decorate

Place a cardboard cake round on a cake turntable. Dot a little bit of buttercream in the center of the round and spread it out with an angled icing spatula. Place the first chilled cake layer in the center. Add a thin layer of the white buttercream. Place the next cake layer on top, then repeat, making sure to line the layers up evenly. After adding the top cake layer, crumb coat the cake by spreading a thin even layer of the buttercream around the entire cake. Use a cake scraper to smooth everything out evenly. Freeze for 2 minutes to set the buttercream.

Using a wooden spoon, beat out any air bubbles in the remaining buttercream. Reserve about 1½ cups of the white buttercream and set aside for the final swirls on top. Spread an even layer of buttercream around the entire cake, using both the green and white buttercream in different places to create the watercolor effect. Use a cake scraper for smooth sides and clean edges.

Using the Wilton 1M tip, pipe 8 even swirls on top of the cake around the outside rim.

Place a maraschino cherry on top of each swirl.

TIP: In the baking section of your grocery store, you might find both peppermint and mint extracts. And yes, they do taste different. Save the peppermint for our winter baking section; you'll need the mint extract for this cake. But make sure to use only a little. Just like almond extract, a little goes a long way. We are walking a fine line between soft mint buttercream and flat-out toothpaste!

HUMMINGBIRD CAKE *with Cream Cheese Buttercream and Candied Pecan Crumble*

What exactly is a hummingbird cake? It's a gorgeous cake that's made with banana, pineapple, cinnamon, and pecans. My version also adds an addicting candied pecan crumble around the whole outside of the cake. While the pineapple and bananas create a beautifully soft cake, the crumble really takes the texture and flavor home. For the best results, choose your brownest bananas.

Banana Pineapple Cake

- 9 ounces ripe banana, mashed (2 medium bananas)
- 6 ounces crushed pineapple, drained (⅔ cup)
- ½ cup buttermilk (room temperature)
- ⅓ cup sour cream (room temperature)
- 4 egg whites (room temperature)
- ⅓ cup vegetable oil
- 1 tablespoon pure vanilla extract
- 1 box white cake mix

Cream Cheese Buttercream

- 1 cup (2 sticks) unsalted butter
- 8 ounces (1 brick) cream cheese
- ⅛ cup heavy cream (plus more if needed)
- 1 tablespoon pure vanilla extract
- Pinch of salt
- 7 to 8 cups powdered sugar

Candied Pecan Crumble

- 4 cups chopped pecans
- 1 cup packed brown sugar
- 1 cup granulated sugar
- Pinch of ground cinnamon

For Decorating

- Pecan halves
- Piping bag
- Wilton 1A (circle) piping tip

For the Banana Pineapple Cake

Preheat the oven to 325°F, then prep three 6-inch round cake pans with a swipe of shortening and dusting of flour to prevent sticking.

In a large bowl, whisk together the mashed bananas, pineapple, buttermilk, sour cream, egg whites, oil, and vanilla until thoroughly combined.

Sift in the cake mix and whisk until just combined. Do not overmix. Split the batter evenly among the prepared pans.

Bake for 30 to 35 minutes, until the center is baked through. Let the cakes cool in the pan for a minute before flipping them out onto a wire rack to cool completely. (Keep the oven on for the pecan crumble.) Wrap and freeze the cakes before assembly.

For the Cream Cheese Buttercream

In the bowl of a stand mixer fitted with a paddle attachment, beat the butter on medium speed until it's light and fluffy, then add the cream cheese and beat until fully incorporated. Add the heavy cream, vanilla, and salt and beat again until combined, then scrape down the sides with a spatula.

With the mixer on low speed, add the powdered sugar about ½ cup at a time. The buttercream will be thick. Add a little more heavy cream, 1 tablespoon at a time, to thin it out if needed, and then flip the mixer to high speed and beat until the buttercream is lighter in color and texture, about 2 minutes.

For the Candied Pecan Crumble

Preheat the oven to 325°F, if needed. Line a cookie sheet with parchment paper.

In a medium bowl, stir together the pecans, brown sugar, granulated sugar, and cinnamon. Spread out evenly on the prepared cookie sheet. Bake for 5 minutes, then stir. Repeat until the sugar has slightly caramelized and bubbles on the pecans, 10 to 15 minutes total. Let cool

completely. Stir to create a crumble that can be easily applied to the side of the cake later.

To Assemble and Decorate

Place a cardboard cake round on a cake turntable. Dot a little bit of buttercream in the center of the round and spread it out with an angled icing spatula. Place the first chilled cake layer in the center. Add a layer of buttercream. Place the next cake layer on top, then repeat, making sure to line the layers up evenly. After adding the top cake layer, crumb coat the cake by spreading a thin layer of buttercream around the entire cake. Freeze for 2 minutes to set the buttercream.

Using a wooden spoon, beat out any air bubbles in the remaining buttercream. Spread a final layer of buttercream around the entire cake, using a cake scraper for smooth sides and clean edges. Place a cookie sheet under the cake on the turntable. Immediately press a layer of the candied pecans around the entire cake, letting the cookie sheet catch any that fall as you work.

When the cake is completely coated, transfer the remaining buttercream to a piping bag fitted with the Wilton 1A tip. Pipe small dollops of buttercream on the top of the cake around the outside rim. Gently press a pecan half on each buttercream dollop.

TIP: For an extra treat, double the batch of the candied pecan crumble and sprinkle it on salads, stir it into yogurt, or even use it as topping for ice cream.

LEMON CAKE *with Lemon Cream Cheese Buttercream*

Cakes with all the bells and whistles are fun, but every baker needs a few simple classics that they can always come back to in a pinch for a baby shower, birthday, wedding, or even Sunday dinner with family. Everyone needs a good lemon cream cake, and this one has been my favorite for years and years. I'll never turn down a slice of zesty lemon cake frosted with a thick cream cheese buttercream. This one is also perfect for decorating with fresh berries, candied lemons (if not using fresh like I do here), or a few white chocolate shavings to make it extra fancy. I also love turning this recipe into cupcakes or even a Bundt cake. It simply can't be beat, and with fresh lemon juice and zest right in the cake batter, your whole kitchen will smell like a lemon orchard by the time your oven finishes preheating.

Lemon Cake

- ¾ cup buttermilk (room temperature)
- ⅔ cup sour cream (room temperature)
- 3 large eggs plus 1 egg white (room temperature)
- ⅓ cup vegetable oil
- 1 tablespoon pure vanilla extract
- Zest and juice of 1 large lemon
- ¼ cup flour
- 1 box lemon cake mix

Lemon Cream Cheese Buttercream

- 1 cup (2 sticks) unsalted butter
- 8 ounces (1 brick) cream cheese
- ⅛ cup heavy cream (plus more if needed)
- 2 tablespoons lemon zest
- 1 tablespoon pure vanilla extract
- 1 teaspoon lemon extract (optional)
- Pinch of salt
- 7 to 8 cups powdered sugar

For Decorating

Lemon slices

For the Lemon Cake

Preheat the oven to 325°F, then prep three 6-inch round cake pans with a swipe of shortening and dusting of flour to prevent sticking.

In a large bowl, whisk together the buttermilk, sour cream, eggs, oil, vanilla, and lemon zest and juice until thoroughly combined. Sift in the flour and cake mix and whisk until just combined. Do not overmix. Split the batter evenly among the prepared pans.

Bake for 30 to 32 minutes, until the center is baked through. Let the cakes cool in the pan for a minute before flipping them out onto a wire rack to cool completely. Wrap and freeze the cakes before assembly.

For the Lemon Cream Cheese Buttercream

In the bowl of a stand mixer fitted with a paddle attachment, beat the butter on medium speed until it's light and fluffy, then add the cream cheese and beat until fully incorporated. Add the heavy cream, lemon zest, vanilla, lemon extract (if using), and salt and beat again until combined, then scrape down the sides with a spatula.

With the mixer on low speed, add the powdered sugar about ½ cup at a time. The buttercream will be thick. Add a little more heavy cream, 1 tablespoon at a time, to thin it out if needed, then flip the mixer to high speed and beat until the buttercream is lighter in color and texture, about 2 minutes.

To Assemble and Decorate

Place a cardboard cake round on a cake turntable. Dot a little bit of buttercream in the center of the round and spread it out with an angled icing spatula. Place the first chilled cake layer in the center. Add a layer of buttercream. Place the next cake layer on top, then repeat, making sure to line the layers up evenly. After adding the top cake layer, crumb coat the cake by spreading a thin layer of buttercream around the entire cake. Freeze for 2 minutes to set the buttercream.

Using a wooden spoon, beat out any air bubbles in the remaining buttercream. Spread a final layer of buttercream around the entire cake, using a cake scraper for smooth sides, swirling the top using an angled icing spatula and turntable, and leaving the top edge uneven for a more rustic look.

With a straight icing spatula, drag the buttercream up to make vertical lines, starting at the bottom of the cake and stopping at various heights.

Just before serving, place a few lemon slices on top as garnish.

 TIP: If using fresh lemons on your cake as garnish, let them sit on a paper towel for a bit to remove some of the moisture, and hold off on putting them on your cake until right before serving. That way, the acid in the lemon juice doesn't ruin the buttercream.

CARROT CAKE *with Almond Cream Cheese Buttercream*

If there's one cake my dad always requested, it would be my carrot cake. For birthdays, Father's Day, or Easter Sunday—he loved my carrot cake so very much. Now that he's not here to enjoy it with us, I feel like it's become almost sacred to me. The memory, the taste, the way he'd tell me how delicious it always was—these things will never fade in my mind, and I hope they never do. I love how a particular cake can hold a memory tight and keep it safe until I'm ready to flip on the oven again.

Hey, Dad, this one's for you.

Carrot Cake

- ¾ cup buttermilk (room temperature)
- ⅔ cup sour cream (room temperature)
- 3 large eggs (room temperature)
- 2 medium carrots, finely grated (about ½ cup packed; see Tip)
- ⅓ cup vegetable oil
- 1 tablespoon pure vanilla extract
- 1 box carrot cake or spice cake mix

Almond Cream Cheese Buttercream

- 1 cup (2 sticks) unsalted butter
- 8 ounces (1 brick) cream cheese
- ⅛ cup heavy cream (plus more if needed)
- 1 tablespoon pure vanilla extract
- ¼ teaspoon almond extract
- Pinch of salt
- 7 to 8 cups powdered sugar

For Decorating

- Light green gel coloring
- Orange gel coloring
- Piping bag
- Wilton 5 piping tip (or any fine, round tip)
- Wilton 10 piping tip (or any pearl-size round tip)

For the Carrot Cake

Preheat the oven to 325°F, then prep three 6-inch round cake pans with a swipe of shortening and dusting of flour to prevent sticking.

In a large bowl, whisk together the buttermilk, sour cream, eggs, grated carrots, oil, and vanilla until thoroughly combined. Sift in the cake mix and whisk until just combined. Do not overmix. Split the batter evenly among the prepared pans.

Bake for 50 to 52 minutes, until the center is baked through. Let the cakes cool in the pan for a minute before flipping them out onto a wire rack to cool completely. Slice each cake round in half horizontally to create 6 layers. Wrap and freeze the cakes before assembly.

For the Almond Cream Cheese Buttercream

In the bowl of a stand mixer fitted with a paddle attachment, beat the butter on medium speed until it's light and fluffy, then add the cream cheese and beat until fully incorporated. Add the heavy cream, vanilla, almond extract, and salt and beat again until combined, then scrape down the sides with a spatula.

With the mixer on low speed, add the powdered sugar about ½ cup at a time. The buttercream will be thick. Add a little more heavy cream, 1 tablespoon at a time, to thin it out if needed, and then flip the mixer to high speed and beat until the buttercream is lighter in color and texture, about 2 minutes.

To Assemble and Decorate

Place a cardboard cake round on a cake turntable. Dot a little bit of buttercream in the center of the round and spread it out with an angled icing spatula. Place the first chilled cake layer in the center. Add a layer of buttercream.

Place the next cake layer on top, then repeat, making sure to line the layers up evenly. After adding the top cake layer, crumb coat the cake by spreading a thin layer of buttercream around the entire cake. Freeze for 2 minutes to set the buttercream.

Using a wooden spoon, beat out any air bubbles in the remaining buttercream. Spread a final layer of buttercream around the entire cake, using a cake scraper for smooth sides. Leave the top edge uneven for a more rustic look.

Divide the remaining buttercream into two small bowls and tint one with a drop of light green gel coloring for a soft green and the other with a small drop of orange for light orange. Transfer the green buttercream to a piping bag fitted with a very small circle piping tip (Wilton 5) for the carrot fronds, and the orange buttercream to another piping bag fitted with a small piping tip (Wilton 10) for the carrots.

To pipe the carrots, using the orange buttercream, pipe a small circle of buttercream and gently drag the tail while still squeezing. Gently release the buttercream to make a pointed tip on the tail (the end of the carrot). Repeat in a random pattern all around the side of the cake. Using the green buttercream, pipe small fronds coming off the top of the carrots in three small lines.

TIP: When you grate your carrots, use the smallest holes possible on your grater to ensure the carrots bake through all the way.

SAINT PATRICK'S DAY
RAINBOW RUFFLE CAKE

What You'll Need

- 1 batch Vanilla Buttercream (page xvii)
- Gel coloring in pastel pink, orange, yellow, green, blue, and purple
- 1 cake, stacked and crumb coated (see page xxiv)
- ½ teaspoon metallic gold luster dust
- 2 tablespoons any clear extract or alcohol
- 6 Wilton 127 piping tips plus 6 piping bags
- Cake turntable
- Paintbrush

1. Divide the buttercream into 6 portions (about 1½ cups each), tint with the 6 colors, and scoop into the piping bags fitted with the Wilton 127 tips. Place the cake on the turntable.

2. To pipe the first ruffle, hold the bag with the pointed end of the piping tip at the top and the larger end against the cake, with the tip tilted slightly away from the cake. Pipe the ruffle around the top in a continuous swoop, rotating the turntable as you go. As you finish, slightly overlap the end of the ruffle over the beginning—this seam will be the back of the cake.

3. Repeat step 2 with the other colors to make additional ruffles.

4. Mix the luster dust with the extract until it's thick.

5. Freeze the cake to firm up the buttercream, about 5 minutes, then use the paintbrush to paint the metallic color on the edges of the ruffles. If the buttercream starts to soften, put the cake back in the freezer to firm up again before continuing.

SAINT PATRICK'S DAY RAINBOW STRIPE CAKE

What You'll Need

- 1 batch Classic White Cake batter (page 251)
- 2 batches Vanilla Buttercream (page xvii)
- Gel colorings in pink, orange, yellow, green, blue, and purple
- 6-inch and 8-inch cake boards
- Cake turntable
- Angled icing spatula
- Thin-stripe cake comb
- Flat cake scraper
- Plastic wrap
- Scissors
- Wilton 1M piping tip
- 7 piping bags

1. Divide the cake batter into six 6-inch cake pans and tint them with each of the 6 colors. Bake, cool, then wrap the layers in plastic wrap and freeze for at least an hour before stacking.

2. Tape the 6-inch cake board to the 8-inch cake board and set it on a turntable. Dot a little bit of buttercream in the center of the round and spread it out with an angled icing spatula.

3. Stack the cake layers in this order, adding a layer of white buttercream between each layer: purple, blue, green, yellow, orange, and pink. Frost with a crumb coat (see page xxiv). Freeze for 2 minutes to set the buttercream.

4. Spread a final layer of white buttercream around the entire cake. Use the thin-stripe cake comb to make clean indents on the side of the cake (see the photo on page 174 for how to hold the comb). Freeze the cake for at least 10 minutes. Meanwhile, divide the remaining buttercream into 6 portions, tint them with the gel colors, and scoop them into 6 piping bags. Snip the tiny tip off the piping bags, then pipe the individual colors in the clean indents on the side of the cake.

6. To make the multicolored rosettes on top of the cake, lay out a sheet of plastic wrap. Pipe a line of red buttercream, followed by orange, yellow, green, blue, and purple. Make sure they're all the same amount and length.

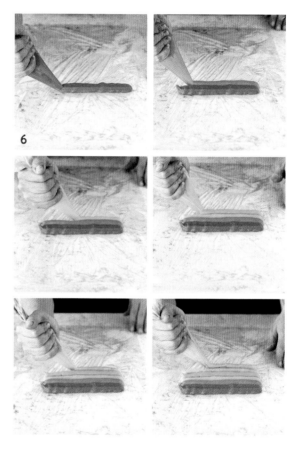

5. Working quickly, use a flat cake scraper to smooth out the stripes. It will look messy before it gets better! Apply a little bit of pressure and scrape until the clean stripes start to show through. On the final turn, heat the cake scraper with hot water to make a clean finish.

7. Carefully roll the plastic wrap over the buttercream so that the purple buttercream meets the red, creating a log. Pinch the sides and twist the ends to close.

8. Snip off one end of the log with scissors.

9. Place the log in the piping bag fitted with the Wilton 1M piping tip, with the snipped-off end at the tip of the bag.

10. Holding the piping bag perpendicular to the cake, start squeezing out the buttercream in a steady stream. Slowly start to wrap the buttercream swirl around the middle and pull up. Gently release when the swirl is finished. You may need to make another rainbow buttercream log, depending on how many swirls you add to the top of your cake. Just remove the plastic wrap from the piping bag and add the new log.

EASTER
ROBIN'S EGG SPECKLED CAKE

What You'll Need

- 2 tablespoons pure vanilla extract
- 1 teaspoon cocoa powder
- 1 drop black gel coloring
- 1 cake, stacked and frosted (see page xxii) with light blue buttercream

Cadbury Mini Eggs

Variety of white sprinkles

Silver sprinkle rods

Paintbrush

1. Mix together the vanilla, cocoa, and gel coloring to make a liquid paint. Dip the tip of the paintbrush into the paint mixture. Flick the end of the paintbrush with your thumb to make black speckles on the sides and top of the cake.

2. Place the Cadbury eggs around the outside rim of the top of the cake, then fill in the rest of the top of the cake.

3. Press a few more eggs around the sides. Place on a few white sprinkles and silver rods to finish.

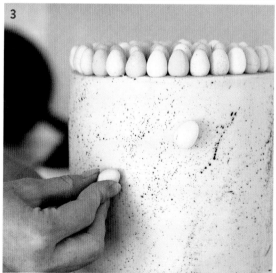

EASTER
BUNNY SPRINKLE CAKE

What You'll Need

- 1 cake, stacked and crumb coated (see page xxiv)
- 1 batch Vanilla Buttercream (page xvii)
- Gel coloring in pastel green, yellow, blue, pink, and purple
- Pastel nonpareils
- Parchment paper
- Cake turntable
- Thin-stripe cake comb
- Flat cake scraper
- 5 piping bags

1. Draw or trace a bunny-head shape on a piece of parchment paper, then cut it out.

2. Spread a final layer of white buttercream around the entire cake. Use the thin-stripe cake comb to make clean indents on the side of the cake (see the photo on page 174 for how to hold the comb). Freeze the cake for at least 10 minutes. Meanwhile, divide the remaining buttercream into 5 portions, tint them with the gel colors, and scoop them into the piping bags. Snip the tiny tips off the piping bags, then pipe the individual colors in the clean indents on the side of the cake.

3. Working quickly, use the flat cake scraper to smooth out the stripes (see page 54). It will look messy before it gets better! Apply a little bit of pressure and scrape until the clean stripes start to show through. On the final turn, heat the cake scraper with hot water to make a clean finish.

4. While the buttercream is still wet, carefully place the parchment bunny cutout on top of the cake. Make sure the edges are sealed so the sprinkles don't sneak underneath.

5. Sprinkle on the nonpareils, then freeze the cake for 5 minutes. Carefully peel away the parchment paper to reveal the bunny shape.

MOTHER'S DAY
LAMBETH CAKE

What You'll Need

- 1 batch Vanilla Buttercream (page xvii), tinted with pink gel coloring
- 1 cake, stacked and frosted (see page xxii) with light pink buttercream

Pearl sprinkles

- 2 piping bags Wilton piping tips 1M, 32, 10, 15, 3, 104
- 6 couplers Cake turntable

1. Fit one piping bag with the Wilton 1M tip and another with a coupler, and fill both bags with buttercream. With the 1M tip, pipe a shell border around the bottom of the cake.

2. Attach the #32 piping tip to the coupler and pipe a shell border right above the 1M border.

3. Switch to the #10 piping tip. Hold the wider end of the piping tip against the cake with the pointed end pointing down at a 20- to 30-degree angle. Carefully swoop the buttercream down into a ruffle while pulling in one direction.

4. Repeat step 3 to make a second ruffle right above the first.

5. Switch to the #15 piping tip and pipe rosettes right above the peaks of the ruffles.

6. With the #3 piping tip, pipe a braid border right over where the top ruffle meets the cake.

7. Next, pipe a small fleur-de-lis above the roses and below the ruffle.

8. Pipe small dots to the left and right of the fleurs-de-lis above the roses.

9. Switch to the #104 piping tip. Repeat step 3 to make another ruffle at the top of the cake, making sure the swoops line up with the ones below and the peaks reach the top of the cake.

10. With the #3 piping tip, pipe a braid above the ruffle, as you did in step 6.

11. With the same tip, pipe a thin swag below the ruffle. The best way to get a smooth line is to press the buttercream right under the ruffle at the point, then keep squeezing while pulling the bag away from the cake slightly—the buttercream should hold firm in the air—then carefully press it back to the cake at the next point underneath the ruffle.

12. Switch to the #32 piping tip and pipe a small star dollop in the eave of the ruffles.

13. With the #15 piping tip, pipe a shell border right under the smooth line swoops.

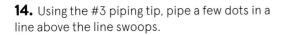

14. Using the #3 piping tip, pipe a few dots in a line above the line swoops.

15. Switch to the #32 piping tip and pipe a shell border around the top rim of the cake.

16. With the other piping bag with the 1M piping tip, pipe a border right inside the small shell border.

17. Fit the other piping bag with the #3 piping tip. Pipe a connected-dot border under the shell swoop from step #16. Place a few pearl sprinkles in various places.

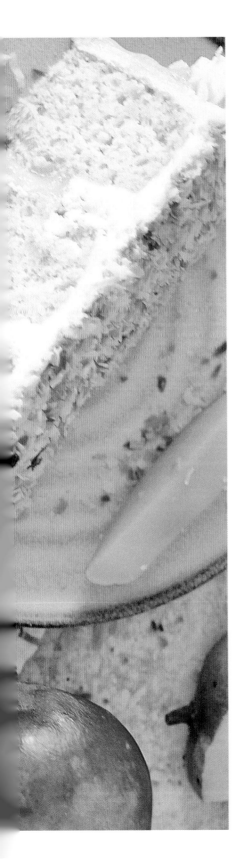

Chapter 2

SUMMER SWEETS

Our summer days are packed with beautiful hikes in the Rocky Mountains, which surround our valley. We love sipping on thick, creamy shakes from our favorite burger places after our long runs, as well as soaking in outdoor movie nights with s'mores under the stars in our backyard. Ryan and I often enjoy twilight walks around the neighborhood when the air is still warm. Around the Fourth of July, the sky fills with bright fireworks, and all my nieces and nephews gather together for a decorated bike parade. We frequent carnivals and festivals with friends and family. Farmers' markets are filled to the brim with fresh fruits, and our days are filled with shaded picnics by the park or playing at the splash pad with our boys. Although summertime isn't when most would want turn on their oven, the beautiful flavors of the season baked into a delicious cake are worth not missing out on for any celebration.

APRICOT UPSIDE-DOWN CAKE *with Honey Brown Sugar Buttercream*

When I created this cake, it reminded me of our time in our first house in Provo, Utah, as new parents. We had the nicest friends in the neighborhood, and a couple of times someone brought over a giant bowl of juicy apricots, which I had never had before. I remember carefully slicing them up and baking them into pancakes and muffins, finding ways to sneak them into a smoothie, making pureed baby food for our little guy, and even trying (and failing miserably) to make a tart out of them. This cake brings me right back to those days, when I was getting a better grasp on baking, finding my way through the kitchen, and not wanting to see a single apricot again for weeks.

For these beautiful cake layers, you can use either fresh or canned apricots. The top apricot layer will be exposed, so take care in lining them up when placing them into the butter and brown sugar layer in the bottom of the pan. The honey cake batter is baked right into the apricots, seeping up all their rich flavor.

Apricot Upside-Down Cake

- ¼ cup (½ stick) unsalted butter, melted
- ⅔ cup packed brown sugar
- 2 (15-ounce) cans apricot halves, drained and sliced
- ¾ cup buttermilk (room temperature)
- ⅔ cup sour cream (room temperature)
- 2 large eggs plus 2 egg whites (room temperature)
- ⅓ cup vegetable oil
- 2 tablespoons honey
- 1 tablespoon pure vanilla extract
- ½ teaspoon almond extract
- 1 box white cake mix

Honey Brown Sugar Buttercream

- 1½ cups (3 sticks) unsalted butter
- ½ cup packed brown sugar
- ¼ cup heavy cream (plus more if needed)
- ¼ cup honey
- 1 tablespoon pure vanilla extract
- Pinch of salt
- 7 to 8 cups powdered sugar

For the Apricot Upside-Down Cake
Preheat the oven to 325°F, then prep three 6-inch round cake pans with a swipe of shortening and dusting of flour to prevent sticking.

Divide the melted butter and brown sugar evenly among the prepared pans. Arrange the apricot slices right on top of the butter and brown sugar in an even layer.

In a large bowl, whisk together the buttermilk, sour cream, eggs, oil, honey, vanilla, and almond extract until thoroughly combined. Sift in the cake mix and whisk until just combined. Do not overmix. Split the batter evenly among the prepared pans.

Bake for 27 to 30 minutes, until the center is baked through. Let the cakes cool in the pan for a minute before carefully flipping them out onto a wire rack to cool completely. Wrap and freeze the cakes before assembly.

For the Honey Brown Sugar Buttercream
In the bowl of a stand mixer fitted with a paddle attachment, beat together the butter and brown sugar on medium speed until light and fluffy, about 2 minutes. Add the heavy cream, honey, vanilla, and salt and beat again until combined, then scrape down the sides with a spatula.

With the mixer on low speed, add the powdered sugar about ½ cup at a time. The buttercream will be thick. Add more heavy cream to thin it out if needed, and then flip the mixer to high speed and beat until the buttercream is lighter in color and texture, about 2 minutes.

To Assemble

Place a cardboard cake round on a cake turntable. Dot a little bit of buttercream in the center of the round and spread it out with an angled icing spatula. Place the first chilled cake layer in the center (fruit side up). Add a layer of buttercream. Place the next cake layer on top, then repeat, making sure to line the layers up evenly. After adding the top cake layer, crumb coat the sides of the cake (leaving the fruit exposed on top) by spreading on a thin layer of buttercream. Freeze for 2 minutes to set the buttercream.

Using a wooden spoon, beat out any air bubbles in the remaining buttercream. Spread a thick final layer of buttercream on the sides of the cake, using a cake scraper for smooth sides. Leave the top edge uneven to create a rustic look.

TIP: For the buttercream to really soak up the flavor of the brown sugar without the texture being too grainy, make sure to take your time and whip up the butter and brown sugar longer than you think. Also, good-quality honey will give you a richer flavor in both the cake and the buttercream.

DARK CHOCOLATE RASPBERRY CAKE *with*
Raspberry Buttercream and Chocolate Ganache

This cake boasts not only chocolate in the cake layers but also as a delightful filling, curls around the outside, and let's not forget that the entire cake is covered in chocolate ganache! The raspberry buttercream hiding underneath is made with raspberry emulsion, so the taste is a bit more like what you'd expect in a raspberry-cream dessert. The sweetness pairs beautifully with the dark chocolate shell. It's perfect for any fancy occasion or just about any day you need to satisfy your raspberry-chocolate sweet tooth.

Dark Chocolate Raspberry Cake

- 1 cup buttermilk (room temperature)
- ½ cup sour cream (room temperature)
- 3 large eggs plus 1 egg white (room temperature)
- ⅓ cup vegetable oil
- 2 tablespoons raspberry emulsion
- 1 tablespoon pure vanilla extract
- ¼ cup dark cocoa powder, such as Hershey's Special Dark
- ¼ cup flour
- 1 box dark chocolate cake mix

Raspberry Filling

- 12 ounces frozen raspberries, thawed (or fresh)
- ¼ cup plus 1 tablespoon granulated sugar
- 1½ tablespoons lemon juice
- 1 tablespoon cornstarch

Raspberry Buttercream

- 1½ cups (3 sticks) unsalted butter
- ¼ cup heavy cream (plus more if needed)
- 1 tablespoon pure vanilla extract
- 1 tablespoon raspberry emulsion
- Pinch of salt
- 1 drop red gel coloring
- 7 to 8 cups powdered sugar

Chocolate Ganache

- 3 cups dark chocolate melts
- 1 cup heavy cream

For Decorating

- Chocolate shavings
- Fresh raspberries

For the Dark Chocolate Raspberry Cake

Preheat the oven to 325°F, then prep three 6-inch round cake pans with a swipe of shortening and dusting of flour to prevent sticking.

In a large bowl, whisk together the buttermilk, sour cream, eggs, oil, raspberry emulsion, and vanilla until thoroughly combined. Sift in the cocoa, flour, and cake mix and whisk until just combined. Do not overmix. Split the batter evenly among the prepared pans.

Bake for 27 to 30 minutes, until the center is baked through. Let the cakes cool in the pan for a minute before carefully flipping out onto a wire rack to cool completely. Wrap and freeze the cakes before assembly.

For the Raspberry Filling

Put the raspberries in a food processor and pulse until a thick puree forms. Strain the puree to remove the seeds if desired. You should have about 1 cup puree.

In a small saucepan over medium heat, stir together the raspberry puree, sugar, and lemon juice and cook until bubbly, 3 to 4 minutes. Whisk together the cornstarch and 1 tablespoon of water in a small bowl to make a slurry, then add it to the raspberry mixture and cook until it thickens, about 2 minutes. Place the filling in a bowl, cover, and refrigerate until thickened and cooled completely (about an hour or so).

For the Raspberry Buttercream

In the bowl of a stand mixer fitted with a paddle attachment, beat the butter on medium speed until it's light and fluffy, about 2 minutes. Add the heavy cream, vanilla, raspberry emulsion, and salt and beat again until combined, then scrape down the sides with a spatula. Add the gel coloring and mix to add a soft-pink hue to the buttercream.

With the mixer on low speed, add the powdered sugar about ½ cup at a time. The buttercream will be thick. Add more heavy cream to thin it out if needed, and then flip the mixer to high speed and beat until the buttercream is lighter in color and texture, about 2 minutes.

For the Chocolate Ganache

In a medium microwave-safe bowl, stir together the chocolate melts and heavy cream. Microwave for 1 minute, then stir until there are no lumps and the ganache is thick and creamy. Set aside to cool for about 10 minutes, until easily spreadable with a cake knife.

To Assemble and Decorate

Place a cardboard cake round on a cake turntable. Dot a little bit of buttercream in the center of the round and spread it out with an angled icing spatula. Place the first chilled cake layer in the center. Add a thin layer of buttercream. Pipe a buttercream dam around the outside rim of the frosted cake layer, then fill with about ½ cup of the raspberry filling. Place the next cake layer on top, then repeat, making sure to line the layers up evenly. After adding the top cake layer, crumb coat the cake by spreading a thin layer of buttercream around the entire cake. Freeze for 2 minutes to set the buttercream.

Using a wooden spoon, beat out any air bubbles in the remaining buttercream. Spread a thick final layer of buttercream just on the sides of the cake, using a cake scraper for smooth sides and clean edges. Freeze for about 5 minutes to fully set the buttercream.

Working quickly (the ganache will cool quickly when you add it to the chilled cake), spread a generous layer of ganache around the entire cake using your cake spatula, then smooth everything out with a cake scraper. Gently apply the chocolate shavings along the bottom of the cake.

When the ganache has hardened, cover the top of the cake with fresh raspberries.

TIP: This cake has two layers of coating on the outside, which makes chilling the cake vital. First, frost the cake with the raspberry buttercream, creating smooth sides and edges. Then, freeze the entire cake until it's firm (about 5 minutes). Next, slather on the thick chocolate ganache coating and use a cake scraper for clean sides. You will need to work quickly because the cold buttercream will cool the ganache. The more even your buttercream and ganache layers are here, the neater the cake slice will look at the end. It's worth it!

PASSION FRUIT COCONUT CAKE *with*
Coconut Buttercream and Passion Fruit Curd

This cake is perfect for warm summer days, or even for when you're wishing for warm days ahead. If you want your kitchen to smell like a tropical oasis, this cake will take you there. My soft coconut layers filled with passion fruit curd, frosted with coconut passion fruit buttercream, and topped with even more passion fruit curd will have you ready for summer no matter what month it is. I knew I wanted to use fresh passion fruit in my curd, so I was happy to find a few of them at a specialty grocery store near us. Have you ever sliced into a passion fruit before? The inside is . . . different! My sons thought I had found an alien egg or something. But my goodness, does that passion fruit sure make a tasty curd! I wanted to spread it on toast and drizzle it on pancakes as soon as I tasted it.

Coconut Cake

- ¾ cup buttermilk (room temperature)
- ⅔ cup sour cream (room temperature)
- 4 egg whites (room temperature)
- ⅓ cup vegetable oil
- 2 tablespoons coconut emulsion
- 1 tablespoon pure vanilla extract
- 1 box white cake mix

Passion Fruit Curd

- 4 passion fruits, pulp only (about ¼ cup total), seeds left in
- 2 tablespoons granulated sugar
- 1 teaspoon lemon juice
- 2 egg yolks
- 3 tablespoons butter

Coconut Passion Fruit Buttercream

- 1½ cups (3 sticks) unsalted butter
- ½ cup 100 percent passion fruit juice
- 4 passion fruits, pulp only, seeds strained and removed (a little less than ¼ cup strained pulp)
- 1 tablespoon pure vanilla extract
- 1 teaspoon coconut emulsion
- Pinch of salt
- 7 to 8 cups powdered sugar
- 3 tablespoons heavy cream (if needed)

For Decorating

- Passion fruit halves

For the Coconut Cake

Preheat the oven to 325°F, then prep three 6-inch round cake pans with a swipe of shortening and dusting of flour to prevent sticking.

In a large bowl, whisk together the buttermilk, sour cream, egg whites, oil, coconut emulsion, and vanilla until thoroughly combined. Sift in the cake mix and whisk until just combined. Do not overmix. Split the batter evenly among the prepared pans.

Bake for 27 to 30 minutes, until the center is baked through. Let the cakes cool in the pan for a minute before carefully flipping them out onto a wire rack to cool completely. Wrap and freeze the cakes before assembly.

For the Passion Fruit Curd

In a small saucepan over low heat, whisk together the passion fruit pulp, sugar, lemon juice, and egg yolks until slightly bubbling, 3 to 5 minutes. Add the butter, 1 tablespoon at a time, and stir until it melts completely into the filling. Transfer to a glass dish, cover, and refrigerate until thickened and cooled completely.

For the Coconut Passion Fruit Buttercream

In the bowl of a stand mixer fitted with a paddle attachment, beat the butter on medium speed until it's light and fluffy, about 2 minutes. Add

the passion fruit juice and pulp, vanilla, coconut emulsion, and salt and beat again until combined, then scrape down the sides with a spatula.

With the mixer on low speed, add the powdered sugar about ½ cup at a time. Add the heavy cream if needed to thin it out, and then flip the mixer to high speed and beat until the buttercream is lighter in color and texture, about 2 minutes.

To Assemble and Decorate

Place a cardboard cake round on a cake turntable. Dot a little bit of buttercream in the center of the round and spread it out with an angled icing spatula. Place the first chilled cake layer in the center. Add a thin layer of buttercream. Pipe a buttercream dam around the outside rim of the frosted cake layer, and then fill with about ½ cup of the curd. Place the next cake layer on top, then repeat, making sure to line the layers up evenly. After adding the top cake layer, crumb coat the cake by spreading a thin layer of buttercream around the entire cake. Freeze for 2 minutes to set the buttercream.

Using a wooden spoon, beat out any air bubbles in the remaining buttercream. Spread a thick final layer of buttercream on the sides of the cake, using a cake scraper for smooth sides and clean edges. Add a little crown of the remaining passion fruit curd around the top rim in a circle.

Place sliced passion fruit on top as garnish.

TIP: The riper your passion fruits are, the sweeter your curd will be. If you prefer to have no seeds (they seemed less crunchy after they were cooked), you can strain them out. However, you may need to grab a few more passion fruits so you still have plenty of pulp to work with. If you'd like to use frozen passion fruit, that will work just as well here.

TOASTED COCONUT LIME CAKE *with Toasted Coconut Buttercream and Lime Curd*

Each summer, little shaved ice stands seem to pop up in almost every grocery store parking lot around us. One particular place my family loves to visit has an option of adding ice cream in the middle of the shaved ice cone or even toasted coconut on top. Now that was a game changer! The list of flavorings to choose from is long, but I always come back to coconut and lime (in addition to some kind of mango, pineapple, guava, or peach flavor). It tastes like a piña colada Slurpee I used to drink when I was younger and will always remind me of summertime.

Coconut Lime Cake

- ¾ cup buttermilk (room temperature)
- ⅔ cup sour cream (room temperature)
- 4 egg whites (room temperature)
- ⅓ cup vegetable oil
- 2 tablespoons coconut emulsion
- 1 tablespoon pure vanilla extract
- 1 tablespoon lime juice
- Zest of 2 limes (1 teaspoon zest)
- 1 box white cake mix

Lime Curd

- ¾ cup granulated sugar
- 3 large egg yolks
- ½ cup lime juice
- Zest of 1 to 2 limes
- 4 tablespoons unsalted butter
- 1 drop lime-green gel coloring

Toasted Coconut Buttercream

- 1½ cups (3 sticks) unsalted butter
- 1 cup crushed toasted sweetened shredded coconut (see Tip)
- ¼ cup heavy cream (plus more if needed)
- 1 tablespoon pure vanilla extract
- 2 teaspoons coconut emulsion
- Pinch of salt
- 7 to 8 cups powdered sugar

For Decorating

- Limes, a mix of halved, sliced, and quartered plus curls of zest

For the Coconut Lime Cake

Preheat the oven to 325°F, then prep three 6-inch round cake pans with a swipe of shortening and dusting of flour to prevent sticking.

In a large bowl, whisk together the buttermilk, sour cream, egg whites, oil, coconut emulsion, vanilla, and lime juice and zest until thoroughly combined. Sift in the cake mix and whisk until just combined. Do not overmix. Split the batter evenly among the prepared pans.

Bake for 27 to 30 minutes, until the center is baked through. Let the cakes cool in the pan for a minute before carefully flipping them out onto a wire rack to cool completely. Wrap and freeze the cakes before assembly.

For the Lime Curd

In a medium saucepan over low heat, whisk together the sugar, egg yolks, and lime juice and zest until thick and bubbly, 3 to 5 minutes. Add the butter, 1 tablespoon at a time, and stir until it melts completely into the filling. Add the gel coloring for a soft green hue. Transfer the curd to a glass bowl, cover, and refrigerate until thickened and cooled completely.

For the Toasted Coconut Buttercream

In the bowl of a stand mixer fitted with a paddle attachment, beat the butter on medium speed until it's light and fluffy, about 2 minutes. Add the toasted coconut, heavy cream, vanilla, coconut emulsion, and salt and beat again until combined, then scrape down the sides with a spatula.

With the mixer on low speed, add the powdered sugar about ½ cup at a time. The buttercream will be thick. Add a little more heavy cream, 1 tablespoon at a time, to thin it out if needed, and then flip the mixer to high speed and beat until the buttercream is lighter in color and texture, about 2 minutes.

To Assemble and Decorate

Place a cardboard cake round on a cake turntable. Dot a little bit of buttercream in the center of the round and spread it out with an angled icing spatula. Place the first chilled cake layer in the center. Add a thin layer of buttercream. Pipe a buttercream dam around the outside rim of the frosted cake layer, and then fill with about ½ cup of the curd. Place the next cake layer on top, then repeat, making sure to line the layers up evenly. After adding the top cake layer, crumb coat the cake by spreading a thin layer of buttercream around the entire cake. Freeze for 2 minutes to set the buttercream.

Using a wooden spoon, beat out any air bubbles in the remaining buttercream. Spread a thick final layer of buttercream around the entire cake, using a cake scraper for smooth sides. Leave the top edge uneven for a more rustic look.

Place the limes and lime zest curls on top of the cake for garnish.

TIP: To make an evenly toasted batch of coconut all at once, spread the coconut in an even layer on a cookie sheet and bake slowly at 325°F in the oven. Stir when you see the coconut start to look a little toasted, and then bake for another 30 seconds. Repeat until the coconut is golden brown all over. Let cool completely, then add it to your buttercream.

STRAWBERRY CHEESECAKE CAKE *with*
Graham Cracker Crust and Strawberry Filling

Sometimes my favorite way to come up with a new cake flavor is to use another famous dessert as my inspiration. I borrow elements we all know and love from the dessert and transform it right into a cake. In this cake, I took a strawberry cheesecake and made the best cake version I could think of. It was an instant hit! With a graham cracker crust on the bottom, cheesecake cake layers, strawberry filling, cream cheese buttercream, and fresh strawberries on top, it was love at first bite. The cream-cheese cake batter is baked right onto the graham cracker crust, and the cake looks almost like a cheesecake when it comes out of the oven. The smell and taste will certainly remind you of one, too.

Strawberry Cheesecake Cake with Graham Cracker Crust

- 9 whole graham crackers
- ¼ cup packed brown sugar
- 6 tablespoons unsalted butter, melted
- 1 cup buttermilk (room temperature)
- ⅓ cup sour cream (room temperature)
- 4 egg whites (room temperature)
- 4 ounces cream cheese, softened
- ½ cup vegetable oil
- 1 tablespoon pure vanilla extract
- 1 tablespoon cream cheese emulsion (optional)
- 1 box white cake mix

Strawberry Sauce/ Filling

- 1 cup granulated sugar
- 2 tablespoons cornstarch
- 1 (3-ounce) package strawberry Jell-O, with 1 tablespoon of the mix removed

Cream Cheese Buttercream

- 1 cup (2 sticks) unsalted butter
- 8 ounces (1 brick) cream cheese
- ¼ cup heavy cream
- 1 tablespoon pure vanilla extract
- Pinch of salt
- 7 to 8 cups powdered sugar

For Decorating

- 1 cup sliced strawberries, plus enough whole strawberries to cover the top of the cake
- Red gel coloring
- Crumbled graham crackers
- Piping bag
- Wilton 1M piping tip

For the Strawberry Cheesecake Cake with Graham Cracker Crust

Preheat the oven to 325°F, then prep three 6-inch round cake pans with a swipe of shortening and dusting of flour to prevent sticking.

In a food processor, pulse together the graham crackers, brown sugar, and butter until a crust forms. Split the crust mixture evenly among the prepared pans and press to firm with the bottom of a glass or flat measuring cup.

In a large bowl, whisk together the buttermilk, sour cream, egg whites, cream cheese, oil, vanilla, and cream cheese emulsion (if using) until thoroughly combined. Sift in the cake mix and whisk until just combined. Do not overmix. Split the batter evenly among the pans.

Bake for 30 to 32 minutes, until the center is baked through. Let the cakes cool in the pan for a minute before flipping them out onto a wire rack to cool completely. Wrap and freeze the cakes before assembly.

For the Strawberry Sauce/Filling

In a small saucepan over medium heat, stir together the sugar and 1 cup of water and heat until boiling. Add the cornstarch and Jell-O. (Remember to remove 1 tablespoon of the Jell-O mix!)

Remove from the heat and stir until combined. The mixture should thicken slightly as it cools. Transfer to a glass container, cover, and

refrigerate until cooled completely. You want it to have a thick, sauce-like texture. If it sets up too firm (more like Jell-O), you can microwave it for 10 seconds to get it back to the right consistency.

For the Cream Cheese Buttercream

In the bowl of a stand mixer fitted with a paddle attachment, beat the butter on medium speed until it's light and fluffy, then add the cream cheese and beat until fully incorporated. Add the heavy cream, vanilla, and salt and beat again until combined, then scrape down the sides with a spatula.

With the mixer on low speed, add the powdered sugar about ½ cup at a time. The buttercream will be thick. Add a little more heavy cream, 1 tablespoon at a time, to thin it out if needed, and then flip the mixer to high speed and beat until the buttercream is lighter in color and texture, about 2 minutes.

Transfer ⅔ cup buttercream to a small bowl, add 1 drop of red gel coloring, and stir until incorporated. Set aside.

To Assemble

Place a cardboard cake round on a cake turntable. Dot a little bit of the buttercream in the center of the round and spread it out with an angled icing spatula. Place the first chilled cake layer in the center, crust side down. Add a thin layer of buttercream. Pipe a buttercream dam around the outside rim of the frosted cake layer, fill with about ½ cup of the strawberry filling, and then place thinly sliced strawberries in an even layer. Place the next cake layer on top and repeat, making sure to line the layers up evenly. After adding the top cake layer, crumb coat the cake

by spreading a thin layer of buttercream around the entire cake. Freeze for 2 minutes to set the buttercream.

Using a wooden spoon, beat out any air bubbles in the remaining buttercream. Finish frosting the cake as desired or follow the decorating instructions below.

To Decorate the Cake

Spread a final layer of buttercream around the entire cake, using a cake scraper for smooth sides and clean edges. With a straight icing spatula, spread the red buttercream along the bottom edge of the cake, then gently pull the red buttercream upward all around the sides. Press a thin layer of graham cracker crumbles onto the cake along the bottom edge.

Using the Wilton 1M tip, pipe a shell border around the top outside rim of the cake. Sprinkle graham cracker crumbles over the shell border.

Add whole sliced strawberries on the top of the cake inside the border, then drizzle on the strawberry sauce.

TIP: The filling and topping get that classic strawberry-sauce texture and flavor from Jell-O. I remove 1 tablespoon from the package to make the mixture saucier (otherwise it gets too firm). If you don't have time for Jell-O, you can use premade strawberry sauce as a quick substitute.

ORANGE MERINGUE CAKE *with Orange Vanilla Buttercream and Orange Curd Filling*

After driving past an orange orchard in California and taking in that tangy, sweet smell, I wished I could bottle up the scent and keep it with me forever. I created this dreamy orange meringue cake with that moment in mind. The orange cake layers, which use fresh orange juice and zest, will fill your kitchen with that dreamy fragrance. And the orange curd—*oh, this orange curd!* It is heaven-sent with its almost-marmalade texture. I slice the cake layers horizontally (into 6 layers) in order to get double the filling in this cake. An airy meringue on top looks gorgeous and tastes perfect with the orange cake, filling, and buttercream underneath.

Orange Cake

- ¾ cup buttermilk (room temperature)
- ⅔ cup sour cream (room temperature)
- 4 egg whites (room temperature)
- ⅓ cup vegetable oil
- 1 tablespoon pure vanilla extract
- ¼ cup orange juice
- Zest of 1 orange (1 tablespoon)
- ¼ cup flour
- 1 box white cake mix

Orange Curd

- ½ cup sugar
- ½ cup orange juice
- Zest of 2 oranges (2 tablespoons)
- 2 egg yolks
- 1 tablespoon cornstarch
- 1 teaspoon lemon juice
- 2 tablespoons unsalted butter

Orange Vanilla Bean Buttercream

- 1 batch Vanilla Buttercream (page xvii; use only 2 teaspoons pure vanilla extract)
- Zest of 1 orange (1 tablespoon)
- 2 teaspoons orange juice
- 1 teaspoon vanilla bean paste

Toasted Meringue

- 4 egg whites
- ¾ cup sugar
- 1 teaspoon pure vanilla extract
- Pinch of salt

For Decorating

- Kitchen blowtorch

For the Orange Cake

Preheat the oven to 325°F, then prep three 6-inch round cake pans with a swipe of shortening and dusting of flour to prevent sticking.

In a large bowl, whisk together the buttermilk, sour cream, egg whites, oil, vanilla, and orange juice and zest until thoroughly combined. Sift in the flour and cake mix and whisk until just combined. Do not overmix. Split the batter evenly among the prepared pans.

Bake for 27 to 30 minutes, until the center is baked through. Let the cakes cool in the pan for a minute before flipping them out onto a wire rack to cool completely. Slice each cake round in half horizontally to create 6 layers. Wrap and freeze the cakes before assembly.

For the Orange Curd

In a medium saucepan over medium heat, whisk together the sugar, orange juice and zest, egg yolks, cornstarch, and lemon juice until thick and bubbly, about 3 minutes. Add the butter and stir until it melts completely. Pour the curd into a glass container, cover, and refrigerate until thickened and cooled completely.

For the Orange Vanilla Bean Buttercream

In the bowl of a stand mixer fitted with a paddle attachment, beat together the buttercream, orange zest and juice, and vanilla bean paste until combined, then scrape down the sides with a spatula.

To Assemble

Place a cardboard cake round on a cake turntable. Dot a little bit of buttercream in the center of the round and spread it out with an angled icing spatula. Place the first chilled cake layer in the center. Add a thin layer of buttercream. Pipe a buttercream dam around the outside rim of the frosted cake layer, and then fill with about ¼ cup of the orange curd. Place the next cake layer on top, then repeat, making sure to line the layers up evenly. After adding the top cake layer, crumb coat the cake by spreading a thin layer of buttercream around the entire cake. Freeze for 2 minutes to set the buttercream.

Using a wooden spoon, beat out any air bubbles in the remaining buttercream. Spread a final layer of buttercream around the entire cake, using a cake scraper for smooth sides and clean edges. Freeze for 2 minutes to firm.

For the Toasted Meringue

Once the cake is frosted, place the metal bowl of a stand mixer with the egg whites and sugar over a double boiler (a small pan with about an inch of boiling water). Whisk constantly until the sugar dissolves, about 3 minutes. Place the bowl back on the stand mixer fitted with a whisk attachment and whip on medium speed until soft peaks form. Increase the speed to high and whip until stiff peaks form. Add the vanilla and salt, then whip again until combined.

Spread the meringue over the entire cake, using a straight icing spatula on the sides and top to make a rustic design. Freeze the meringue for 3 minutes, then carefully use a kitchen torch to lightly toast the meringue.

TIP: If you're making this cake in advance, I suggest waiting to make the meringue until the day of your gathering. This way you can keep the texture of the meringue at its peak (no pun intended).

STRAWBERRY-PEACH CAKE

This cake is inspired by one of my favorite desserts to make: my strawberry-peach crumb bars. Although this one doesn't have the crumb (which you could always add, following the recipe from some of my other cakes, such as Peach Cobbler Cupcakes from *Cake Confidence* or Apple Pie Cake from my blog), I love how well the peach and strawberry come together. To preserve the peach flavor in the buttercream without sacrificing the smooth consistency, I puree some of the peach filling and add it to the buttercream.

Strawberry Cake
- ⅔ cup buttermilk (room temperature)
- ⅔ cup sour cream (room temperature)
- 3 large eggs plus 1 egg white (room temperature)
- ⅓ cup vegetable oil
- ¼ cup freeze-dried strawberries, pulsed into a fine powder
- 1 tablespoon pure vanilla extract
- 1 tablespoon strawberry emulsion
- 1 box strawberry cake mix

Peach Filling
- 3 to 4 large ripe peaches (2 cups chopped or 16 ounces frozen peaches), diced small
- ½ cup packed brown sugar
- 1 tablespoon lemon juice
- 1 teaspoon ground cinnamon
- Pinch of ground nutmeg
- 1 teaspoon cornstarch

Peach Buttercream
- 1½ cups (3 sticks) unsalted butter
- ½ cup pureed Peach Filling (recipe above)
- ¼ cup heavy cream (plus more if needed)
- 1 tablespoon pure vanilla extract
- ½ teaspoon peach flavoring (optional)
- Pinch of salt
- 7 to 8 cups powdered sugar

For Decorating
- Peach slices and fresh strawberries

For the Strawberry Cake
Preheat the oven to 325°F, then prep three 6-inch round cake pans with a swipe of shortening and dusting of flour to prevent sticking.

In a large bowl, whisk together the buttermilk, sour cream, eggs, oil, freeze-dried strawberry powder, vanilla, and strawberry emulsion until thoroughly combined. Sift in the cake mix and whisk until just combined. Do not overmix. Split the batter evenly among the prepared pans.

Bake for 27 to 30 minutes, until the center is baked through. Let the cakes cool in the pan for a minute before flipping them out onto a wire rack to cool completely. Wrap and freeze the cakes before assembly.

For the Peach Filling
In a medium saucepan over medium heat, stir together the diced peaches, brown sugar, lemon juice, cinnamon, and nutmeg until the filling is thick and bubbly, 3 to 5 minutes. In a small cup, stir together the cornstarch with 2 tablespoons of water to make a slurry. Add the slurry to the peach filling and stir until thickened, about 2 minutes. Transfer to a glass dish, cover, and refrigerate until cooled completely.

For the Peach Buttercream
In the bowl of a stand mixer fitted with a paddle attachment, beat the butter on medium speed until it's light and fluffy. Add the peach puree, heavy cream, vanilla, peach flavoring (if using), and salt and beat again until combined, then scrape down the sides with a spatula.

With the mixer on low speed, add the powdered sugar about ½ cup at a time. The buttercream will be thick. Add a little more heavy cream, 1 tablespoon at a time, to thin it out if needed, and then flip the mixer to high speed and

beat until the buttercream is lighter in color and texture, about 2 minutes.

To Assemble

Place a cardboard cake round on a cake turntable. Dot a little bit of buttercream in the center of the round and spread it out with an angled icing spatula. Place the first chilled cake layer in the center. Add a thin layer of buttercream. Pipe a buttercream dam around the outside rim of the frosted cake layer, then add about ½ cup of the peach filling. Place the next cake layer on top, then repeat, making sure to line the layers up evenly. After adding on the top cake layer, crumb coat the cake by spreading a thin layer of buttercream around the entire cake. Freeze for 2 minutes to set the buttercream.

Using a wooden spoon, beat out any air bubbles in the remaining buttercream. Spread a final layer of buttercream around the entire cake, using a straight icing spatula to make rustic swoops on the side.

Place peach slices and fresh strawberries on the top.

TIP: You don't need fancy cake tools to frost a cake. Although they are most certainly helpful, they aren't always essential. I used a straight icing spatula but you can use a regular knife to get this rustic buttercream look and added on fresh strawberries and peaches. When it comes to rustic cakes, straight sides and clean edges are out, and lines and buttercream ridges are in.

PIÑA COLADA CAKE *with Coconut Buttercream and Pineapple Curd*

For our honeymoon, my husband and I were lucky enough to go to Molokai, a small, lesser-visited island in Hawaii. One afternoon we decided to find a couple of pineapples to snack on. Everyone isn't kidding when they say that pineapple tastes different in Hawaii. They were right! It was almost like it was an entirely different fruit. The flavor was so deep and much more intense than I had ever experienced before. It tasted like pineapple, but every bite was something I'll never forget. This cake, inspired by that memory, stars pineapple, surrounded by what I like to call a tropical-cake oasis.

Pineapple Cake
- ⅔ cup buttermilk (room temperature)
- ⅔ cup sour cream (room temperature)
- 3 egg whites (room temperature)
- ⅓ cup vegetable oil
- 1 tablespoon pure vanilla extract
- 1 box pineapple cake mix

Pineapple Curd
- 1 cup diced pineapple (fresh or canned), pureed
- ¼ cup granulated sugar
- 2 egg yolks
- 1 teaspoon cornstarch
- 2 tablespoons unsalted butter

Coconut Buttercream
- 1½ cups (3 sticks) unsalted butter
- ¼ cup coconut milk
- ¼ cup heavy cream (plus more if needed)
- 1 tablespoon pure vanilla extract
- 1 tablespoon coconut emulsion
- Pinch of salt
- 7 to 8 cups powdered sugar

For Decorating
- 8 maraschino cherries with stems (see Tip)
- 8 fresh pineapple wedges
- Piping bag
- Wilton 1A circle piping tip

For the Pineapple Cake
Preheat the oven to 325°F, then prep three 6-inch round cake pans with a swipe of shortening and dusting of flour to prevent sticking.

In a large bowl, whisk together the buttermilk, sour cream, egg whites, oil, and vanilla until thoroughly combined. Sift in the cake mix and whisk until just combined. Do not overmix. Split the batter evenly among the prepared pans.

Bake for 27 to 30 minutes, until the center is baked through. Let the cakes cool in the pan for a minute before flipping them out onto a wire rack to cool completely. Wrap and freeze the cakes before assembly.

For the Pineapple Curd
In a medium saucepan over medium heat, whisk together the pineapple puree, sugar, and egg yolks until bubbly, 2 to 5 minutes. In a small cup, whisk together the cornstarch and 1 tablespoon of water to make a slurry. Add to the pineapple curd and cook, stirring, until thickened, about 1 minute. Remove from the heat.

Add the butter, 1 tablespoon at a time, stirring between each addition. Transfer to a glass dish, cover, and refrigerate until thickened and cooled completely.

For the Coconut Buttercream
In the bowl of a stand mixer fitted with a paddle attachment, beat the butter on medium speed until it's light and fluffy. Add the coconut milk, heavy cream, vanilla, coconut emulsion, and salt and beat again until combined, then scrape down the sides with a spatula.

With the mixer on low speed, add the powdered sugar about ½ cup at a time. The buttercream will be thick. Add a little more heavy

cream, 1 tablespoon at a time, to thin it out if needed, and then flip the mixer to high speed and beat until the buttercream is lighter in color and texture, about 2 minutes.

To Assemble and Decorate

Place a cardboard cake round on a cake turntable. Dot a little bit of buttercream in the center of the round and spread it out with an angled icing spatula. Place the first chilled cake layer in the center. Add a thin layer of buttercream. Pipe a buttercream dam around the outside rim of the frosted cake layer, and then add about ½ cup of the pineapple curd. Place the next cake layer on top, then repeat, making sure to line the layers up evenly. After adding the top cake layer, crumb coat the cake by spreading a thin layer of buttercream around the entire cake. Freeze for 2 minutes to set the buttercream.

Using a wooden spoon, beat out any air bubbles in the remaining buttercream. Spread a final layer of buttercream around the entire cake, using a cake scraper for smooth sides and clean edges.

Fit a piping bag with the Wilton 1A tip, fill it with buttercream, and pipe 8 small swirls of buttercream on top of the cake, then gently place a maraschino cherry on each swirl. Place a fresh pineapple wedge between each swirl.

TIP: Using fresh (versus canned) pineapple will give you different results for the curd. The flavor of fresh is so much better, but the acid tends to react differently with the other curd ingredients. Make sure to let the pineapple curd thicken enough before storing it to cool. The flavor will also have more of an opportunity to intensify—a win-win.

To avoid the maraschino cherries dripping onto your white buttercream, drain them, then let them finish draining on a paper towel before placing them on the cake.

CHERRY LIME SWIRL CAKE

I love baking with fresh ingredients like cherries and limes, but sometimes it's fun to switch things up and use other mediums to achieve a similar (and sometimes more candy-like) flavor. This cake is inspired by some cherry lime cookies I used to make: pink cookies flavored with cherry Jell-O, frosted with lime buttercream made with lime Jell-O (yes, lots of Jell-O happening with this one), and topped off with maraschino cherries. They were bright and bold and tasted almost like a cherry limeade. I used both Jell-O flavorings in this cake to echo those cookies, but you can always use cherry emulsion and lime zest if you'd prefer to go that route. Since the flavors are so playful, I gave it an equally whimsical design. The stripes on the outside and the swirls on the inside really make it something fun not only to make but to eat.

Cherry Lime Swirl Cake

- ¾ cup buttermilk (room temperature)
- ⅔ cup sour cream (room temperature)
- 4 egg whites (room temperature)
- ⅓ cup vegetable oil
- 1 tablespoon pure vanilla extract
- 1 box white cake mix
- 1 (3-ounce) package lime Jell-O, 1 tablespoon removed (or 2 tablespoons lime zest plus 1 tablespoon lime juice)
- 1 (3-ounce) package cherry Jell-O, 1 tablespoon removed (or 1 tablespoon cherry emulsion)
- 1 drop light green gel coloring (optional)
- 2 drops red gel coloring (optional)

Cherry and Lime Stripe Buttercream

- ¾ cup heavy cream (plus more if needed)
- 2 tablespoons lime Jell-O powder
- 2 tablespoons cherry Jell-O powder
- 1½ cups (3 sticks) unsalted butter
- 1 tablespoon pure vanilla extract
- Pinch of salt
- 7 to 8 cups powdered sugar
- 1 drop light green gel coloring
- 2 drops red gel coloring

For Decorating

- 12 maraschino cherries with stems
- Thick-stripe cake comb
- Piping bag
- Wilton 21 piping tip (or any small French tip)

For the Cherry Lime Swirl Cake

Preheat the oven to 325°F, then prep three 6-inch round cake pans with a swipe of shortening and dusting of flour to prevent sticking.

In a large bowl, whisk together the buttermilk, sour cream, egg whites, oil, and vanilla until thoroughly combined. Sift in the cake mix and whisk until just combined. Do not overmix. Split the batter in half, and add the lime Jell-O powder (or lime zest) to one bowl and the cherry Jell-O powder (or cherry emulsion) to the other. (Don't forget to remove a tablespoon from each Jell-O.) Add gel coloring to the respective flavors (green to lime, red to cherry) and stir gently.

Split the batter evenly among the prepared pans, alternating scoops of red and green batter. With a toothpick, gently swirl the batter in a figure-eight pattern to create the marbled effect.

Bake for 27 to 30 minutes, until the center is baked through. Let the cakes cool in the pan for a minute before flipping them out onto a wire rack to cool completely. Wrap and freeze the cakes before assembly.

For the Cherry and Lime Stripe Buttercream

Whisk together ¼ cup of the heavy cream and the lime Jell-O in a small cup and ¼ cup of heavy cream and the cherry Jell-O in another. Let sit for 5 minutes to hydrate the powder. Set aside until after the buttercream is mixed.

In the bowl of a stand mixer fitted with a paddle attachment, beat the butter on medium speed until it's light and fluffy. Add the remaining ¼ cup heavy cream, the vanilla, and salt and beat again until combined, then scrape down the sides with a spatula.

With the mixer on low speed, add the powdered sugar about ½ cup at a time. The buttercream will be thick. Add a little more heavy cream, 1 tablespoon at a time, to thin out if needed, and then flip the mixer to high speed and beat until the buttercream is lighter in color and texture, about 2 minutes.

In two separate bowls, transfer about 1½ cups of buttercream in each. In one bowl, stir in the cherry mixture. To the other, stir in the lime mixture. Add the gel coloring to the respective flavors. Transfer the cherry buttercream to a piping bag without a tip.

To Assemble and Decorate

Place a cardboard cake round on a cake turntable. Dot a little bit of lime buttercream in the center of the round and spread it out with an angled icing spatula. Place the first chilled cake layer in the center. Add a thin layer of lime buttercream. Place the next cake layer on top, then repeat, making sure to line the layers up evenly. After adding the top cake layer, crumb coat the cake by spreading a thin layer of lime buttercream around the entire cake. Freeze for 2 minutes to set the buttercream.

Using a wooden spoon, beat out any air bubbles in the remaining buttercream flavors. Spread a final layer of lime buttercream around the entire cake, using a cake scraper for an even coat. Using the thick-stripe cake comb, scrape stripe indents into the cake. The cleaner the stripe indents, the neater the stripes. Freeze for 10 minutes. Pipe the cherry buttercream in the indents, then use a cake scraper to slowly smooth and reveal the stripes. Keep scraping and apply a bit of pressure to get clean stripes.

Transfer the remaining cherry buttercream to a piping bag fitted with the Wilton 21 tip and pipe small swirls of buttercream in a crown around the top rim of the cake. Gently place a maraschino cherry on each swirl.

TIP: The longer the Jell-O powder sits in the cake batter or buttercream, the better the flavor and the less grainy the texture.

Don't use the full package of Jell-O. A little bit goes a long way, and too much will overpower the cake.

The Jell-O creates the softest shades of pink and green, but if you'd like to have a little more color, add a single drop of green or pink gel coloring to make those colors really sing!

CHERRY PIE CAKE *with Graham Cracker Buttercream and Cherry Pie Filling*

Doesn't this cake just scream summertime barbecues or the Fourth of July? I packed some really fun textures and flavors into this cake to make it hopefully stand up to the quintessential cherry pie.

First, we have the cherry pie cake, with lovely pockets of cherries throughout the white cake batter. Next, we have the graham cracker buttercream. I love this stuff. To evoke summer picnics and gatherings, I opted for a basketweave design on the sides and, of course, a classic lattice pattern on top.

Cherry Pie Filling

- 2 cups pitted fresh cherries
- 1 cup granulated sugar
- 2 teaspoons lemon juice
- ½ teaspoon lemon zest
- Pinch of salt
- 1 tablespoon cornstarch

Cherry Pie Cake

- ¾ cup buttermilk (room temperature)
- ⅔ cup sour cream (room temperature)
- 1 large egg plus 3 egg whites (room temperature)
- ⅓ cup vegetable oil
- 1 tablespoon pure vanilla extract
- 1 box white cake mix

- ⅔ cup Cherry Pie Filling (recipe above; see Tip)

Graham Cracker Buttercream

- 1½ cups (3 sticks) unsalted butter
- 8 graham crackers, pulsed to a fine powder (see Tip)
- ¼ cup heavy cream (plus more if needed)
- 1 tablespoon vanilla bean paste
- 2 teaspoons pure vanilla extract
- Pinch of salt
- 7 to 8 cups powdered sugar

For Decorating

- Piping bags
- Wilton 2B (basketweave), 6B (French), and 10 (small circle) piping tips

For the Cherry Pie Filling

In a medium saucepan over medium heat, stir together the cherries, 1 cup of water, the sugar, lemon juice and zest, and salt and simmer until the mixture thickens slightly, 5 to 7 minutes. In a small cup, whisk together the cornstarch and 1 tablespoon of water to make a slurry. Add to the cherry pie mixture and continue to cook until thickened, about 2 minutes. Transfer to a glass dish, cover, then refrigerate until thickened and cooled completely.

For the Cherry Pie Cake

Preheat the oven to 325°F, then prep three 6-inch round cake pans with a swipe of shortening and dusting of flour to prevent sticking.

In a large bowl, whisk together the buttermilk, sour cream, eggs, oil, and vanilla until thoroughly combined. Sift in the cake mix and whisk until just combined. Do not overmix. Gently fold in the cherry pie filling. Split the batter evenly among the prepared pans.

Bake for 30 to 32 minutes, until the center is baked through. Let the cakes cool in the pan for a minute before flipping them out onto a wire rack to cool completely. Wrap and freeze the cakes before assembly.

For the Graham Cracker Buttercream

In the bowl of a stand mixer fitted with a paddle attachment, beat the butter on medium speed until it's light and fluffy. Add the graham cracker powder, heavy cream, vanilla bean paste, vanilla, and salt and beat again until combined, then scrape down the sides with a spatula.

With the mixer on low speed, add the powdered sugar about ½ cup at a time. The buttercream will be thick. Add a little more heavy cream, 1 tablespoon at a time, to thin it out if needed, and then flip the mixer to high speed and beat until the buttercream is lighter in color and texture, about 2 minutes.

To Assemble

Place a cardboard cake round on a cake turntable. Dot a little bit of buttercream in the center of the round and spread it out with an angled icing spatula. Place the first chilled cake layer in the center. Add a thin layer of buttercream. Pipe a buttercream dam around the outside rim of the frosted cake layer, then add about ½ cup of the cherry pie filling. Place the next cake layer on top, then repeat, making sure to line the layers up evenly. After adding the top cake layer, crumb coat the cake by spreading a thin layer of buttercream around the entire cake. Freeze for 2 minutes to set the buttercream.

Using a wooden spoon, beat out any air bubbles in the remaining buttercream. Finish frosting the cake as desired or follow the decorating instructions below.

To Decorate the Cake

Fit a piping bag with the Wilton 2B tip and fill with buttercream. Pipe a straight line vertically from the bottom to the top of the side of the cake. Pipe a series of 1-inch horizontal lines over the vertical line, with a little less than an inch between them. Pipe another vertical line next to the first, then add another set of horizontal lines, staggered between the previous ones. Repeat the pattern until it goes around the entire cake.

Around the top rim, pipe a shell border using the #6B tip. Add the remaining cherry pie filling to the center of the top of the cake. Switch to the #10 tip and carefully pipe parallel lines on top of the cherry filling. Pipe another set of parallel lines perpendicular to the first ones to create a lattice look on top.

TIP: When making your graham cracker buttercream, make sure to process the graham crackers into a very fine powder. This will enable the buttercream to flow freely through the intricate piping tips on the side and top of your cake without getting stuck.

You can practice piping the buttercream design on a sheet of parchment paper before trying it on your actual cake. When you're comfortable with the technique, simply scrape the buttercream off the parchment and back into your piping bag. Now you're ready to go!

If you're in a crunch for time, replace the homemade cherry pie filling with canned cherry pie filling from the baking section of your local grocery store.

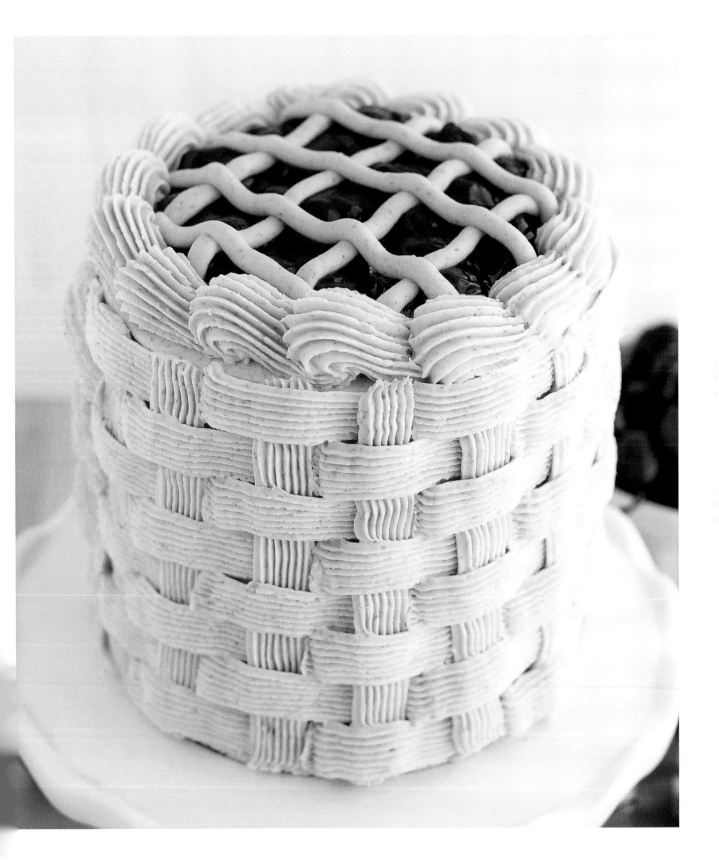

BLUEBERRY SHORTBREAD CRUMBLE CAKE

I challenge you to reread that title without salivating. It's not possible. Every part of this cake is my new favorite. With a fresh blueberry cake (isn't that color gorgeous?) baked right onto a shortbread crust, a fresh blueberry filling, blueberry buttercream, and a shortbread crumble on top, you might already be headed out the door to find as many blueberries as you can to make this cake immediately! The different textures and flavor combinations really create something special. This is now officially one of my top-five favorite cakes!

Blueberry Cake with Shortbread Crust

- 24 shortbread cookies (14 ounces, such as Sandies)
- 4 tablespoons unsalted butter, melted
- ½ cup buttermilk (room temperature)
- ½ cup sour cream (room temperature)
- ½ cup fresh blueberries, pureed
- 3 large eggs plus 1 egg white (room temperature)
- ⅓ cup vegetable oil
- 1 tablespoon pure vanilla extract
- 1 tablespoon blueberry emulsion
- 1 box white cake mix

Blueberry Filling

- 1 cup fresh blueberries
- ¼ cup plus 1 tablespoon granulated sugar
- 3 tablespoons lemon juice
- 2 teaspoons cornstarch

Blueberry Buttercream

- 1½ cups (3 sticks) unsalted butter
- ¼ cup heavy cream (plus more if needed)
- 1 tablespoon blueberry emulsion
- 1 tablespoon pure vanilla extract
- Pinch of salt
- 7 to 8 cups powdered sugar

Shortbread Crumble

- ⅔ cup reserved prepared shortbread crumble (from the cake; see below)

For Decorating

- Fresh blueberries
- Leaves from a blueberry plant, or small mint leaves (see Tip)

For the Blueberry Cake with Shortbread Crust

Preheat the oven to 325°F, then prep three 6-inch round cake pans with a swipe of shortening and dusting of flour to prevent sticking.

In a food processor, pulse together the shortbread cookies and melted butter until a fine crust forms. Reserve ⅔ cup of the shortbread crumble and set aside.

Split the rest of the crust mixture evenly among the prepared pans and press to firm with the bottom of a glass or flat measuring cup.

In a large bowl, whisk together the buttermilk, sour cream, blueberry puree, eggs, oil, vanilla, and blueberry emulsion until thoroughly combined. Sift in the cake mix and whisk until just combined. Do not overmix. Split the batter evenly among the prepared pans.

Bake for 32 to 35 minutes, until the center is baked through. Let the cakes cool in the pan for a minute before flipping them out onto a wire rack to cool completely. Wrap and freeze the cakes before assembly.

For the Blueberry Filling

In a small saucepan over medium heat, stir together the blueberries, sugar, and lemon juice and cook, stirring, until thick and bubbly, about 5 minutes. Sift in the cornstarch and stir until thickened, 2 to 3 minutes. Transfer the filling to a bowl, cover, and refrigerate until thickened and cooled completely.

For the Blueberry Buttercream

In the bowl of a stand mixer fitted with a paddle attachment, beat the butter on medium speed until it's light and fluffy. Add the heavy cream, blueberry emulsion, vanilla, and salt and beat again until combined, then scrape down the sides with a spatula.

With the mixer on low speed, add the powdered sugar about ½ cup at a time. The buttercream will be thick. Add a little more heavy cream, 1 tablespoon at a time, to thin it out if needed, and then flip the mixer to high speed and beat until the buttercream is lighter in color and texture, about 2 minutes.

For the Shortbread Crumble

Preheat the oven to 350°F. Spread out the reserved crumble on a cookie sheet lined with parchment paper. Bake for 7 to 10 minutes, until toasted and golden. Set aside to cool completely before adding to the cake.

To Assemble

Place a cardboard cake round on a cake turntable. Dot a little bit of buttercream in the center of the round and spread it out with an angled icing spatula. Place the first chilled cake layer in the center (crust side up). Add a thin layer of buttercream. Pipe a buttercream dam around the outside rim of the frosted cake layer, then add about ½ cup of the blueberry filling. Place the next cake layer on top, then repeat, making sure to line the layers up evenly. After adding the top cake layer, crumb coat the cake by spreading a thin layer of buttercream around the entire cake. Freeze for 2 minutes to set the buttercream.

Using a wooden spoon, beat out any air bubbles in the remaining buttercream. Finish frosting the cake as desired or follow the decorating instructions below.

To Decorate the Cake

Spread a final layer of buttercream around the entire cake, using a cake scraper for smooth sides. Leave the top edge uneven for a rustic look.

Press the blueberries in groups of three into the buttercream and add one leaf per trio. Sprinkle the reserved baked crumble over the top.

TIP: When decorating a cake with fresh leaves, make sure to research what is cake-safe, wash and dry the leaves thoroughly, and remind your guests that they're just for garnish. I used blueberry leaves from our blueberry plant in the garden, and they looked cute as a button next to the trio of blueberries pressed into the side of the cake.

RASPBERRY LEMONADE SWIRL CAKE *with*
Raspberry Lemonade Buttercream, Lemon Curd, and Raspberry Filling

This cake is double the fun with double the filling between each layer. I couldn't decide between lemon curd or raspberry filling, so I decided that using both would easily solve the problem. I was right! They are equally delicious, and both really enhance the lemon and raspberry flavors in this cake. I also slice my three cake rounds in half horizontally, creating six thin layers and therefore *more* space for the delicious fillings. If you're short on time, use store-bought lemon curd.

Raspberry Lemonade Swirl Cake

- ¾ cup buttermilk (room temperature)
- ⅔ cup sour cream (room temperature)
- 3 large eggs plus 1 egg white (room temperature)
- ⅓ cup vegetable oil
- 1 tablespoon pure vanilla extract
- Zest and juice of 1 lemon
- ¼ cup flour
- 1 box lemon cake mix
- 2 tablespoons raspberry emulsion
- 2 drops soft-pink gel coloring

Lemon Curd

- 1 large egg plus 3 egg yolks
- ¾ cup granulated sugar
- ½ cup lemon juice
- Zest of 2 lemons
- 4 tablespoons unsalted butter

Raspberry Filling

- 1 cup raspberry jam (homemade or store-bought)

Raspberry Lemonade Buttercream

- 1½ cups (3 sticks) unsalted butter
- ¼ cup heavy cream (plus more if needed)
- 1 tablespoon pure vanilla extract
- Pinch of salt
- 7 to 8 cups powdered sugar
- 1 teaspoon lemon extract
- 1 drop yellow gel coloring
- 1 teaspoon raspberry emulsion
- 1 drop red gel coloring

For Decorating

- Lemon slices
- Fresh raspberries
- Wavy cake scraper
- Piping bags
- Wilton 6B piping tip

For the Raspberry Lemonade Swirl Cake

Preheat the oven to 325°F, then prep three 6-inch round cake pans with a swipe of shortening and dusting of flour to prevent sticking.

In a large bowl, whisk together the buttermilk, sour cream, eggs, oil, vanilla, and lemon zest and juice until thoroughly combined. Sift in the flour and cake mix and whisk until just combined. Do not overmix. Divide the batter in half in two bowls, then gently fold the raspberry emulsion and gel coloring into one bowl. Split the batter evenly among the prepared pans, alternating between scoops of lemon and raspberry cake batter.

Bake for 30 to 32 minutes, until the center is baked through. Let the cakes cool in the pan for a minute before flipping them out onto a wire rack to cool completely. Slice each cake round in half horizontally so there are 6 layers. Wrap and freeze the cakes before assembly.

For the Lemon Curd

In a medium saucepan over medium heat, whisk together the eggs, sugar, lemon juice, and zest until the mixture thickens, 3 to 5 minutes. Remove the curd from the heat and add the butter, 1 tablespoon at a time. Strain the curd to remove the zest. Transfer to a glass dish, cover, and refrigerate until thickened and cooled completely.

For the Raspberry Lemonade Buttercream

In the bowl of a stand mixer fitted with a paddle attachment, beat the butter on medium speed until it's light and fluffy. Add the heavy cream, vanilla, and salt and beat again until combined, then scrape down the sides with a spatula.

With the mixer on low speed, add the powdered sugar about ½ cup at a time. The buttercream will be thick. Add a little more heavy cream, 1 tablespoon at a time, to thin it out if needed, and then flip the mixer to high speed and beat until the buttercream is lighter in color and texture, about 2 minutes.

Divide the buttercream between two bowls. Add the lemon extract and yellow gel coloring to one bowl and the raspberry emulsion and red gel coloring to the other. Fill one piping bag with lemon buttercream and one with raspberry buttercream.

To Assemble

Place a cardboard cake round on a cake turntable. Dot a little bit of buttercream in the center of the round and spread it out with an angled icing spatula. Place the first chilled cake layer in the center. Add a thin layer of either lemon or raspberry buttercream. Pipe a buttercream dam of the same flavor around the outside rim of the frosted cake layer, then add about ⅓ cup of the same flavor filling to match the buttercream. Place the next cake layer on top, then repeat, alternating flavors each time and making sure to line the layers up evenly. After adding the top cake layer, crumb coat the cake (use the lemon on the top half and the raspberry on the bottom) by spreading a thin layer of buttercream around the entire cake. Freeze for 2 minutes to set the buttercream.

Using a wooden spoon, beat out any air bubbles in the remaining buttercreams. Finish frosting the cake as desired or follow the decorating instructions below.

To Decorate the Cake

Spread a thick final layer of lemon buttercream on the top half of the cake and raspberry along the bottom. Use a wavy cake scraper to make the decorative pattern on the sides and use an angled icing spatula on top to flatten and clean up the edges (see the Tip on page 264).

Fill a piping bag fitted with a Wilton 6B tip with the remaining buttercream, then pipe dollops around the top rim of the cake in a crown. Place a lemon slice between each dollop and a raspberry on top of each one.

MANGO COCONUT CAKE *with Coconut Buttercream and Mango Curd*

All the brightest flavors of summertime have been sweetly combined in this delicious tropical cake. Tender coconut cake layers are filled with mango curd, frosted in soft coconut buttercream, and coated in toasted coconut for a touch of warmth and mouthwatering texture. You will not be able to resist this one, especially the mango curd.

Coconut Cake

- ¾ cup buttermilk (room temperature)
- ⅔ cup sour cream (room temperature)
- 4 egg whites (room temperature)
- ⅓ cup vegetable oil
- 2 to 3 tablespoons coconut emulsion
- 1 tablespoon pure vanilla extract
- 1 box white cake mix

Mango Curd

- 1 cup plus 3 tablespoons mango puree (from about 2 ripe mangoes; see Tip)
- ¼ cup sugar
- 1 tablespoon lime juice
- 2 egg yolks
- 2 tablespoons unsalted butter
  - Coconut Buttercream (page 89)

For Decorating

- 1 14-ounce bag sweetened shredded coconut
  Piping bag
  Wilton 1M piping tip

For the Coconut Cake

Preheat the oven to 325°F, then prep three 6-inch round cake pans with a swipe of shortening and dusting of flour to prevent sticking.

In a large bowl, whisk together the buttermilk, sour cream, egg whites, oil, coconut emulsion, and vanilla until thoroughly combined. Sift in the cake mix and whisk until just combined. Do not overmix. Split the batter evenly among the prepared pans.

Bake for 27 to 30 minutes, until the center is baked through. Let the cakes cool in the pan for a minute before flipping them out onto a wire rack to cool completely. Wrap and freeze the cakes before assembly.

For the Mango Curd

In a small saucepan over medium heat, combine 1 cup of the mango puree, the sugar, lime juice, and egg yolks and cook, stirring constantly, until the mixture thickens, 3 to 5 minutes. Add the butter, 1 tablespoon at a time, stirring until melted between each addition. Stir in the remaining 3 tablespoons mango puree. Transfer to a glass dish, cover, and refrigerate until thickened and cooled completely.

For the Toasted Coconut

Preheat the oven to 350°F. Line a cookie sheet with parchment paper. Spread the shredded coconut in an even layer on the cookie sheet. Bake for 2 to 5 minutes, stir, then bake again for 1 minute and stir again. Repeat until it's toasted to your satisfaction. Keep a close eye on it because it may burn quickly. Let cool completely before using.

To Assemble

Place a cardboard cake round on a cake turntable. Dot a little bit of buttercream in the center of the round and spread it out with an angled icing spatula. Place the first chilled cake layer in the center. Add a thin layer of

buttercream. Pipe a buttercream dam around the outside rim of the frosted cake layer, then add about ½ cup of the mango curd. Place the next cake layer on top, then repeat, making sure to line the layers up evenly. After adding the top cake layer, crumb coat the cake by spreading a thin layer of buttercream around the entire cake. Freeze for 2 minutes to set the buttercream.

Using a wooden spoon, beat out any air bubbles in the remaining buttercream. Finish frosting the cake as desired or follow the decorating instructions below.

To Decorate the Cake

Spread a final layer of buttercream, using a cake scraper for smooth sides and clean edges. Place the cake on a cookie sheet on the cake turntable. Press an even layer of toasted coconut right onto the buttercream around the sides of the cake, letting the excess fall onto the cookie sheet.

Fit a piping bag with a Wilton 1M tip, fill with the remaining buttercream, and pipe a shell crown around the outside rim of the top of the cake. Spread the rest of the mango puree on top in the center.

TIP: Use fresh mangoes. Frozen mango might work just as well, but I always go for fresh when I can so I don't have to worry about additional moisture watering down the curd. I used the mangoes with the green-and-red skins, but I can imagine the other varieties doing the job. Slice your mango (it can be tricky, but once you figure out where that pesky pit is, you're in business) with a knife, or scrape off the skin using the edge of a glass to easily separate the skin from the actual mango inside. Puree it in a small blender so it looks as smooth as applesauce, and you'll be ready to make your mango curd.

TRIPLE BERRY COBBLER CAKE *with Cinnamon Vanilla Bean Buttercream, Berry Filling, and Oatmeal Crumble*

This cake is a must-make for summer. With soft almond and vanilla bean cake layers studded with pockets of fresh berries, a gorgeous berry compote filling, an oatmeal crumble layer baked right into the cake and spread around the outside for garnish, whipped vanilla bean buttercream with a touch of cinnamon, and a handful of fresh berries on top, it has everything I love about berry cobbler. Try it with a scoop of vanilla bean ice cream (you won't regret it, I promise).

Oatmeal Crumble
- 1 cup old-fashioned oats
- 1 cup flour
- ½ cup packed brown sugar
- 3 tablespoons granulated sugar
- ½ teaspoon ground cinnamon
- Pinch of ground nutmeg
- Pinch of salt
- ½ cup (1 stick) butter, softened

Berry Cobbler Cake
- ¾ cup buttermilk (room temperature)
- ⅔ cup sour cream (room temperature)
- 1 large egg plus 3 egg whites (room temperature)
- ⅓ cup vegetable oil
- 1 tablespoon vanilla bean paste
- 2 teaspoons pure vanilla extract
- ½ teaspoon almond extract
- 1 box white cake mix
- 1½ cups fresh berries (such as raspberries, blackberries, blueberries, and strawberries), chopped
- ¼ cup flour

Berry Filling
- 1½ cups mixed berries (such as raspberries, blackberries, blueberries, and strawberries)
- ¼ cup granulated sugar
- 1 tablespoon lemon juice
- 2 tablespoons cornstarch

Cinnamon Vanilla Bean Buttercream
- 1½ cups (3 sticks) unsalted butter
- ¼ cup heavy cream (plus more if needed)
- 1 tablespoon vanilla bean paste
- 1 teaspoon pure vanilla extract
- 1 teaspoon ground cinnamon
- Pinch of salt
- 7 to 8 cups powdered sugar

For Decorating
- Fresh berries
- Reserved baked oatmeal crumble

For the Oatmeal Crumble
Preheat the oven to 350°F and line a cookie sheet with parchment paper.

In a bowl of a stand mixer fitted with a paddle attachment, mix together the oats, flour, brown sugar, sugar, cinnamon, nutmeg, and salt. Cut in the softened butter and mix until combined. Reserve 1 cup of the unbaked oatmeal crumble and set aside (you will use it in your cake layers).

Spread the rest of the crumble on the prepared cookie sheet in an even layer. Bake for about 15 minutes, stirring every 5 minutes, until evenly golden brown. Let cool completely. Store in an airtight container until you're ready to assemble the cake.

For the Berry Cobbler Cake
Preheat the oven to 325°F, then prep three 6-inch round cake pans with a swipe of shortening and dusting of flour to prevent sticking.

In a large bowl, whisk together the buttermilk, sour cream, eggs, oil, vanilla bean paste, vanilla,

and almond extract until thoroughly combined. Sift in the cake mix and whisk until just combined. Do not overmix. In a separate bowl, toss together the berries and flour. Gently fold them into the cake batter. Split the batter evenly among the prepared pans. Sprinkle the reserved 1 cup of crumble among the three pans (making sure the crumbles are spread out evenly on the surface).

Bake for 30 to 32 minutes, until the center is baked through. Let the cakes cool in the pan for a minute before flipping them out onto a wire rack to cool completely. Wrap and freeze the cakes before assembly.

For the Berry Filling
In a medium saucepan over medium heat, bring the berries, sugar, and lemon juice to a simmer and cook, stirring, until the berries are cooked through and the mixture reduces slightly and thickens, about 5 minutes. You can then either leave it chunky or pulse the mixture with an immersion blender to make a more even compote.

In a small bowl, whisk together the cornstarch and ¾ cup water to make a watery slurry. Pour the slurry over the berries in the saucepan and let thicken while stirring over low heat, about 2 minutes. Transfer to a glass dish, cover, and refrigerate until thickened and cooled completely.

For the Cinnamon Vanilla Bean Buttercream
In the bowl of a stand mixer fitted with a paddle attachment, beat the butter until it's light and fluffy. Add the heavy cream, vanilla bean paste, vanilla, cinnamon, and salt and beat again until combined, then scrape down the sides with a spatula.

With the mixer on low speed, add the powdered sugar about ½ cup at a time. The buttercream will be thick. Add a little more heavy cream, 1 tablespoon at a time, to thin it out if needed, and then flip the mixer to high speed and beat until the buttercream is lighter in color and texture, about 2 minutes.

To Assemble and Decorate
Place a cardboard cake round on a cake turntable. Dot a little bit of buttercream in the center of the round and spread it out with an angled icing spatula. Place the first chilled cake layer in the center. Add a thin layer of buttercream. Pipe a buttercream dam around the outside rim of the frosted cake layer, add about ½ cup of the berry filling, then sprinkle on a bit of the crumble. Place the next cake layer on top, then repeat, making sure to line the layers up evenly. After adding the top cake layer, crumb coat the cake by spreading a thin layer of buttercream around the entire cake. Freeze for 2 minutes to set the buttercream.

Using a wooden spoon, beat out any air bubbles in the remaining buttercream. Spread a final layer of buttercream around the entire cake, using a cake scraper for smooth sides. Leave the top edge raw for a more rustic look.

Place the cake on a cookie sheet on the cake turntable. Gently press the crumble around the bottom quarter of the entire cake, letting the excess crumble pieces fall onto the cookie sheet. Place fresh berries on the top of the cake and add a sprinkle of the crumble.

 TIP: Whenever I make a cake with many different components, I love to split up the recipe over a few days. For this one, I suggest baking the cake layers and crumble and making the filling one day, and then making the buttercream on the next. You can either assemble everything that day or even wait until the following day to put it all together.

GRAPEFRUIT POPPY SEED CAKE *with*
Grapefruit Poppy Seed Buttercream and Grapefruit Curd

When I was pregnant with my two boys, I craved grapefruit. I could eat slices of grapefruit and drink grapefruit juice without wincing at the tartness. These days I can't even think about doing that without making a sour face. However, grapefruit cake with grapefruit curd? Now *that's* a grapefruit obsession I can get on board with.

This cake is a twist on the usual citrus and poppy seed combination, starring grapefruit rather than lemon. Using grapefruit zest and juice really brings out such a bright flavor in both the cake batter and the buttercream. Speaking of buttercream, have you ever had poppy seed buttercream before? It's delightful! I didn't think the cake batter should have all the fun, so on a whim I tossed some poppy seeds into the buttercream and I loved not only how it looked but how it tasted.

Grapefruit Poppy Seed Cake

- ¾ cup buttermilk (room temperature)
- ⅔ cup sour cream (room temperature)
- 4 egg whites (room temperature)
- ½ cup vegetable oil
- ¼ cup flour
- ¼ cup grapefruit juice
- Zest of 1 grapefruit (1½ tablespoons)
- 1 tablespoon pure vanilla extract
- 1 tablespoon poppy seeds
- 1 box white cake mix

Grapefruit Curd

- ½ cup granulated sugar
- 2 egg yolks
- ½ cup grapefruit juice
- 1 tablespoon grapefruit zest
- 3 tablespoons unsalted butter
- 1 drop soft-pink gel coloring

Grapefruit Poppy Seed Buttercream

- 1½ cups (3 sticks) unsalted butter
- ¼ cup heavy cream (plus more if needed)
- 2 teaspoons poppy seeds
- 1 tablespoon grapefruit zest
- 1 tablespoon grapefruit juice
- 1 tablespoon pure vanilla extract
- Pinch of salt
- 7 to 8 cups powdered sugar

For Decorating

- Grapefruit slices
- Grapefruit zest curls

For the Grapefruit Poppy Seed Cake

Preheat the oven to 325°F, then prep three 6-inch round cake pans with a swipe of shortening and dusting of flour to prevent sticking.

In a large bowl, whisk together the buttermilk, sour cream, egg whites, oil, flour, grapefruit juice and zest, vanilla, and poppy seeds until thoroughly combined. Sift in the cake mix and whisk until just combined. Do not overmix. Split the batter evenly among the prepared pans.

Bake for 27 to 30 minutes, until the center is baked through. Let the cakes cool in the pan for a minute before flipping them out onto a wire rack to cool completely. Wrap and freeze the cakes before assembly.

For the Grapefruit Curd

In a medium saucepan over medium heat, whisk together the sugar, egg yolks, and grapefruit juice and zest until thickened, about 5 minutes. Remove from the heat, then add the butter, 1 tablespoon at a time, letting it melt after each addition. Add the gel coloring, then strain the

curd to remove the zest. Transfer to a glass dish, cover, and refrigerate until thickened and cooled completely.

For the Grapefruit Poppy Seed Buttercream

In the bowl of a stand mixer fitted with a paddle attachment, beat the butter on medium speed until it's light and fluffy. Add the heavy cream, poppy seeds, grapefruit zest and juice, vanilla, and salt and beat again until combined, then scrape down the sides with a spatula.

With the mixer on low speed, add the powdered sugar about ½ cup at a time. The buttercream will be thick. Add a little more heavy cream, 1 tablespoon at a time, to thin it out if needed, and then flip the mixer to high speed and beat until the buttercream is lighter in color and texture, about 2 minutes.

To Assemble and Decorate

Place a cardboard cake round on a cake turntable. Dot a little bit of buttercream in the center of the round and spread it out with an angled icing spatula. Place the first chilled cake layer in the center. Add a thin layer of buttercream. Pipe a buttercream dam around the outside rim of the frosted cake layer, then add about ½ cup of the grapefruit curd. Place the next cake layer on top, then repeat, making sure to line the layers up evenly. After adding the top cake layer, crumb coat the cake by spreading a thin layer of buttercream around the entire cake. Freeze for 2 minutes to set the buttercream.

Using a wooden spoon, beat out any air bubbles in the remaining buttercream. Spread a final layer of buttercream around the entire cake, using a cake scraper for smooth sides and clean edges.

Garnish with grapefruit slices and zest curls.

TIP: When a recipe calls for both zest and juice, make sure to get all the zest off the fruit before slicing it open for the juice. It seems like something so simple, but it makes a huge difference and helps you get the most flavor out of your citrus.

GUAVA CAKE *with Guava Curd and Cream Cheese Buttercream*

I used to fly to the Burbank, California, area quite often for TV segments on the Hallmark Channel. On one of my first visits, I asked my readers where I should grab a quick pastry or bite to eat. A resounding recommendation to go to Porto's flooded my messages. I walked into the bakery and immediately filled a box with all kinds of tasty treats. Everything was delicious, but the one dessert that I fell hard for was the guava-and-cheese pastry. The dough was perfectly flaky, and the inside was filled with cream cheese and a guava spread. It was divine. On my next visit, I left with an entire box of only guava-and-cheese pastries. I was hooked and have never looked back.

Although this cake doesn't have the signature puff-pastry exterior, the guava curd filling and cream cheese buttercream remind me so much of Porto's.

Guava Cake
- ¾ cup buttermilk (room temperature)
- ⅔ cup sour cream (room temperature)
- 3 large eggs (room temperature)
- ⅓ cup vegetable oil
- 4 ripe small white guava fruits, pulp pureed and strained to remove seeds (2 to 3 tablespoons strained puree)
- 1 tablespoon pure vanilla extract
- 1 box white cake mix

Guava Curd
- 3 to 4 ripe guava fruits, pureed (1 cup puree, or use 1 cup frozen pulp)

- ¼ cup sugar
- 2 egg yolks
- 2 tablespoons lemon juice
- 1 teaspoon cornstarch
- 1 tablespoon unsalted butter
- 1 drop soft-pink gel coloring

  Cream Cheese Buttercream (page 41)

For Decorating
- Soft-pink gel coloring
- Piping bag
- Wilton 104 (petal) piping tip (3 tips are recommended but not essential)

For the Guava Cake

Preheat the oven to 325°F, then prep three 6-inch round cake pans with a swipe of shortening and dusting of flour to prevent sticking.

In a large bowl, whisk together the buttermilk, sour cream, eggs, oil, guava puree, and vanilla until thoroughly combined. Sift in the cake mix and whisk until just combined. Do not overmix. Split the batter evenly among the prepared pans.

Bake for 27 to 30 minutes, until the center is baked through. Let the cakes cool in the pan for a minute before flipping them out onto a wire rack to cool completely. Wrap and freeze the cakes before assembly.

For the Guava Curd

In a medium saucepan over medium heat, whisk together the guava puree, sugar, egg yolks, and lemon juice until thickened, about 5 minutes. In a separate small cup, whisk together the cornstarch with 1 tablespoon of water to make a slurry. Add the slurry to the guava curd and cook, whisking, until thickened, about 2 minutes.

Remove from the heat, then add the butter. Stir, then add the gel coloring. Transfer to a glass dish, cover, and refrigerate until thickened and cooled completely.

To Assemble

Place a cardboard cake round on a cake turntable. Dot a little bit of buttercream in the center of the round and spread it out with an angled icing spatula. Place the first chilled cake layer in the center. Add a thin layer of buttercream. Pipe a buttercream dam around the outside rim of the frosted cake layer, and then add about ½ cup of the guava curd. Place the next cake layer on top, then repeat, making sure to line the layers up evenly. After adding the top cake layer, crumb coat the cake by spreading a thin layer of buttercream around the entire cake. Freeze for 2 minutes to set the buttercream.

Using a wooden spoon, beat out any air bubbles in the remaining buttercream. Finish frosting the cake as desired or follow the decorating instructions below.

To Decorate the Cake

Split the remaining buttercream into three bowls. Tint one section darker pink by adding 2 drops of the soft-pink gel coloring, then tint the second section light pink with 1 drop. Leave the last section white. Add the three colors to three separate piping bags fitted with the Wilton 104 tips. (If you have only one petal tip, use a coupler in each of the piping bags so you can switch the tip to the next bag when you're done with the first.)

With the darkest shade of pink buttercream, pipe overlapping ribbons starting at the bottom of the cake, holding the wider end of the piping tip against the cake and turning the turntable as you pipe. About a third of the way up the cake, switch to the light pink. Repeat on the top third with the white buttercream. On the top of the cake, start on the outside rim of the cake and slowly (using your cake turntable) pipe a steady rim of buttercream continuously while bringing it to the center.

> **TIP:** To make the guava filling, you can use frozen guava pulp or fresh guavas like I did. If you're using fresh guavas, grab a few extra: there isn't a lot of fruit in the guavas themselves, so you'll need plenty on hand for the delicious filling.

FOURTH OF JULY FLAG CAKE

What You'll Need

- 1 batch Classic White Cake batter (page 251)
- Red and blue gel coloring
- 1 batch Vanilla Buttercream (page xvii)
- Gold and white sphere sprinkles
- Four 6-inch cake pans (see Note)
- Small circle cookie cutter (or knife)
- Cardboard cake round
- Angled icing spatula
- Cake turntable
- Piping bag
- Cake scraper
- Wilton 3 piping tip

NOTE: The flag effect will only work using 6-inch cake pans; 8-inch or 9-inch cake rounds will be too thin.

To serve, slice the cake cold with a hot knife for the cleanest slices.

1. Divide the cake batter into four bowls (see Note). Use the gel color to tint the batter in three of the bowls red and one blue. Transfer the batter to four cake pans. Bake and let cool completely. Wrap and freeze the cakes before assembly. Carefully slice the red cake rounds in half horizontally to create 6 thin layers. Leave the blue cake round whole for now.

2. Using a cookie cutter, cut three small circles, each about 2½ inches wide, from one of the red cake rounds.

3. Cut a circle (the same size as the thin red circles) out of the center of the blue cake round.

4. Place a cardboard cake round on a cake turntable. Spread a little bit of buttercream in the middle of the cake board with an angled icing spatula.

5. Place the first red cake round on the board. Add a layer of buttercream. Repeat with the remaining 5 red cake rounds.

6. Place the blue cake round with the cut-out center on top.

7. Insert the first small red cake cutout, then pipe in a layer of white buttercream. Repeat with another red cake cutout, and then, if needed, another layer of buttercream and the third red cake cutout. Its top should be level with the top of the blue one.

8. Crumb coat, freeze, and then frost the entire cake. Use a cake scraper to create clean sides. Leave the top edge uneven for a more rustic finish.

9. Tint 1 cup of the buttercream red and 1 cup blue. With a piping bag fitted with the Wilton 3 tip and either the red or blue buttercream, pipe small lines coming out of one central point to create fireworks. Add on little dots at the ends of the cascading lines.

10. Repeat with the other color, then place on a few gold and white sprinkles.

FOURTH OF JULY
ROCKET POP PIÑATA CAKE

What You'll Need

- 3 cake rounds, one tinted red, one white, and one tinted blue (see Note)
- 1 batch Vanilla Buttercream (page xvii)
- Red and blue gel coloring
- Fourth of July sprinkles (1 to 2 cups)
- Small circle cookie cutter (or knife)
- 3 piping bags
- Cardboard cake round
- Cake turntable
- Angled icing spatula
- Straight icing spatula
- Cake scraper

NOTE: To tint the cake batter, divide 1 batch Classic White Cake batter (page 251) among three 6-inch cake pans. Use gel colors to tint the batter in one pan red and one blue (leave the third pan plain). Bake as directed in the recipe and let cool completely. Wrap and freeze the cakes before assembly.

To Prep the Cake Rounds

1. Slice the cake rounds in half horizontally, creating two thin layers of each color.

2. Using a cookie cutter, cut a circle from the center of one blue, two red, and two white cake rounds to create a well for the sprinkles. Keep one blue layer whole.

3. Tint 1 cup buttercream red and 1 cup blue using the gel colors and transfer them to piping bags. Transfer 1 cup untinted buttercream to a piping bag as well. You will use the remaining white buttercream for the inside of the cake and the crumb coat. You won't need piping tips; when

you're ready, just slice off the end of the bag to create an opening.

To Assemble the Cake

1. Place a cardboard cake round on a cake turntable. Spread a little bit of buttercream in the middle of the cake board with an angled icing spatula.

2. Place the first thin red cake layer on the board and spread on a thin layer of white buttercream. Add a little bit of buttercream inside the hollowed-out center, but only to barely cover the cake like a crumb coat.

3. Repeat step 2 with the remaining red layer, two white layers, and one blue cake layer, lining up the holes in the middle of the cake.

4. Using a straight icing spatula, spread a little buttercream inside the hollow of the cake.

5. Fill the hollow in the cake with the Fourth of July sprinkles until you reach the top.

6. Top with the last blue cake round (which shouldn't have a hole in it). Crumb coat the entire cake (see page xxiv), then freeze for about 5 minutes.

7. Using your cake turntable and red buttercream, pipe a thick horizontal stripe around the bottom third of the cake.

8. Right above the red stripe, add a white stripe in the middle third of the cake.

9. For the top stripe, pipe the blue buttercream up to the top rim of the cake.

10. Use a cake scraper to slowly smooth out the sides. You may need to go around the cake a few times. Make sure to keep the cake scraper straight and use an easy amount of pressure. Add some blue buttercream on top with the angled icing spatula, then use the cake scraper again on the sides to finish.

Chapter 3

FALL FAVORITES

In the fall, our family plays in piles of crisp amber leaves in our sweaters and boots in Grandma's backyard. We snack on more than a few soft, warm apple cider donuts, get painfully lost in corn mazes at dusk, and walk through pumpkin patch after pumpkin patch to find the best orange and white pumpkins to bring home for our front porch. The warm smells of cinnamon and pumpkin wrap around our home like a cozy blanket while the oven fills with muffins, cakes, cookies, and just about anything else I can find an excuse to bake.

CANNOLI CAKE *with Cinnamon Mascarpone Buttercream and Ricotta Filling*

My cannoli cake is the ultimate homage to the classic Italian dessert, with a fresh ricotta filling, cinnamon mascarpone buttercream, and a few cannoli to top it all off. I love cannoli that are stuffed with as many mini chocolate chips as possible, so naturally, I created a cannoli cake that is covered in them, with little chocolate chips hiding throughout the soft white cake layers. Each element brings something truly decadent to each slice and will have your family saying "perfetto" around the table.

For the Cannoli Cake

- ¾ cup buttermilk (room temperature)
- ⅔ cup sour cream (room temperature)
- 4 egg whites (room temperature)
- ⅓ cup vegetable oil
- 1 tablespoon pure vanilla extract
- 1 teaspoon ground cinnamon
- ½ cup mini chocolate chips
- 1 box white cake mix

For the Cannoli Filling

- 1 cup ricotta cheese, strained in a fine-mesh sieve in the refrigerator for at least 24 hours to remove moisture
- ½ cup powdered sugar
- ½ cup mascarpone
- 1 teaspoon pure vanilla extract
- ¼ cup mini chocolate chips

Cinnamon Mascarpone Buttercream

- 1½ cups (3 sticks) unsalted butter
- ½ cup mascarpone
- ¼ cup heavy cream (plus more if needed)
- 1 tablespoon pure vanilla extract
- 1 teaspoon cinnamon
- Pinch of salt
- 7 to 8 cups powdered sugar

For Decorating

- Mini cannoli shells (see Tip)
- 2 cups mini chocolate chips
- Ground cinnamon
- Piping bag
- Wilton 6B piping tip

For the Cannoli Cake

Preheat the oven to 325°F, then prep three 6-inch round cake pans with a swipe of shortening and dusting of flour to prevent sticking.

In a large bowl, whisk together the buttermilk, sour cream, egg whites, oil, and vanilla until thoroughly combined. Stir in the cinnamon and mini chocolate chips. Sift in the cake mix and whisk until just combined. Do not overmix. Split the batter evenly among the prepared pans.

Bake for 27 to 30 minutes, until the center is baked through. Let the cakes cool in the pan for a minute before flipping them out onto a wire rack to cool completely. Wrap and freeze the cakes before assembly.

For the Cannoli Filling

Gently stir together the drained ricotta, powdered sugar, mascarpone, and vanilla. The mixture should be pipeable. If not, the ricotta is too moist, and you may need to either strain the filling through a cheesecloth until it reaches a pipeable consistency or add a little more powdered sugar if you don't mind more sweetness. Cover and refrigerate until ready to assemble the cake.

For the Cinnamon Mascarpone Buttercream

In the bowl of a stand mixer fitted with a paddle attachment, beat the butter on medium speed until it's light and fluffy. Add the mascarpone, heavy cream, vanilla, cinnamon, and salt and beat

again until combined, then scrape down the sides with a spatula.

With the mixer on low speed, add the powdered sugar about ½ cup at a time. The buttercream will be thick. Add a little more heavy cream, 1 tablespoon at a time, to thin it out if needed, and then flip the mixer to high speed and beat until the buttercream is lighter in color and texture, about 2 minutes.

To Assemble and Decorate

Place a cardboard cake round on a cake turntable. Dot a little bit of buttercream in the center of the round and spread it out with an angled icing spatula. Place the first chilled cake layer in the center. Add a thin layer of buttercream. Pipe a buttercream dam around the outside rim of the frosted cake layer, and then add about ½ cup of the cannoli filling. Sprinkle on some mini chocolate chips. Place the next cake layer on top, then repeat, making sure to line the layers up evenly. After adding the top cake layer, crumb coat the cake by spreading a thin layer of buttercream around the entire cake. Freeze for 2 minutes to set the buttercream.

Meanwhile, pipe the cannoli filling into the cannoli shells. Place a few mini chocolate chips on the ends. Store in the refrigerator until ready to add to the cake.

Using a wooden spoon, beat out any air bubbles in the remaining buttercream. Spread a final layer of buttercream around the entire cake, using a cake scraper for smooth sides and clean edges.

Place the cake on a cookie sheet and set the cookie sheet on a cake turntable. Press a layer of mini chocolate chips onto the sides of the cake.

Add the remaining buttercream to a piping bag fitted with a Wilton 6B tip. Pipe a shell border around the top of the cake and sprinkle with a little bit of cinnamon. Place a few cannolis on top as garnish.

TIP: Empty cannoli shells are easy to find online. Just fill them with your own ricotta filling.

CHOCOLATE ZUCCHINI CAKE *with Dark Chocolate Buttercream*

If you've ever grown a zucchini plant in your backyard garden, you know how quickly your harvest can go from one zucchini to five large ones in what seems like only a few days! Coming up with new, inventive ways to use them can be a challenge. Your kitchen fills with zucchini muffins, zucchini bread, zucchini noodles, zucchini casseroles, and maybe a few failed attempts at hidden zucchini in your kids' meals. Trust me, though, after trying this cake, you'll be begging your zucchini plant for more. No one will suspect zucchini is one of the main ingredients, and you'll feel like a champ getting another serving of veggies on the plate (although I'm not sure it technically counts if it's covered in chocolate).

Chocolate Zucchini Cake

- ¾ cup buttermilk (room temperature)
- ⅔ cup sour cream (room temperature)
- 3 large eggs plus 1 egg white (room temperature)
- ½ cup mini chocolate chips
- ⅓ cup vegetable oil
- 1 cup finely shredded zucchini (about 1 medium zucchini), drained and compressed to ¼ cup (see Tip)
- 1 tablespoon pure vanilla extract
- ¼ cup cocoa powder
- 1 box dark chocolate cake mix

Dark Chocolate Buttercream

- 1 batch Vanilla Buttercream (page xvii)
- ⅔ cup Dutch-process cocoa powder

For Decorating

Piping bag
Wilton 1M piping tip

For the Chocolate Zucchini Cake

Preheat the oven to 325°F, then prep three 6-inch round cake pans with a swipe of shortening and dusting of flour to prevent sticking.

In a large bowl, whisk together the buttermilk, sour cream, eggs, mini chocolate chips, oil, zucchini, and vanilla until thoroughly combined. Sift in the cocoa powder and cake mix and whisk until just combined. Do not overmix. Split the batter evenly among the prepared pans.

Bake for 30 to 32 minutes, until the center is baked through. Let the cakes cool in the pan for a minute before flipping them out onto a wire rack to cool completely. Wrap and freeze the cakes before assembly.

For the Dark Chocolate Buttercream

In the bowl of a stand mixer fitted with a paddle attachment, beat the buttercream and cocoa powder until combined and then scrape down the sides with a spatula.

To Assemble and Decorate

Place a cardboard cake round on a cake turntable. Dot a little bit of buttercream in the center of the round and spread it out with an angled icing spatula. Place the first chilled cake layer in the center. Add a layer of buttercream. Place the next cake layer on top, then repeat, making sure to line the layers up evenly. After adding the top cake layer, crumb coat the cake by spreading a thin layer of buttercream around the entire cake. Freeze for 2 minutes to set the buttercream.

Using a wooden spoon, beat out any air bubbles in the remaining buttercream. Add a little buttercream on top of the cake and add a swirl using the cake turntable and straight icing spatula. Add the buttercream to a piping bag fitted with a Wilton 1M tip. Starting at the bottom, squeeze the buttercream into rosettes in rows, hiding the ending "tail" behind the next rosette. Repeat until the rosettes cover the entire side of the cake.

 TIP: Zucchini is a very watery vegetable. To help the cake layers bake up beautifully without adding in too much extra liquid, grate the zucchini on the smallest holes of your grater, then squeeze the excess moisture from the shreds with either a strong paper towel or cheesecloth. You can also press it into a fine-mesh sieve with your hands to remove some of the liquid, too.

POACHED PEAR CARAMEL CAKE *with*
Mascarpone Buttercream

This cake looks as stunning as it tastes. It's a showstopper with poached pears towering on top, a caramel drip, dreamy mascarpone buttercream, and poached pears baked right into soft caramel cake layers. Poached pears are much easier to make than you would think. All it takes is a little patience as they soak in the cinnamon liquid until they're perfectly soft. Your kitchen will smell just like fall, and you'll wish you could bottle up that scent forever.

For the Pear Caramel Cake
- ⅔ cup packed brown sugar
- 1 large pear, peeled and thinly sliced (see Tip)
- ¾ cup buttermilk (room temperature)
- ⅔ cup sour cream (room temperature)
- 4 egg whites (room temperature)
- ⅓ cup vegetable oil
- 1 tablespoon pure vanilla extract
- 2 teaspoons caramel extract
- 1 box white cake mix

Mascarpone Buttercream
- 1 cup (2 sticks) unsalted butter
- ½ cup mascarpone
- 2 to 3 tablespoons heavy cream (plus more if needed)
- 1 tablespoon pure vanilla extract
- Pinch of salt
- 6 cups powdered sugar

Poached Pears
- 1 cup granulated sugar
- 1 tablespoon pure vanilla extract
- 2 cinnamon sticks
- 1 teaspoon lemon or orange zest
- ¼ teaspoon ground cloves
- 3 whole pears, peeled, stem left on (see Tip)

Caramel Drip
- 1 cup Wilton Salted Caramel Candy Melts (see Tip)
- ¼ cup heavy cream

For the Pear Caramel Cake
Preheat the oven to 325°F, then prep three 6-inch round cake pans with a swipe of shortening and dusting of flour to prevent sticking.

Evenly sprinkle the brown sugar into the prepared pans and then lay the pear slices on top in an even layer with the points of the slices meeting in the middle.

In a large bowl, whisk together the buttermilk, sour cream, egg whites, oil, vanilla, and caramel extract until thoroughly combined. Sift in the cake mix and whisk until just combined. Do not overmix. Split the batter evenly among the pans.

Bake for 27 to 30 minutes, until the center is baked through. Let the cakes cool in the pan for a minute before flipping them out onto a wire rack to cool completely. Wrap and freeze the cakes before assembly.

For the Mascarpone Buttercream
In the bowl of a stand mixer fitted with a paddle attachment, beat the butter on medium speed until it's light and fluffy. Add the mascarpone, heavy cream, vanilla, and salt and beat again until combined, then scrape down the sides with a spatula.

With the mixer on low speed, add the powdered sugar about ½ cup at a time. The buttercream will be thick. Add a little more heavy cream, 1 tablespoon at a time, to thin it out if needed, and then flip the mixer to high speed and beat until the buttercream is lighter in color and texture, about 2 minutes.

For the Poached Pears
In a medium saucepan over medium heat, stir together 3 cups of water, the sugar, vanilla,

cinnamon sticks, zest, and cloves. Bring the mixture to a boil over medium heat, then add the pears. Cover with a lid, then immediately reduce the heat to low and simmer until tender, 10 to 20 minutes. (The time will vary depending on how thick the pears are.) Carefully remove the pears from the poaching liquid and transfer to a plate. Cover with plastic wrap and store in the refrigerator. You may simmer the remaining liquid into a reduction and serve with the cake slices as a syrup if desired.

For the Caramel Drip

In a microwave-safe bowl, stir together the caramel melts and heavy cream. Microwave for 30 seconds, then stir until smooth. Transfer to a drip bottle and set aside.

To Assemble and Decorate

Place a cardboard cake round on a cake turntable. Dot a little bit of buttercream in the center of the round and spread it out with an angled icing spatula. Place the first chilled cake layer in the center (fruit side up). Add a layer of buttercream. Place the next cake layer on top, then repeat, making sure to line the layers up evenly. After adding the top cake layer, crumb coat the cake by spreading a layer of buttercream around the entire cake. (For this cake a generous crumb coat is the final layer.) Freeze for 2 minutes to set the buttercream.

Add the caramel drip using the drip bottle. Apply on the top edge, letting it pool a bit and then cascade down the side of the cake. Repeat around the entire cake. Squeeze more caramel on the top of the cake, and then use an angled icing spatula to spread the caramel to the edges.

Before serving, place the poached pears on top of the cake, using toothpicks to keep them in place if necessary. To serve, slice the poached pears and place next to each cake slice.

TIP: I've tried this recipe with different kinds of pears, and they all worked beautifully. However, the texture and ripeness of the pears are key. Find the sweet spot by choosing pears that have a little give when you press on the skin but haven't changed color all the way to a fully ripe fruit.

If you can't find the Wilton caramel melts, you can use 1 cup homemade caramel plus ¼ cup white chocolate chips and a pinch of salt for the caramel drip.

SWEET POTATO PECAN PIE CAKE *with*
Brown Butter Maple Pecan Buttercream and Pecan Pie Filling

This cake is a celebration of all those gorgeous fall flavors we love to enjoy around Thanksgiving. I created this autumn-on-a-plate cake with my favorite sweet potato casserole in mind. For the filling, I actually used my pecan pie recipe. I know you'll be tempted to use a lot of this filling between your cake layers, but I promise only ½ cup between the layers is needed. You can always serve more on the side of each cake slice.

Next, for the maple flavoring, you can always use 100 percent maple syrup, or you can skip it and add maple extract for a stronger flavor. You can often find maple extract at your local grocery store next to the other extracts and emulsions. I use only 1 teaspoon here, but if you want a stronger maple flavor, add a second teaspoon. Whip it all up together, and you'll fall in love with the smell alone before you even taste the cake.

Sweet Potato Cake

- 20 ounces (about 3 small) sweet potatoes, baked, skins removed (see Tip)
- ½ cup buttermilk (room temperature)
- ½ cup sour cream (room temperature)
- 3 large eggs (room temperature)
- ½ cup vegetable oil
- 1 tablespoon pure vanilla extract
- 1 teaspoon ground cinnamon
- 1 box yellow cake mix

Pecan Pie Filling

- 1 cup crushed pecans (see Tip)
- 1 large egg
- ¼ cup light corn syrup

- ¼ cup packed brown sugar
- 1 teaspoon pure vanilla extract
- ½ teaspoon ground cinnamon
- Pinch of salt
- 3 tablespoons unsalted butter

Brown Butter Maple Pecan Buttercream

- 2 cups (4 sticks) unsalted butter
- 1 cup pecans, pulsed to a fine powder (see Tip)
- ¼ cup heavy cream (plus more if needed)
- 1 tablespoon pure vanilla extract
- 1 teaspoon maple extract (or 3 tablespoons pure maple syrup)
- 1 teaspoon ground cinnamon

- Pinch of salt
- 7 to 8 cups powdered sugar

For Decorating

- Pecan halves and crumbles
- Large piping bag
- Wilton 127D (large petal) piping tip

For the Sweet Potato Cake

Preheat the oven to 325°F, then prep three 6-inch round cake pans with a swipe of shortening and dusting of flour to prevent sticking.

In a large bowl, mash the baked sweet potato. Add in the buttermilk, sour cream, eggs, oil, vanilla, and cinnamon and whisk together until thoroughly combined. Sift in the cake mix and whisk until just combined. Do not overmix. Split the batter evenly among the prepared pans.

Bake for 30 to 32 minutes, until the center is baked through. Let the cakes cool in the pan for a minute before flipping them out onto a wire rack to cool completely. Wrap and freeze the cakes before assembly.

For the Pecan Pie Filling

In a small saucepan over medium heat, stir together the crushed pecans, egg, corn syrup, brown sugar, vanilla, cinnamon, and salt and cook, stirring, until the mixture comes together and bubbles, about 5 minutes. Stir in the butter. Continue cooking until thickened, about a minute. Transfer to a glass bowl, cover, and refrigerate until thickened and cooled completely.

For the Brown Butter Maple Pecan Buttercream

Make the browned butter in advance: In a small saucepan over medium heat, melt ½ cup (1 stick) of the butter. Stir until the butter foams. It will then begin to brown. Watch very closely and keep stirring. Don't let it burn! It can go from brown to burned very quickly. When the butter has reached a dark amber color and has a nutty aroma, immediately remove from the heat and transfer it to a glass bowl (make sure to scrape out all the brown bits—those have a lot of flavor). Cover, then refrigerate until it cools completely.

In the bowl of a stand mixer fitted with a paddle attachment, beat the remaining 1½ cups (3 sticks) butter and the prepared browned butter on medium speed until light and fluffy. Add the pecans, heavy cream, vanilla, maple extract, cinnamon, and salt and beat again until combined, then scrape down the sides with a spatula.

With the mixer on low speed, add the powdered sugar about ½ cup at a time. The buttercream will be thick. Add a little more heavy cream, 1 tablespoon at a time, to thin it out if needed, and then flip the mixer to high speed and beat until the buttercream is lighter in color and texture, about 2 minutes.

To Assemble

Place a cardboard cake round on a cake turntable. Dot a little bit of buttercream in the center of the round and spread it out with an angled icing spatula. Place the first chilled cake layer in the center. Add a thin layer of buttercream. Pipe a buttercream dam around the outside rim of the frosted cake layer, then add about ½ cup of the pecan pie filling. Place the next cake layer on top, then repeat, making sure to line the layers up evenly. After adding the top cake layer, crumb coat the cake by spreading a thin layer of buttercream around the entire cake. Freeze for 2 minutes to set the buttercream.

Using a wooden spoon, beat out any air bubbles in the remaining buttercream. Finish frosting the cake as desired or follow the decorating instructions below.

To Decorate the Cake

Spread a layer of buttercream on the top of the cake.

Fit a large piping bag with the Wilton 127D tip and fill it with buttercream. Starting at the top, holding the thick end of the tip against the cake, pipe a single ribbon around the cake, slightly overlapping the end of the ribbon in the back. Pipe a second ribbon right under the first one. Continue until the entire cake is coated top to bottom.

Place pecan pieces on the top of the cake in a pattern. Sprinkle on pecan crumbles as well.

TIP: You are more than welcome to bake the sweet potatoes in the oven, but I love to save time and just heat them up in the microwave for about 5 minutes. Just make sure they're cooked through and super soft. For extra flavor, toast up your pecans on the stove over medium heat for 2 to 5 minutes, or in the oven at 350°F for 5 to 7 minutes before adding them to your filling and buttercream.

PUMPKIN CAKE *with Gingersnap Crust and Gingersnap Buttercream*

In my grandma June's kitchen, there was always a cookie jar next to the sink. It was crammed to the top with ginger cookies, and those cookies will always remind me of her. I think this cake—with its gingersnap crust, gingersnap buttercream, and gingersnap cookies all around—would have made her smile as much as I did while making it. Pairing gingersnap with pumpkin is also a home run for fall baking.

Pumpkin Cake with Gingersnap Crust

- 30 gingersnap cookies (8 ounces)
- 6 tablespoons unsalted butter, melted
- 15 ounces canned pumpkin
- ⅓ cup buttermilk (room temperature)
- ½ cup sour cream (room temperature)
- 3 large eggs (room temperature)
- ⅓ cup vegetable oil
- 1 tablespoon pumpkin pie spice
- 1 tablespoon pure vanilla extract
- 1 box yellow cake mix

Gingersnap Buttercream

- 1 batch Vanilla Buttercream (page xvii)
- 25 gingersnap cookies (6⅔ ounces), pulsed into a fine powder
- 3 tablespoons molasses

For Decorating

- Gingersnap cookies

For the Pumpkin Cake with Gingersnap Crust

Preheat the oven to 325°F, then prep three 6-inch round cake pans with a swipe of shortening and dusting of flour to prevent sticking.

In a food processor, process the gingersnaps and melted butter until a fine crust forms. Split the crust mixture evenly into the prepared baking pans and press to firm with the bottom of a glass or flat measuring cup.

In a large bowl, whisk together the pumpkin, buttermilk, sour cream, eggs, oil, pumpkin pie spice, and vanilla until thoroughly combined. Sift in the cake mix and whisk until just combined. Do not overmix. Split the batter evenly among the prepared pans.

Bake for 32 to 35 minutes, until the center is baked through. Let the cakes cool in the pan for a minute before flipping them out onto a wire rack to cool completely. Wrap and freeze the cakes before assembly.

For the Gingersnap Buttercream

In the bowl of a stand mixer fitted with a paddle attachment, beat together the buttercream, gingersnap powder, and molasses until evenly combined, then scrape down the sides with a spatula.

To Assemble and Decorate

Place a cardboard cake round on a cake turntable. Dot a little bit of buttercream in the center of the round and spread it out with an angled icing spatula. Place the first chilled cake layer in the center (crust side up). Add a layer of buttercream. Place the next cake layer on top, then repeat, making sure to line the layers up evenly. After adding the top cake layer, crumb coat the cake by spreading a thin layer of buttercream around the entire cake. Freeze for 2 minutes to set the buttercream.

Using a wooden spoon, beat out any air bubbles in the remaining buttercream. Spread a final layer of buttercream around the entire cake, using a cake scraper for smooth sides. Leave the top edge raw for a more rustic look.

Right before serving, place ginger cookie halves and pieces all around the cake. Place cookie halves around the bottom of the cake and in a pattern on top starting with large cookies and working down to cookie fragments.

TIP: It's very important to use crisp gingersnaps for the buttercream. They crumble up to a fine powder perfectly in the food processor and make the most charming specks all around the outside of the cake.

Hold off on adding the gingersnap cookies until right before your gathering. Cookies tend to soak up moisture from the buttercream and soften quite a bit. So finish your cake, then place those delicious cookies right before serving.

BLACK FOREST CAKE *with Whipped Cream Frosting and Cherry Filling*

If you haven't tasted a Black Forest cake before, let me introduce you to what I'm sure will be one of your new favorites. Rich dark chocolate cake, a sweet and tart cherry compote filling, and soft whipped cream frosting are the classic components of this dessert. But why on earth is it called a "Black Forest cake" anyway? I always thought the name came from the mountain range in Germany, but some say the cake is named after a cherry liqueur called Schwarzwälder Kirschwasser (Black Forest Kirsch from the Black Forest region). Still others say it's named after the traditional women's clothing there (dark clothes, white shirts, and hats with red pom-poms that look like cherries). Either way, it's a very traditional German cake.

Although my version of the cake doesn't have any cherry liqueur in it (for religious reasons), I still think we have a really yummy version of this cake on our hands. If you'd love to add Kirsch or cherry schnapps or liqueur to the cake, I suggest adding it to the compote one tablespoon at a time or brushing the cake layers with it as one would with a simple syrup.

Dark Chocolate Cake

- ¾ cup buttermilk (room temperature)
- ⅔ cup sour cream (room temperature)
- 3 large eggs plus 1 egg white (room temperature)
- ⅓ cup vegetable oil
- ½ cup semisweet mini chocolate chips
- 1 tablespoon pure vanilla extract
- ½ cup Dutch-process cocoa powder
- ¼ cup flour
- 1 box dark chocolate cake mix

Cherry Filling

- 1½ cups fresh cherries, pitted and roughly chopped

- ¼ cup granulated sugar
- 1 tablespoon lemon juice
- 1 tablespoon cornstarch
- 1 teaspoon pure vanilla extract
- ⅛ teaspoon almond extract (optional)

Chocolate Ganache Drip

- 1 cup dark chocolate candy melts
- ¼ cup heavy cream

Stabilized Whipped Cream Frosting

- 3 cups heavy whipping cream
- 1 tablespoon unflavored powdered gelatin (one 1.8-gram packet)

- 3 ounces cream cheese (room temperature)
- 1 tablespoon pure vanilla extract
- 2 cups powdered sugar

For Decorating

- 12 fresh cherries with stems
  - Piping bag
  - Wilton 1M piping tip

For the Dark Chocolate Cake

Preheat the oven to 325°F, then prep three 6-inch round cake pans with a swipe of shortening and dusting of flour to prevent sticking.

In a large bowl, whisk together the buttermilk, sour cream, eggs, oil, chocolate chips, and vanilla until thoroughly combined. Sift in the cocoa, flour, and cake mix and whisk until just combined. Do not overmix. Split the batter evenly among the prepared pans.

Bake for 30 to 32 minutes, until the center is baked through. Let the cakes cool in the pan for a minute before flipping them out onto a wire rack to cool completely. Wrap and freeze the cakes before assembly.

For the Cherry Filling

In a small saucepan over medium heat, stir together the cherries, ½ cup of water, the sugar, lemon juice, and cornstarch. Bring the mixture to a boil, then reduce the heat and cook, stirring, until thickened, about 10 minutes. Stir in the vanilla and almond extracts and stir until thickened again, about 2 minutes. Transfer to a glass dish, cover, and refrigerate until thickened and cooled completely.

For the Chocolate Ganache Drip
In a small microwave-safe bowl, stir together the chocolate melts and heavy cream and heat in the microwave for 30 seconds. Stir until smooth, then transfer to a drip bottle.

For the Stabilized Whipped Cream Frosting
Place the metal bowl of a stand mixer and the stand mixer's whisk attachment in the freezer to chill for about 10 minutes. Attach them to the stand mixer and beat the heavy whipping cream and gelatin together on low speed, medium speed, then high speed, each for about a minute until stiff peaks form.

When at stiff peaks, add the cream cheese, vanilla, and powdered sugar and whip up again. It's important to work quickly so that the whipped cream doesn't deflate.

To Assemble
Place a cardboard cake round on a cake turntable. Spread on a little bit of whipped cream in the center of the round and spread it out with an angled icing spatula. Place the first chilled cake layer in the center. Add a thin layer of whipped cream. Pipe a whipped cream dam around the outside rim of the frosted cake layer, then add about ½ cup of the cherry filling. Place the next cake layer on top, then repeat, making sure to line the layers up evenly. After adding the top cake layer, crumb coat the cake by spreading a thin layer of whipped cream around the entire cake. Freeze for 2 minutes to set. Finish frosting the cake as desired or follow the decorating instructions below.

To Decorate the Cake
Pipe the ganache drips on the top of the chilled cake, letting the drips cascade down the sides about an inch apart from each other. Add more ganache in the center and spread to the edges with an angled icing spatula. Freeze for 1 minute to set the ganache drips.

Fit a piping bag with the Wilton 1M tip and fill with the remaining whipped cream. Pipe small dollops on top of the chilled ganache around the top outside rim of the cake. Place a cherry on each of the dollops. Freeze until the day of your event, then move to the fridge and refrigerate for about an hour before serving.

TIP: You're going to need a cherry pitter for those juicy fresh cherries, and your sanity. Alternatively, you could use canned cherry pie filling.

Whipped cream naturally wants to deflate after an hour or two—not ideal for a stacked cake and soft filling. But with my surefire technique, which incorporates gelatin and cream cheese, the whipped cream will not only be stackable but pipeable, and it will hold up the weight of the cakes and filling. Make sure the gelatin has time to set up in the whipped cream and that you keep the cake very cold for the best results.

WHITE CHOCOLATE MACADAMIA NUT CAKE

When I was a kid, I loathed a popular sandwich shop—I avoided the place at all costs, and the only thing I could stomach was their white chocolate chip macadamia nut cookies. They were always soft and chewy and had just the right amount of white chocolate as well as little pieces of nuts throughout. Fast-forward to now, and I love getting quick sandwiches there with my boys after hiking, and I still find myself getting a white chocolate chip macadamia nut cookie (or three) to share. While creating this cake, I tried to pack in as much white chocolate and macadamia nut flavor as I could, just like those delicious cookies. I hope you love it just as much as I do.

Macadamia Nut Cake

- ¾ cup buttermilk (room temperature)
- ⅔ cup sour cream (room temperature)
- 4 egg whites (room temperature)
- 4 ounces (about 1 cup) macadamia nuts, toasted and pureed into nut butter
- ⅓ cup vegetable oil
- 1 tablespoon pure vanilla extract
- 1 box white cake mix

White Chocolate Macadamia Nut Buttercream

- ½ cup white chocolate chips
- 2 tablespoons plus ¼ cup heavy cream (plus more if needed)
- 1½ cups (3 sticks) unsalted butter
- 4 ounces (about 1 cup) macadamia nuts, toasted and pureed into nut butter
- 1 tablespoon pure vanilla extract
- Pinch of salt
- 7 to 8 cups powdered sugar

For Decorating

- White chocolate shavings
- Toasted macadamia nuts, chopped

For the Macadamia Nut Cake

Preheat the oven to 325°F, then prep three 6-inch round cake pans with a swipe of shortening and dusting of flour to prevent sticking.

In a large bowl, whisk together the buttermilk, sour cream, egg whites, macadamia nut butter, oil, and vanilla until thoroughly combined. Sift in the cake mix and whisk until just combined. Do not overmix. Split the batter evenly among the prepared pans.

Bake for 27 to 30 minutes, until the center is baked through. Let the cakes cool in the pan for a minute before flipping them out onto a wire rack to cool completely. Wrap and freeze the cakes before assembly.

For the White Chocolate Macadamia Nut Buttercream

In a small microwave-safe bowl, stir together the white chocolate chips and 2 tablespoons of the heavy cream. Heat in the microwave for 30 seconds, then stir until smooth. Let cool to room temperature.

In the bowl of a stand mixer fitted with a paddle attachment, beat the butter and macadamia nut butter until light and fluffy. Add the white chocolate ganache, the remaining ¼ cup heavy cream, vanilla, and salt and beat again until combined, then scrape down the sides with a spatula.

With the mixer on low speed, add the powdered sugar about ½ cup at a time. The buttercream will be thick. Add a little more heavy cream, 1 tablespoon at a time, to thin it out if needed, then flip the mixer to high speed and beat until the buttercream is lighter in color and texture, about 2 minutes.

To Assemble

Place a cardboard cake round on a cake turntable. Dot a little bit of buttercream in the center of the round and spread it out with an angled icing spatula. Place the first chilled cake layer in the center. Add a layer of buttercream. Place the next cake layer on top, then repeat, making sure to line the layers up evenly. After adding the top cake layer, crumb coat the cake by spreading a thin layer of buttercream around the entire cake. Freeze for 2 minutes to set the buttercream.

Using a wooden spoon, beat out any air bubbles in the remaining buttercream. Finish frosting the cake as desired or follow the decorating instructions below.

To Decorate the Cake

Spread an even layer of buttercream on the sides of the cake, using a cake scraper for smooth sides. Leave the top unfinished. Freeze for 2 minutes.

Next, spread on a second layer of buttercream that only goes halfway up the side of the cake. Use a cake scraper to smooth out that layer, leaving the top edge unfinished (don't smooth it into the cake). It should look like a shelf. Freeze for 2 minutes again. Repeat with a final short layer of buttercream at the bottom (creating three tiered layers of buttercream as shown in the photo).

Sprinkle the top with white chocolate shavings and macadamia nut crumbles.

TIP: Regular macadamia nuts are quite delicious on their own, but toasting them almost transforms them into a completely different nut! The golden roast on the outside makes such a warm comforting flavor that blends really well into the buttercream. To toast, heat the nuts in a pan over medium heat for 2 to 5 minutes until golden brown.

To make the nut butter, toast the nuts and let cool completely. Add the nuts to a high-speed blender and blend until smooth.

TRIPLE CHOCOLATE CAKE

Why have one type of chocolate when you can have three? You will need two different kinds of cocoa for this cake—regular (also called "natural") and Dutch process—plus white chocolate, milk chocolate, and dark chocolate chips for the buttercreams. I know that may sound overwhelming, but you will only be making one batch of cake batter and one batch of buttercream. You will split each of them three ways and change the flavors to white, milk, and dark chocolate by stirring in their respective flavors. Easy peasy, I promise.

Triple Chocolate Cake

- ¾ cup plus 4 tablespoons buttermilk (room temperature)
- ⅔ cup sour cream (room temperature)
- 4 egg whites (room temperature)
- ⅓ cup vegetable oil
- 1 tablespoon pure vanilla extract
- 1 box white cake mix
- ¼ cup regular cocoa powder
- ¼ cup dark cocoa powder, such as Hershey's Special Dark

Triple Chocolate Buttercream

- 9 tablespoons heavy cream
- ½ cup white chocolate chips
- ½ cup milk chocolate chips
- ½ cup dark chocolate chips
- 1 batch Vanilla Buttercream (page xvii)

For Decorating

- Piping bag
- Wilton 1M piping tip

For the Triple Chocolate Cake

Preheat the oven to 325°F, then prep three 6-inch round cake pans with a swipe of shortening and dusting of flour to prevent sticking.

In a large bowl, whisk together the buttermilk, sour cream, egg whites, oil, and vanilla until thoroughly combined. Sift in the cake mix and whisk until just combined. Do not overmix. Split the batter equally into three bowls. Add one-third of the (plain) batter to one of the prepared pans and set aside. In a small bowl, mix together the regular cocoa powder and 2 tablespoons of the buttermilk, then add it to one bowl of batter. In a separate small bowl, mix together the dark cocoa and remaining 2 tablespoons buttermilk and add to the remaining bowl. Stir each separately to combine. Pour each batter into a prepared pan. You should have one white, one brown, and one dark brown.

Bake for 27 to 30 minutes, until the center is baked through. Let the cakes cool in the pan for a minute before flipping them out onto a wire rack to cool completely. Wrap and freeze the cakes before assembly.

For the Triple Chocolate Buttercream

In three separate microwave-safe bowls, stir together the three different chocolates each with 3 tablespoons of heavy cream. Microwave each

bowl, one at a time, for 30 seconds and then stir until smooth. Let cool to room temperature.

Split the buttercream into three separate bowls. Add the white chocolate ganache to one, the milk chocolate to another, and the dark chocolate to the third. Stir to combine.

To Assemble and Decorate

Place a cardboard cake round on a cake turntable. Dot a little bit of dark chocolate buttercream in the center of the round and spread it out with an angled icing spatula. Place the chilled dark chocolate cake layer in the center. Add a layer of dark chocolate buttercream. Place the milk chocolate cake layer on top, then add a layer of milk chocolate buttercream, making sure to line the layers up evenly. Add the white cake layer, then crumb coat the cake by spreading a thin layer of buttercream around the entire cake, using the white chocolate on top, milk chocolate in the middle, and dark chocolate buttercream along the bottom layer. Freeze for 2 minutes to set the buttercream.

Using a wooden spoon, beat out any air bubbles in the remaining buttercreams. Minding the respective chocolate layers, spread a coat of dark chocolate buttercream on the bottom, the milk chocolate in the middle, and the white chocolate on top, using a cake scraper for smooth sides and clean edges.

Fit a piping bag with a Wilton 1M tip and spoon the remaining buttercream—all three flavors—into the bag (there's no need to mix them together; it's better if the buttercream has distinct swirls). Pipe even swirls around the top of the cake.

HORCHATA CAKE

Horchata is a heavenly tasting Mexican rice-milk drink with cinnamon. It offers a good balance, too, if you've ordered a spicy dish and need something cool and milky to calm down your taste buds. I'd always wanted to make an horchata cake, but feared it would end up tasting just like a cinnamon cake. To create that true horchata flavor in both the cake and buttercream, I use a horchata mix (found in the Latin American section at my grocery store, but you could also order it online). The resulting flavor is instantly recognizable.

Horchata Cake

- ⅔ cup buttermilk (room temperature)
- ⅔ cup sour cream (room temperature)
- 4 egg whites (room temperature)
- ½ cup horchata mix (such as Klass)
- ⅓ cup vegetable oil
- 1 tablespoon pure vanilla extract
- 1 teaspoon ground cinnamon
- ¼ cup flour
- 1 box white cake mix

Horchata Buttercream

- ½ cup heavy cream (plus more if needed)
- 3 tablespoons horchata mix (plus more if needed)
- 1½ cups (3 sticks) unsalted butter
- 1 tablespoon pure vanilla extract
- ½ teaspoon ground cinnamon
- Pinch of salt
- 7 to 8 cups powdered sugar

For Decorating

- Cinnamon sticks
- Ground cinnamon

For the Horchata Cake

Preheat the oven to 325°F, then prep three 6-inch round cake pans with a swipe of shortening and dusting of flour to prevent sticking.

In a large bowl, whisk together the buttermilk, sour cream, egg whites, horchata mix, oil, vanilla, and cinnamon until thoroughly combined. Let the mixture sit briefly until the horchata mix has dissolved. Sift in the flour and cake mix and whisk until just combined. Do not overmix. Split the batter evenly among the prepared pans.

Bake for 27 to 30 minutes, until the center is baked through. Let the cakes cool in the pan for a minute before flipping them out onto a wire rack to cool completely. Wrap and freeze the cakes before assembly.

For the Horchata Buttercream

In a cup, stir together the heavy cream and horchata mix. Let soak until all the powder has been dissolved into the cream, about 15 minutes.

In the bowl of a stand mixer fitted with a paddle attachment, beat the butter on medium speed until it's light and fluffy, then add the horchata mixture, vanilla, cinnamon, and salt and beat again until combined, then scrape down the sides with a spatula.

With the mixer on low speed, add the powdered sugar about ½ cup at a time. The buttercream will be thick. Add a little more heavy cream, 1 tablespoon at a time, to thin it out if needed, and then flip the mixer to high speed and beat until the buttercream is lighter in color and texture, about 2 minutes.

To Assemble and Decorate

Place a cardboard cake round on a cake turntable. Dot a little bit of buttercream in the center of the round and spread it out with an angled icing spatula. Place the first chilled cake layer in the center. Add a layer of buttercream. Place the next cake layer on top, then repeat, making sure to line the layers up evenly. After adding the top cake layer, crumb coat the cake by spreading a thin layer of buttercream around

the entire cake. Freeze for 2 minutes to set the buttercream.

Using a wooden spoon, beat out any air bubbles in the remaining buttercream. Spread a final layer of buttercream around the entire cake, using a cake scraper for smooth sides and clean edges. Place a couple of cinnamon sticks on top and dust the rim of the cake with a little ground cinnamon.

TIP: To achieve the best flavor from the horchata mix and to avoid any graininess, make sure the powder has plenty of time to soak in the buttermilk for the cake layers and the heavy cream for the buttercream.

SALTED CARAMEL PRETZEL CAKE

Sweet and salty are a classic duo, so putting them together in a cake by way of caramel and pretzel is something I knew would be extra fun. No need to prebake the crust—it bakes right along with the cake layers. How awesome is that? For max pretzel taste in the buttercream, I pulse them down to a fine powder and then toss them right in. Instead of using caramel in my buttercream (which can change the consistency), I use caramel extract. Place the pretzels on the cake right before your gathering, so they'll stay nice and crunchy for serving.

Salted Caramel Pretzel Cake

- 5 tablespoons unsalted butter
- 5 ounces salted pretzels
- 3 tablespoons packed brown sugar
- ¾ cup buttermilk (room temperature)
- ⅔ cup sour cream (room temperature)
- 3 large eggs plus 1 egg white (room temperature)
- ⅓ cup vegetable oil
- 1 tablespoon pure vanilla extract
- 2 teaspoons caramel extract
- 1 box white cake mix

Caramel Sauce Filling

- 1 cup granulated sugar
- 6 tablespoons salted butter
- ½ cup heavy cream
- ½ teaspoon salt

Caramel Pretzel Buttercream

- 1½ cups (3 sticks) unsalted butter
- 1 cup pretzels, pulsed to a powder in a food processor
- ½ cup heavy cream (plus more if needed)
- 1 tablespoon pure vanilla extract
- 2 teaspoons caramel extract
- Pinch of salt
- 7 to 8 cups powdered sugar

For Decorating

- Pretzels

For the Salted Caramel Pretzel Cake

Preheat the oven to 325°F, then prep three 6-inch round cake pans with a swipe of shortening and dusting of flour to prevent sticking.

In a food processor, blend together the butter, pretzels, and brown sugar until a fine crust forms.

Split the crust mixture evenly into the prepared pans and press to firm with the bottom of a glass or flat measuring cup.

In a large bowl, whisk together the buttermilk, sour cream, eggs, oil, vanilla, and caramel extract until thoroughly combined. Then sift in the cake mix and whisk until just combined. Do not overmix. Split the batter evenly among the prepared pans.

Bake for 30 to 32 minutes, until the center is baked through. Let the cakes cool in the pan for a minute before flipping them out onto a wire rack to cool completely. Wrap and freeze the cakes before assembly.

For the Caramel Sauce Filling

In a medium saucepan over medium heat, cook the sugar, stirring constantly with a wooden spoon, until the sugar clumps melt and form an amber liquid, 2 to 5 minutes. Add the butter, 1 tablespoon at a time, until melted. It will bubble a lot, so be careful and continue to stir. When all the butter has been added, let the mixture bubble for about a minute without stirring.

Slowly add the heavy cream and let boil for a minute without stirring—it will bubble high in the pan. Remove from the heat and add the salt. Let cool. Gently stir. Cover and refrigerate until ready to use.

For the Caramel Pretzel Buttercream

In the bowl of a stand mixer fitted with a paddle attachment, beat the butter on medium speed until it's light and fluffy, then add the pretzel

powder, heavy cream, vanilla, caramel extract, and salt and beat again until combined, then scrape down the sides with a spatula.

With the mixer on low speed, add the powdered sugar about ½ cup at a time. The buttercream will be thick. Add a little more heavy cream, 1 tablespoon at a time, to thin it out if needed, and then flip the mixer to high speed and beat until the buttercream is lighter in color and texture, about 2 minutes.

To Assemble and Decorate

Place a cardboard cake round on a cake turntable. Dot a little bit of buttercream in the center of the round and spread it out with an angled icing spatula. Place the first chilled cake layer in the center (crust side up). Add a thin layer of buttercream. Pipe a buttercream dam around the outside rim of the frosted cake layer, then add about ½ cup of the caramel sauce filling. Place the next cake layer on top, then repeat, making sure to line the layers up evenly. After adding the top cake layer, crumb coat the cake by spreading a thin layer of buttercream around the entire cake. Freeze for 2 minutes to set the buttercream.

Using a wooden spoon, beat out any air bubbles in the remaining buttercream. Spread a final layer of buttercream around the entire cake, using a cake scraper for smooth sides. Leave the top edge raw for a more rustic look.

Place a double line of pretzels along the bottom of the cake. Gently pour a pool of caramel sauce on top.

TIP: Plain caramel hardens when chilled, so I add a bit of heavy cream to soften it into a slice-friendly consistency and allow it to ooze around the plate in a really mouthwatering way.

If homemade caramel is too much effort, feel free to use store-bought caramel sauce for the filling.

BANANA CAKE *with Hazelnut Buttercream and Nutella Filling*

When he was in kindergarten, my son Liam preferred to make his own toast in the morning, *thank you very much*. However, the amount of Nutella he loved to spread on it still kept me in the kitchen to make sure the rest of the jar could be spared for next time. He felt so grown-up, and I didn't mind how cute his little face looked with a touch of Nutella on his cheeks. As expected, Nutella is very delicious in a cake, too, and goes especially well with bananas, as in this heavenly version.

This cake is a great way to use up any ripe bananas, and you could also add a few slices between the cake layers for even more banana flavor.

Banana Cake
- 2 medium ripe bananas, mashed
- ⅔ cup buttermilk (room temperature)
- ⅔ cup sour cream (room temperature)
- 3 large eggs (room temperature)
- ⅓ cup vegetable oil
- 1 tablespoon pure vanilla extract
- 1 teaspoon banana extract (optional)
- 1 box white cake mix

Hazelnut Filling
- ½ cup Nutella hazelnut spread (see Tip)

Hazelnut Buttercream
- 1½ cups (3 sticks) unsalted butter
- ½ cup Nutella hazelnut spread
- ¼ cup heavy cream (plus more if needed)
- 1 tablespoon pure vanilla extract
- 1 teaspoon hazelnut emulsion (optional)
- Pinch of salt
- 7 to 8 cups powdered sugar

For Decorating
- Piping bag
- Wilton 124 (petal) piping tip
- Chocolate shavings or curls

For the Banana Cake
Preheat the oven to 325°F, then prep three 6-inch round cake pans with a swipe of shortening and dusting of flour to prevent sticking.

In a large bowl, whisk together the mashed bananas, buttermilk, sour cream, eggs, oil, vanilla, and banana extract (if using) until thoroughly combined. Sift in the cake mix and whisk until just combined. Do not overmix. Split the batter evenly among the prepared pans.

Bake for 27 to 30 minutes, until the center is baked through. Let the cakes cool in the pan for a minute before flipping them out onto a wire rack to cool completely. Wrap and freeze the cakes before assembly.

For the Hazelnut Buttercream
In the bowl of a stand mixer fitted with a paddle attachment, whip the butter over medium speed until it's light and fluffy. Add the Nutella, heavy cream, vanilla, hazelnut emulsion (if using), and salt and beat again until combined, then scrape down the sides with a spatula.

With the mixer on low speed, add the powdered sugar about ½ cup at a time. The buttercream will be thick. Add a little more heavy cream, 1 tablespoon at a time, to thin it out if needed, and then flip the mixer to high speed and beat until the buttercream is lighter in color and texture, about 2 minutes.

To Assemble
Place a cardboard cake round on a cake turntable. Dot a little bit of buttercream in the center of the round and spread it out with an angled icing spatula. Place the first chilled cake layer in the center. Spread on half (¼ cup) of the Nutella filling. Add a layer of buttercream, spreading it evenly with an angled icing spatula.

Place the next cake layer on top, then repeat, making sure to line the layers up evenly. After adding the top cake layer, crumb coat the cake by spreading a thin layer of buttercream around the entire cake. Freeze for 2 minutes to set the buttercream.

Using a wooden spoon, beat out any air bubbles in the remaining buttercream. Finish frosting the cake as desired or follow the decorating instructions below.

To Decorate the Cake

Spread a final layer of buttercream around the entire cake, using a cake scraper for smooth sides and clean edges.

Add the remaining buttercream to a piping bag fitted with the Wilton 124 tip. Holding the wide end of the piping tip against the cake, pipe ribbons on the top of the cake, starting at the outer rim and working your way in until the top is covered. Sprinkle on some chocolate shavings.

TIP: If you can't find Nutella or another kind of hazelnut spread, add 1 tablespoon of hazelnut emulsion or extract and ½ cup of cocoa powder in the buttercream to achieve a similar taste.

The Nutella filling will be easier to spread between the cake layers when it's slightly melted. Transfer it to a small microwave-safe bowl and heat for a few seconds.

PUMPKIN CHOCOLATE CHIP CAKE *with*
Chocolate Buttercream and Ganache Drip

Do you have any fall baking recipes that you can't wait to make every single year? Soft pumpkin chocolate chip cookies are that recipe for me. It's just not officially fall until I smell that sweet aroma of pumpkin and chocolate baking together in the oven and filling my kitchen with the excitement of yet another fall baking season. This cake echoes my favorite part of those cookies. The pumpkin cake is thick and soft in the best way, and each slice has little bits of chocolate chips baked right into the cake batter. The literal icing on the cake is rich with chocolate, and I couldn't help but add a chocolate drip, chocolate jimmies, and a piped herringbone buttercream design on top.

Pumpkin Chocolate Chip Cake

- 15 ounces canned pumpkin
- ½ cup buttermilk (room temperature)
- ½ cup sour cream (room temperature)
- ½ cup semisweet mini chocolate chips
- 3 large eggs (room temperature)
- ⅓ cup vegetable oil
- 1 tablespoon pumpkin pie spice
- 1 teaspoon pure vanilla extract
- 1 box yellow cake mix

Chocolate Ganache Drip

- ½ cup chocolate melts
- ½ cup heavy cream

Chocolate Buttercream

- ½ cup plus ¼ cup heavy cream (plus more if needed)
- ½ cup dark chocolate chips
- 2 cups (4 sticks) unsalted butter
- ½ cup cocoa powder
- 1 tablespoon pure vanilla extract
- Pinch of salt
- 8 to 9 cups powdered sugar

For Decorating

- Chocolate jimmies or sprinkles
- Piping bag
- Wilton 124 piping tip

For the Pumpkin Chocolate Chip Cake

Preheat the oven to 325°F, then prep three 6-inch round cake pans with a swipe of shortening and dusting of flour to prevent sticking.

In a large bowl, whisk together the pumpkin, buttermilk, sour cream, mini chocolate chips, eggs, oil, pumpkin pie spice, and vanilla until thoroughly combined. Sift in the cake mix and whisk until just combined. Do not overmix. Split the batter evenly among the prepared pans.

Bake for 30 to 35 minutes, until the center is baked through. Let the cakes cool in the pan for a minute before flipping them out onto a wire rack to cool completely. Wrap and freeze the cakes before assembly.

For the Chocolate Ganache Drip

In a small microwave-safe bowl, stir together the chocolate melts and heavy cream and heat in the microwave for 30 seconds. Stir until smooth, then transfer to a drip bottle.

For the Chocolate Buttercream

In a small microwave-safe bowl, stir together ½ cup of the heavy cream and the dark chocolate chips and heat in the microwave for 30 seconds. Stir until smooth, then let cool to room temperature before adding to your buttercream.

In the bowl of a stand mixer fitted with a paddle attachment, beat the butter on medium speed until it's light and fluffy. Add the cooled ganache,

cocoa, the remaining ¼ cup heavy cream, vanilla, and salt and beat again until combined, then scrape down the sides with a spatula.

With the mixer on low speed, add the powdered sugar about ½ cup at a time. The buttercream will be thick. Add a little more heavy cream, 1 tablespoon at a time, to thin it out if needed, and then flip the mixer to high speed and beat until the buttercream is lighter in color and texture, about 2 minutes.

To Assemble

Place a cardboard cake round on a cake turntable. Dot a little bit of buttercream in the center of the round and spread it out with an angled icing spatula. Place the first chilled cake layer in the center. Add a layer of buttercream. Place the next cake layer on top, then repeat, making sure to line the layers up evenly. After adding the top cake layer, crumb coat the cake by spreading a thin layer of buttercream around the entire cake. Freeze for 2 minutes to set the buttercream.

Using a wooden spoon, beat out any air bubbles in the remaining buttercream. Finish frosting the cake as desired or follow the decorating instructions below.

To Decorate the Cake

Spread a final layer of buttercream around the entire cake, using a cake scraper for smooth sides and clean edges.

Place the cake on a cookie sheet on the cake turntable. Carefully add chocolate jimmies along the bottom of the cake by gently pressing them on with your hand. Freeze for 2 minutes to set.

Pipe the ganache drips on the top of the chilled cake, letting the drips cascade down the sides about an inch apart from each other. Add more ganache in the center and spread to the edges with an angled icing spatula. Freeze for 1 minute to set the ganache drips.

Add the remaining buttercream to a piping bag fitted with the Wilton 124 tip. Holding the

bag with the wide end of the piping tip against the cake, pipe a herringbone pattern with little buttercream lines in a crown around the top of the cake. Sprinkle more chocolate jimmies around the top.

TIP: This cake bakes up tall and has a different texture than my other cakes. Using an entire can of pumpkin puree in the cake batter creates a delightfully dense consistency (kind of like pumpkin pie), but it is still very cake-like. You can split the batter into four pans instead of three for less-towering rounds to work with.

ULTIMATE CARAMEL CAKE *with Brown Butter Salted Caramel Buttercream and Caramel Filling*

This cake is perfect for the ultimate caramel lover. The idea came to me while trying to create a caramel popcorn–inspired cake, and I ended up grabbing some stroopwafels at the grocery store in the meantime for a future cake idea. I married the two ideas in this ultimate caramel cake, and it was magic. Caramel corn, caramels, and those heavenly stroopwafels really make this cake come to life on the outside, matching the really incredible flavor on the inside.

Caramel Cake

- ¾ cup buttermilk (room temperature)
- ⅔ cup sour cream (room temperature)
- 3 large eggs plus 1 egg white (room temperature)
- ⅓ cup vegetable oil
- ¼ cup packed brown sugar
- 1 tablespoon caramel extract
- 2 teaspoons pure vanilla extract
- 1 box white or butter golden cake mix
- ¼ cup flour

Brown Butter Salted Caramel Buttercream

- 2 cups (4 sticks) unsalted butter
- ¼ cup heavy cream (plus more if needed)
- 2 teaspoons pure vanilla extract
- 2 teaspoons caramel extract
- 2 pinches salt
- 7 to 8 cups powdered sugar

For Decorating

Caramel Sauce Filling (page 153)

Caramel popcorn

Caramels

Mini stroopwafels

For the Caramel Cake

Preheat the oven to 325°F, then prep three 6-inch round cake pans with a swipe of shortening and dusting of flour to prevent sticking.

In a large bowl, whisk together the buttermilk, sour cream, eggs, oil, brown sugar, caramel extract, and vanilla until thoroughly combined. Sift in the cake mix and flour and whisk until just combined. Do not overmix. Split the batter evenly among the prepared pans.

Bake for 27 to 30 minutes, until the center is baked through. Let the cakes cool in the pan for a minute before flipping them out onto a wire rack to cool completely. Wrap and freeze the cakes before assembly.

For the Brown Butter Salted Caramel Buttercream

Make the browned butter in advance: In a medium saucepan over medium heat, melt 1 cup (2 sticks) of the butter. Stir until the butter foams. It will then begin to brown. Watch very closely and keep stirring. Don't let it burn! It can go from brown to burned very quickly. When the butter has reached a dark amber color and has a nutty aroma, immediately remove it from the heat and transfer it to a glass bowl (make sure to scrape out all the brown bits—those have a lot of flavor). Cover, then refrigerate until it cools completely.

In the bowl of a stand mixer fitted with a paddle attachment, beat the remaining 1 cup (2 sticks) butter and browned butter over medium speed until light and fluffy. Add the heavy cream, vanilla, caramel extract, and salt and beat again until combined, then scrape down the sides with a spatula.

With the mixer on low speed, add the powdered sugar about ½ cup at a time. The buttercream will be thick. Add a little more heavy cream, 1 tablespoon at a time, to thin it out if needed, and then flip the mixer to high speed and beat until the buttercream is lighter in color and texture, about 2 minutes.

To Assemble and Decorate

Place a cardboard cake round on a cake turntable. Dot a little bit of buttercream in the center of the round and spread it out with an angled icing spatula. Place the first chilled cake layer in the center. Add a thin layer of buttercream. Pipe a buttercream dam around the outside rim of the frosted cake layer, then add about ½ cup of the caramel sauce filling. Place the next cake layer on top, then repeat, making sure to line the layers up evenly. After adding the top cake layer, crumb coat the cake by spreading a thin layer of buttercream around the entire cake. Freeze for 2 minutes to set the buttercream.

Using a wooden spoon, beat out any air bubbles in the remaining buttercream. Spread a final layer of buttercream around the entire cake, using a cake scraper for smooth sides and clean edges. Holding a straight icing spatula vertically against the bottom of the cake while turning the turntable, carefully create horizontal stripes on the side of the cake from the bottom to the top.

Transfer some of the caramel filling to a drip bottle and add some caramel drip to one side of the cake. Press the caramel popcorn, caramels, and mini stroopwafels all over the top and down the other side of the cake in a decorative pattern.

TIP: Don't be afraid to add all kinds of toppings onto a cake. The more, the better! We can't let sprinkles have all the fun! When you're looking for fun things to top your cake with, start with the candy and cookie section. I guarantee you'll find something exciting (and a few more things) to decorate with.

If you prefer, you can use store-bought caramel sauce or Wilton Salted Caramel Candy Melts instead of making the caramel sauce filling.

CHOCOLATE BISCOFF CAKE

Have you ever had cookie butter spread? If so, then you probably have the same problem that I do: you can't get enough and are always coming up with excuses to spread it on a snack or two. Cookie butter (or speculoos) is made from Biscoff cookies, and I love to use that signature cinnamon and brown sugar flavor in my cakes. Pairing it with chocolate was my son Jake's idea. I let my sons choose their cake flavors for their birthdays, and one year this combo—rich chocolate cake layers and Biscoff buttercream—was Jake's pick.

Chocolate Cookie Butter Cake

- ¾ cup buttermilk (room temperature)
- ⅔ cup sour cream (room temperature)
- ½ cup Biscoff cookie butter spread
- ½ cup crumbled Biscoff cookies
- 3 large eggs plus 1 egg white (room temperature)
- ⅓ cup vegetable oil
- 1 tablespoon pure vanilla extract
- 1 box dark chocolate cake mix

Cookie Butter Filling

- 1 cup cookie butter spread

Cookie Butter Buttercream

- 1½ cups (3 sticks) unsalted butter
- ⅔ cup cookie butter spread
- ½ cup heavy cream (plus more if needed)
- 1 tablespoon pure vanilla extract
- Pinch of salt
- 7 to 8 cups powdered sugar

Cookie Butter Drip

- 1 cup cookie butter spread

For Decorating

- Biscoff cookies, halved
- Biscoff cookie crumbles
- Piping bag
- Wilton 1M piping tip

For the Chocolate Cookie Butter Cake

Preheat the oven to 325°F, then prep three 6-inch round cake pans with a swipe of shortening and dusting of flour to prevent sticking.

In a large bowl, whisk together the buttermilk, sour cream, cookie butter, cookie pieces, eggs, oil, and vanilla until thoroughly combined. Sift in the cake mix and whisk until just combined. Do not overmix. Split the batter evenly among the prepared pans.

Bake for 27 to 30 minutes, until the center is baked through. Let the cakes cool in the pan for a minute before flipping them out onto a wire rack to cool completely. Wrap and freeze the cakes before assembly.

For the Cookie Butter Filling

In a microwave-safe bowl, microwave the cookie butter for about 30 seconds, and then stir.

For the Cookie Butter Buttercream

In the bowl of a stand mixer fitted with a paddle attachment, beat the butter on medium speed until it's light and fluffy. Add the cookie butter, heavy cream, vanilla, and salt and beat again until combined, then scrape down the sides with a spatula.

With the mixer on low speed, add the powdered sugar about ½ cup at a time. The buttercream will be thick. Add a little more heavy cream, 1 tablespoon at a time, to thin it out if needed, and then flip the mixer to high speed and beat until the buttercream is lighter in color and texture, about 2 minutes.

For the Cookie Butter Drip

In a microwave-safe bowl, microwave the cookie butter for about 45 seconds, and then stir. Transfer to a drip bottle and let cool slightly before using.

To Assemble

Place a cardboard cake round on a cake turntable. Dot a little bit of buttercream in the center of the round and spread it out with an angled icing spatula. Place the first chilled cake layer in the center. Add a thin layer of buttercream. Pipe a buttercream dam around the outside rim of the frosted cake layer, then add about ½ cup of the cookie butter filling. Place the next cake layer on top, then repeat with the rest of the layers, making sure to line the layers up evenly. After adding the top cake layer, crumb coat the cake by spreading a thin layer of buttercream around the entire cake. Freeze for 2 minutes to set the buttercream. Finish frosting the cake as desired or follow the decorating instructions below.

To Decorate the Cake

Add the drip to the cake by pooling a bit of it on the top edge and letting the drips cascade down the sides about an inch apart. Freeze for 5 minutes to set.

Add the remaining buttercream to a piping bag fitted with a Wilton 1M tip. Pipe buttercream swirls around the top of the cake. Place half a Biscoff cookie on each buttercream swirl, then sprinkle the top with Biscoff crumbles.

TIP: Biscoff drip is the easiest drip I've ever made. Just transfer the cookie butter to a microwave-safe dish and heat it for about 30 seconds—instant perfect drip!

I made this cake a naked one, but if you'd like to add more buttercream, that's always a good idea, too. It's up to you.

BANANA CARAMEL CAKE *with Peanut Butter Caramel Buttercream*

This cake is so fun. It reminds me of placing banana circles on my peanut butter toast. I'd never thought to add a drizzle of caramel to my toast as well, but after making such a tasty cake with those three flavors, I can't think of any reason why not. The banana cake layers are tender, soft, and have a sweet hint of caramel. And if you haven't tried my peanut butter caramel buttercream yet, you are in for a real treat—it's in my top-five favorites, and one of my secret weapons. The most common review I receive about the peanut butter buttercream is how once people serve it, their guests always request it again and again.

Banana Caramel Cake

- ⅔ cup packed brown sugar
- 2 bananas, sliced
- ¾ cup buttermilk (room temperature)
- ⅔ cup sour cream (room temperature)
- 4 large egg whites (room temperature)
- ⅓ cup vegetable oil
- 1 tablespoon pure vanilla extract
- 2 teaspoons caramel extract
- 1 teaspoon banana extract
- 1 box white cake mix

Peanut Butter Caramel Buttercream

- 1½ cups (3 sticks) unsalted butter
- ⅔ cup creamy peanut butter
- ¼ cup heavy cream (plus more if needed)
- 1 tablespoon pure vanilla extract
- 1 teaspoon caramel extract
- Pinch of salt
- 7 to 8 cups powdered sugar

For Decorating

- ½ cup creamy peanut butter
- Sliced bananas
- Inverted scallop cake comb

For the Banana Caramel Cake

Preheat the oven to 325°F, then prep three 6-inch round cake pans with a swipe of shortening and dusting of flour to prevent sticking.

Sprinkle the brown sugar evenly among the three cake pans. Place the banana slices on top of the brown sugar layer.

In a large bowl, whisk together the buttermilk, sour cream, egg whites, oil, vanilla, caramel extract, and banana extract until thoroughly combined. Sift in the cake mix and whisk until just combined. Do not overmix. Split the batter evenly among the prepared pans.

Bake for 27 to 30 minutes, until the center is baked through. Let the cakes cool in the pan for a minute before flipping them out onto a wire rack to cool completely. Wrap and freeze the cakes before assembly.

For the Peanut Butter Caramel Buttercream

In the bowl of a stand mixer fitted with a paddle attachment, beat the butter on medium speed until it's light and fluffy. Add the peanut butter, heavy cream, vanilla, caramel extract, and salt and beat again to combine, then scrape down the sides with a spatula.

With the mixer on low speed, add the powdered sugar about ½ cup at a time. The buttercream will be thick. Add a little more heavy cream, 1 tablespoon at a time, to thin it out if needed, and then flip the mixer to high speed and beat until the buttercream is lighter in color and texture, about 2 minutes.

To Assemble and Decorate

Place a cardboard cake round on a cake turntable. Dot a little bit of buttercream in the center of the round and spread it out with an

angled icing spatula. Place the first chilled cake layer in the center (fruit side up). Add a layer of buttercream. Place the next cake layer on top, then repeat, making sure to line the layers up evenly. After adding the top cake layer, crumb coat the cake by spreading the buttercream in a thin layer around the entire cake. Freeze for 2 minutes to set the buttercream.

Using a wooden spoon, beat out any air bubbles in the remaining buttercream. Spread a final layer of buttercream around the entire cake, using an inverted scallop cake scraper to make decorative edges and sides, leaving the top edge raw for a more rustic look.

In a microwave-safe bowl, heat the peanut butter until melted. Let cool slightly, then spread it on the top of the cake, using an angled icing spatula and cake turntable to make the swirl design.

Right before serving, place banana slices on top of the cake in a half circle.

TIP: If you're worried about the bananas browning, you can sprinkle on a bit of lemon juice to slow the process, use dried banana chips, or simply wait until right before serving to add the banana slices.

HALLOWEEN
WITCHES' BREW ICE CREAM CONE CAKE

What You'll Need

- 1 cake, stacked and frosted (see Note) with light green buttercream
- Halloween sprinkles
- 1 cup black fondant
- 1 batch Small-Batch Vanilla Buttercream (page xvii)
- 8 sugar cones
- 1 cup white chocolate candy melts
- Sixlets candy
- Decorative sugar eyes
- Piping bag
- Wilton 1M piping tip

NOTE: Frost and decorate the cake before adding the ice cream cones, using a cake scraper for smooth sides and clean edges. Press a rim of Halloween sprinkles around the side of the cake at the bottom. Using a piping bag fitted with a Wilton 1M tip and filled with purple buttercream, pipe swirls in a ring on top of the cake. Press a small ball of black fondant onto each buttercream swirl, add on some decorative eyes, and add more Halloween sprinkles.

1. Use a knife to cut the tip ends of the sugar cones to make 1- to 2-inch smaller ones.

2. Slice off one side of each cone near the top so that it can lay flat against the cake.

3. Heat the candy melts in the microwave until they are melted, then dip the end of the cone into the candy.

4. Before the melted candy sets, dip the cone into the sprinkles.

5. Let the cones dry on a sheet of parchment paper.

6. Press the decorated cones onto the side of the cake.

7. Fit a piping bag with the Wilton 1M tip and fill it with untinted buttercream. Swirl on a little bit of white buttercream on top of the cones to look like ice cream.

8. Place a few sixlets on the tip of the swirls and sprinkles on the swirl.

HALLOWEEN
CANDY CORN STRIPE CAKE

What You'll Need

1 cake, stacked and crumb coated (see page xxiv) with black buttercream

1 batch Vanilla Buttercream (page xvii), divided into fourths and tinted black, orange, and yellow (leave one-fourth white)

About ½ cup each white, orange, and yellow fondant

Cake turntable

Thin-stripe cake comb

7 piping bags

Cake scraper

3 Wilton 1A piping tips

Rolling pin

1. Place your cake on the turntable. After frosting your cake with black buttercream, use a thin-stripe cake comb to create clean indents in the side of the cake. The crisper the indents, the cleaner the stripes will be later on. Freeze the cake for 10 minutes.

3. Count down to the third indent and pipe a white stripe in the indent. Count down another three indents and repeat.

4. Right underneath each white stripe, pipe an orange one.

2. Fill piping bags with black, orange, yellow, and white buttercreams and snip off the ends to create tiny openings the size of the stripes.

5. Underneath the orange stripes, pipe a yellow stripe.

6. In the rest of the stripe indents, pipe in the black buttercream.

7. Immediately use a cake scraper to begin to smooth out the stripes. Keep scraping and applying a bit of pressure, and the stripes will slowly start to reveal themselves. Pipe in more color wherever needed. Hold the cake scraper under hot water for a little bit, then use the warmed scraper on the side of the cake for a finished look.

8. Fit three piping bags with Wilton 1A tips and fill with yellow, white, and orange buttercream.

9. Holding the piping bag perpendicular to the cake, squeeze out a little circle and quickly release while pulling the piping bag up to create a "Hershey kiss" on top. Switch piping bags and repeat around the top outside rim of the cake.

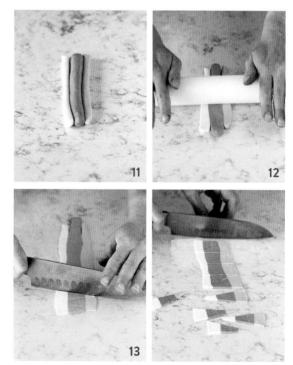

10. To make fondant candy corns, start with a small ball of white, orange, and yellow fondant.

11. Using the rolling pin, roll each ball out into a log, with the orange log a little bigger than the others. Line them up next to each other with the orange log in the middle.

12. Roll them out together to create a striped piece of fondant.

13. Slice the fondant at an angle to create thin triangles. Half the triangles will have the colors in the right order (with yellow at the bottom), and the other half won't. Use the correct ones on the top of your cake as decor.

THANKSGIVING FALL FOLIAGE CAKE

What You'll Need

1 cake, stacked and frosted (see page xxv; I used a scalloped cake comb for the sides), frozen until firm

1 batch Vanilla Buttercream (page xvii), divided and tinted maroon, burnt orange, golden yellow, green, and eggplant

Gold, orange, and purple sphere sprinkles

5 piping bags

4 couplers

Piping tips:

Wilton 1M, 13 (burnt orange)

6B, 3 (eggplant)

104, 2A (golden yellow)

32 (maroon)

352 (green)

1. Fit the piping bags with couplers and fill with the different-colored buttercreams.

2. Attach a Wilton 1M piping tip to the bag of orange buttercream and pipe rosettes in random places in the center of the sides of the cake.

3. Attach a #104 tip to the bag of yellow buttercream and pipe ruffles around one side of each rosette.

4. Attach a #32 tip to the bag of red buttercream and pipe a few stars in groups around the rosettes.

5. Attach a 6B tip to the bag of purple buttercream and pipe a few larger stars around the red stars.

6. Attach the #352 tip to the bag of green buttercream and add on the leaves.

7. Change the tip on the yellow buttercream to #2A and pipe a few circles.

8. Switch the tip on the purple buttercream to #3 and pipe on a few little spots in clusters around the bigger groups of buttercream.

9. Change the tip on the orange buttercream to #13 and pipe tiny rosettes around the bigger ones. Then fill in any white spots with more buttercream designs.

10. Place a few of the sprinkles in various spots.

Chapter 4

WHIMSICAL WINTER BAKES

I grew up in what sometimes felt like a Hallmark Channel movie set. Every winter we decorated bright-colored cookies and sugar-loaded gingerbread houses with Christmas music playing in the background; all the while thick Utah snow fell gently outside our home nestled near the Rocky Mountains. We ice skated, trimmed our home with bright-white Christmas lights, mailed off Christmas cards to friends and family, put up our flocked white-and-gold tree, and hung fluffy stockings over the fireplace. The smell of my grandma's molasses cookies filled the air as we came back inside to warm up after an afternoon of sledding and snowball fights.

MEXICAN HOT CHOCOLATE CAKE *with* *Marshmallow Filling*

I love seeing spicy and sweet—two ends of the taste spectrum—come together. Here, the spiciness of the chili powder is wrapped around the chocolate flavor in a way that is not only strangely pleasant (meaning, it's just not what you'd first expect) but almost downright addicting. To get that classic hint of spice, I used a Mexican hot chocolate mix and added in a pinch of cayenne and cinnamon to really bring out the flavor in both the cake and buttercream.

Mexican Hot Chocolate Cake

- 1 cup buttermilk (room temperature)
- ½ cup sour cream (room temperature)
- ½ cup vegetable oil
- ½ cup Mexican hot chocolate mix (such as Abuelita)
- 3 large eggs (room temperature)
- 1 tablespoon pure vanilla extract
- 1 teaspoon ground cinnamon
- 2 pinches cayenne
- 1 box dark chocolate or devil's food cake mix

Marshmallow Filling

- 1½ cups granulated sugar
- ½ cup cold water
- 2 egg whites
- 1 teaspoon corn syrup
- 1 cup mini marshmallows

- 1 teaspoon pure vanilla extract

Mexican Hot Chocolate Buttercream

- 1½ cups (3 sticks) unsalted butter
- ½ cup Mexican hot chocolate mix
- ¼ cup heavy cream (plus more if needed)
- ¼ cup cocoa powder
- 1 tablespoon pure vanilla extract
- 1 teaspoon ground cinnamon
- Pinch of cayenne
- Pinch of salt
- 7 to 8 cups powdered sugar

For Decorating

- 2 dried red chili peppers
- Piping bag
- Wilton 10 (small circle) piping tip

For the Mexican Hot Chocolate Cake

Preheat the oven to 325°F, then prep three 6-inch round cake pans with a swipe of shortening and dusting of flour to prevent sticking.

In a large bowl, whisk together the buttermilk, sour cream, oil, hot chocolate mix, eggs, vanilla, cinnamon, and cayenne until thoroughly combined. Sift in the cake mix and whisk until just combined. Do not overmix. Split the batter evenly among the prepared pans.

Bake for 27 to 30 minutes, until the center is baked through. Let the cakes cool in the pan for a minute before flipping them out onto a wire rack to cool completely. Wrap and freeze the cakes before assembly.

For the Marshmallow Filling

Over a double boiler (or metal stand mixer bowl over a small saucepan of boiling water), whisk together the sugar, cold water, egg whites, and corn syrup with an electric mixer until stiff peaks form. Remove from the heat. Attach the mixer bowl to a stand mixer fitted with a whisk attachment. Add the mini marshmallows and vanilla and keep whisking until stiff peaks form. Let cool completely to thicken, then transfer to a piping bag.

For the Mexican Hot Chocolate Buttercream

In the bowl of a stand mixer fitted with a paddle attachment, beat the butter on medium speed until it's light and fluffy. Add the hot chocolate mix, heavy cream, cocoa, vanilla, cinnamon, cayenne, and salt, then scrape down the sides with a spatula.

With the mixer on low speed, add the powdered sugar about ½ cup at a time. The buttercream will be thick. Add a little more heavy cream to thin it out if needed, and then flip the mixer to high speed and beat until the buttercream is lighter in color and texture, about 2 minutes.

To Assemble
Place a cardboard cake round on a cake turntable. Dot a little bit of buttercream in the center of the round and spread it out with an angled icing spatula. Place the first chilled cake layer in the center. Add a thin layer of buttercream. Pipe a dam of buttercream around the outside rim of the frosted cake layer, and then pipe the marshmallow filling into the center.

Place the next cake layer on top, then repeat, making sure to line the layers up evenly. After adding the top cake layer, crumb coat the cake by spreading a thin layer of buttercream around the entire cake. Freeze for 2 minutes to set the buttercream.

Using a wooden spoon, beat out any air bubbles in the remaining buttercream. Finish frosting the cake as desired or follow the decorating instructions below.

To Decorate the Cake
Spread a final layer of buttercream around the entire cake, using a cake scraper for smooth sides and clean edges. Freeze for 5 minutes to set.

To make the buttercream pattern on the side of the cake, fill a piping bag fitted with the Wilton 10 piping tip with buttercream.

Pipe a vertical line on the side of the cake from top to bottom, then pipe another one about 2 inches away. Repeat around the entire cake. For the next pattern, pipe a small circle next to one of the vertical lines, dragging the tail downward in a diagonal toward the center. Pipe another circle right next to it, but staggered a little lower, and drag the tail down so it overlaps the previous one. Repeat all the way down the side of the cake to make a braid. Repeat the pattern between each vertical line on the side of the cake.

With the remaining ½ cup marshmallow filling, pipe two circles around the outside rim on the top of the cake. Place the dried chili peppers on top as garnish.

TIP: If you're nervous about the buttercream getting too spicy, add just a tiny bit of the cayenne and taste it. The flavor may intensify, so aim for just under your spiciness tolerance. Also, we're not talking spicy as in spicy chicken wings; it's more of a really fun kind of tickle on your tongue after you're flooded with chocolate-cinnamon flavor.

You could use store-bought marshmallow fluff instead of making your own filling.

WHITE CHOCOLATE CRANBERRY ORANGE CAKE *with Cranberry Filling and Sugared Cranberries*

This cake is all dolled up for a Christmas party and is inspired by the beautiful Christmas spreads from my family's favorite holiday movies. With its hint of orange, the cranberry filling, and the white chocolate, this cake is so lovely to enjoy each year around the holidays.

White Chocolate Orange Cake

- ⅔ cup buttermilk (room temperature)
- ⅔ cup sour cream (room temperature)
- 4 egg whites (room temperature)
- ⅓ cup vegetable oil
- 1 tablespoon pure vanilla extract
- 1 tablespoon orange emulsion
- Zest of 1 orange
- 1 box white cake mix

Cranberry Compote Filling

- 1 cup frozen cranberries, thawed
- ¼ cup plus 1 tablespoon granulated sugar
- 3 tablespoons orange juice
- 1 tablespoon orange zest
- 1 teaspoon pure vanilla extract
- 2 teaspoons cornstarch

White Chocolate Orange Buttercream

- ½ cup white chocolate chips
- ¼ cup plus 3 tablespoons heavy cream (plus more if needed)
- 1½ cups (3 sticks) unsalted butter
- 1 tablespoon pure vanilla extract
- 1 tablespoon orange emulsion
- Pinch of salt
- 7 to 8 cups powdered sugar

Sugared Cranberries

- 1½ cups granulated sugar (plus more if needed)
- 1 cup fresh cranberries

For Decorating

- White sprinkle mix
- Orange
- Piping bag
- Wilton 6B piping tip

For the White Chocolate Orange Cake

Preheat the oven to 325°F, then prep three 6-inch round cake pans with a swipe of shortening and dusting of flour to prevent sticking.

In a large bowl, whisk together the buttermilk, sour cream, egg whites, oil, vanilla, orange emulsion, and orange zest until thoroughly combined. Sift in the cake mix and whisk until just combined. Do not overmix. Split the batter evenly among the prepared pans.

Bake for 27 to 30 minutes, until the center is baked through. Let the cakes cool in the pan for a minute before flipping them out onto a wire rack to cool completely. Wrap and freeze the cakes before assembly.

For the Cranberry Compote Filling

In a small saucepan over medium heat, stir together the cranberries, sugar, orange juice, orange zest, and vanilla and cook until slightly thickened, bubbling, and the cranberries have almost all "popped," about 5 minutes. Sift in the cornstarch and stir until thickened, about 2 minutes. Transfer to a glass dish, cover, and refrigerate until thickened and cooled completely.

For the White Chocolate Orange Buttercream

In a microwave-safe bowl, stir together the white chocolate chips and ¼ cup of the heavy cream, heat for about 30 seconds, and then stir until smooth. Let cool until the ganache is close to room temperature.

In the bowl of a stand mixer fitted with a paddle attachment, beat the butter on medium speed until it's light and fluffy. Add the white chocolate ganache, the remaining 3 tablespoons heavy cream, the vanilla, orange emulsion, and salt and beat again until combined, then scrape down the sides with a spatula.

With the mixer on low speed, add the powdered sugar about ½ cup at a time. The buttercream will be thick. Add a little more heavy cream, 1 tablespoon at a time, to thin it out if needed, and then flip the mixer to high speed and beat until the buttercream is lighter in color and texture, about 2 minutes.

For the Sugared Cranberries

In a small saucepan over medium heat, whisk together ½ cup of water and ½ cup of the sugar and then simmer until the sugar is dissolved. Stir in the cranberries, making sure they're coated in the simple syrup.

Cover the pot and remove from the heat. Steep for about 10 minutes.

Place the remaining 1 cup sugar on a plate. Drain the cranberries, then roll them in the sugar (you may add more sugar if needed). Transfer the sugared cranberries to a piece of parchment paper to dry for 10 minutes.

To Assemble

Place a cardboard cake round on a cake turntable. Dot a little bit of buttercream in the center of the round and spread it out with an angled icing spatula. Place the first chilled cake layer in the center. Add a thin layer of buttercream. Pipe a buttercream dam around the outside rim of the frosted cake layer, then add about ½ cup of the cranberry filling. Place the next cake layer on top, then repeat, making sure to line the layers up evenly. After adding the top cake layer, crumb coat the cake by spreading a thin layer of buttercream around the entire cake. Freeze for 2 minutes to set the buttercream.

Using a wooden spoon, beat out any air bubbles in the remaining buttercream. Finish frosting the cake as desired or follow the decorating instructions below.

To Decorate the Cake

Spread a final layer of buttercream around the entire cake, using a cake scraper for smooth sides and clean edges.

Place the cake on a cookie sheet and set it on the cake turntable. Gently press the white sprinkle mix onto the sides of the cake around the bottom edge, letting the excess sprinkles fall on the cookie sheet.

Slice an orange in half, then slice that half into thin slices. Press the slices into a paper towel to remove as much moisture as possible, then press the orange slices along the top rim of the cake (with the flat side of the slice facing up).

Add the rest of the buttercream to a piping bag fitted with a Wilton 6B tip. Pipe buttercream dollops around the entire top of the cake. Place the sugared cranberries on the dollops around the top outside rim.

TIP: It's a good idea to make an extra handful or two of sugared cranberries; if you're anything like me, it will be hard to not snack on more than a few while assembling the cake.

CHOCOLATE ORANGE CAKE

On Christmas morning, my mother-in-law always makes sure to leave a chocolate orange in the toe of each stocking for her sons, daughters-in-law, and grandchildren. It's a fun tradition we've adopted into our home, too, and it always brings a smile to my face. If you're unfamiliar with chocolate oranges, they're shaped just like real oranges, complete with individual segments, but made out of chocolate. I wish chocolate oranges were available year-round because there's nothing that quite hits the spot for me like a dark chocolate orange slice—and the satisfying smack on the counter to release the slices from their chocolate center.

Chocolate Orange Cake

- ¾ cup buttermilk (room temperature)
- ⅔ cup sour cream (room temperature)
- 3 large eggs plus 1 egg white (room temperature)
- ⅓ cup vegetable oil
- ½ cup mini chocolate chips
- 1 tablespoon pure vanilla extract
- 1 tablespoon orange emulsion
- Zest of 1 orange (about 1 tablespoon)
- ¼ cup flour
- 1 box dark chocolate cake mix

Chocolate Orange Buttercream

- 1 whole chocolate orange (see Tip)
- ½ cup plus 2 tablespoons heavy cream (plus a little more if needed)
- 1½ cups (3 sticks) unsalted butter
- ½ cup cocoa powder
- 1 tablespoon pure vanilla extract
- 1 tablespoon orange emulsion
- Pinch of salt
- 7 to 8 cups powdered sugar

For Decorating

- Piping bag
- Wilton 32 piping tip

For the Chocolate Orange Cake

Preheat the oven to 325°F, then prep three 6-inch round cake pans with a swipe of shortening and dusting of flour to prevent sticking.

In a large bowl, whisk together the buttermilk, sour cream, eggs, oil, chocolate chips, vanilla, orange emulsion, and orange zest until thoroughly combined. Sift in the flour and cake mix and whisk until just combined. Do not overmix. Split the batter among the prepared pans.

Bake for 30 to 32 minutes, until the center is baked through. Let the cakes cool in the pan for a minute before flipping them out onto a wire rack to cool completely. Wrap and freeze the cakes before assembly.

For the Chocolate Orange Buttercream

To a small microwave-safe bowl, add the whole chocolate orange and 2 tablespoons of the heavy cream. Heat for 20 seconds and then stir until smooth. Set aside to cool.

In the bowl of a stand mixer fitted with a paddle attachment, beat the butter on medium speed until it's light and fluffy. Add the chocolate orange ganache, remaining ½ cup heavy cream, cocoa, vanilla, orange emulsion, and salt and beat again until combined, then scrape down the sides of the bowl with a spatula.

With the mixer on low speed, add the powdered sugar about ½ cup at a time. The buttercream will be thick. Add a little more heavy cream, 1 tablespoon at a time, to thin it out if needed, and then flip the mixer to high speed and beat until the buttercream is lighter in color and texture, about 2 minutes.

To Assemble

Place a cardboard cake round on a cake turntable. Dot a little bit of buttercream in the center of the round with an angled icing spatula. Place the first chilled cake layer in the center.

Add a layer of buttercream. Place the next cake layer on top, then repeat, making sure to line the layers up evenly. After adding the top cake layer, crumb coat the cake by spreading a thin layer of buttercream around the entire cake. Add a neat layer of buttercream on the top of the cake (this part will be exposed after adding on the final buttercream braids on the sides). Freeze for 2 minutes to set the buttercream.

Using a wooden spoon, beat out any air bubbles in the remaining buttercream. Finish frosting the cake as desired or follow the decorating instructions below.

To Decorate the Cake

Put the remaining buttercream in a large piping bag fitted with the Wilson 32 tip. Pipe a buttercream braid by piping a shell on the diagonal, with the tail smearing down and to the right. Pipe another shell next to it, with the tail crossing over the previous one diagonally in the opposite direction. Repeat the pattern down the side of the cake. Then repeat the braid pattern in columns next to each other until the entire side of the cake has been covered.

TIP: When I created this cake, I wanted the cake to taste just like a chocolate orange. I learned quickly that the best way for that to happen was to use the real thing. Yes, you will need to melt down an entire chocolate orange to use in the buttercream (if you can't find any in your local stores, you can order them online), but trust me, it will be entirely worth it.

EGGNOG LATTE CAKE

As a little kid, whenever there was a good snow, my siblings and I would put on layer after layer of snow clothes, lace up our snow boots, and drag our orange sleds all the way over to the hill to spend the afternoon sledding. We'd come home just before dusk with red cheeks and frozen fingers, but we always had the time of our lives. Depending on how close it was to Christmas, we'd either make ourselves a cup of hot chocolate with mini marshmallows or sneak a small cup of eggnog from the carton in the fridge. Now, my boys also enjoy a cup of hot cocoa or eggnog at the end of a sledding trip, just as we did so long ago.

Eggnog Latte Cake

- ¾ cup eggnog (room temperature)
- ⅔ cup sour cream (room temperature)
- 4 egg whites (room temperature)
- ⅓ cup vegetable oil
- 1 teaspoon pure vanilla extract
- 1 teaspoon coffee emulsion (or 2 teaspoons instant espresso powder)
- 1 teaspoon ground cinnamon
- Pinch of ground nutmeg
- 1 box white cake mix

Eggnog Latte Buttercream

- 1½ cups (3 sticks) unsalted butter
- ¼ cup eggnog (plus more if needed)
- 1 tablespoon pure vanilla extract
- 1 tablespoon coffee emulsion (or dissolve 1 tablespoon instant espresso powder in the eggnog)
- ½ teaspoon ground cinnamon
- Pinch of ground nutmeg
- Pinch of salt
- 7 to 8 cups powdered sugar
- 1 drop brown gel coloring

For Decorating

- Ground cinnamon
- White sphere sprinkles
- Thin-stripe cake comb
- Parchment paper
- Piping bag
- Wilton 32 piping tip

For the Eggnog Latte Cake

Preheat the oven to 325°F, then prep three 6-inch round cake pans with a swipe of shortening and dusting of flour to prevent sticking.

In a large bowl, whisk together the eggnog, sour cream, egg whites, oil, vanilla, coffee emulsion, cinnamon, and nutmeg until thoroughly combined. Sift in the cake mix and whisk until just combined. Do not overmix. Split the batter evenly among the prepared pans.

Bake for 27 to 30 minutes, until the center is baked through. Let the cakes cool in the pan for a minute before flipping them out onto a wire rack to cool completely. Wrap and freeze the cakes before assembly.

For the Eggnog Latte Buttercream

In the bowl of a stand mixer fitted with a paddle attachment, beat the butter on medium speed until it's light and fluffy. Add the eggnog, vanilla, coffee emulsion, cinnamon, nutmeg, and salt and beat again until combined, then scrape down the sides with a spatula.

With the mixer on low speed, add the powdered sugar about ½ cup at a time. The buttercream will be thick. Add a little more eggnog, 1 tablespoon at a time, to thin it out if needed, and then flip the mixer to high speed and beat until the buttercream is lighter in color and texture, about 2 minutes.

Transfer 1½ cups of the buttercream to a separate bowl and tint it with the brown gel coloring. Add the brown buttercream to a piping bag and snip off the tip to create a tiny opening the size of the stripes.

To Assemble

Place a cardboard cake round on a cake turntable. Dot a little bit of buttercream in the center of the round and spread it out with an angled icing spatula. Place the first chilled cake layer in the center. Add a layer of untinted buttercream. Place the next cake layer on top, then repeat, making sure to line the layers up evenly. After adding the top cake layer, crumb coat the cake by spreading a thin layer of buttercream around the entire cake. Freeze for 2 minutes to set the buttercream.

Using a wooden spoon, beat out any air bubbles in the remaining buttercream. Finish frosting the cake as desired or follow the decorating instructions below.

To Decorate the Cake

Spread a final layer of buttercream around the entire cake, using a thin-stripe cake comb to make clean indents on the side of the cake (see the photo on page 174 for how to hold the comb)

and an angled icing spatula for clean edges on top. The crisper the indents, the cleaner the stripes will be later on. Freeze for at least 10 minutes so that the buttercream is very firm.

Pipe the brown buttercream into the stripe indents and then immediately smooth it out with a flat cake scraper. Apply a little bit of pressure and scrape until the clean stripes start to show through. On the final turn, heat the cake scraper with hot water to make a clean finish.

For the Christmas tree pattern on top of the cake, cut a 6-inch circle of parchment paper (I use a cardboard cake round as my guide). Draw a Christmas tree shape in the center of the circle either freehand or using a cookie cutter as a guide. Cut out the tree shape, and keep both the circle and the tree cutout. Place the circle with the tree cutout on top of the cake and spread a thin layer of the brown buttercream. Smooth it out evenly with a cake scraper or angled icing spatula. Pull up the parchment paper to reveal the tree shape. Next, carefully place the tree cutout on top of the buttercream tree. Sift some cinnamon onto the top of the cake, then freeze for about 3 minutes. Pull up the parchment paper shape and press some white sphere sprinkles on the tree shape.

Add the remaining untinted buttercream to a piping bag fitted with the Wilton 32 tip. Pipe a swirl shell pattern (like a shell, but swirling at the beginning almost like a rosette) around the top and bottom rim of the cake.

TIP: I'm not a coffee drinker for religious reasons, so I don't have it on hand in the house; I use coffee emulsion instead. If you have coffee granules, though, feel free to use those for this cake.

I love how this turned out with the Christmas tree on top, but it would also be darling to do a gingerbread man, stocking, reindeer, or even a candy cane.

FUNFETTI LOFTHOUSE SUGAR COOKIE CAKE *with Vanilla Almond Buttercream and Cookie Dough Filling*

There were sprinkles everywhere. I'd spent the afternoon baking cut-out sugar cookies shaped like gingerbread men, stars, candy canes, and reindeer heads, prepping piping bags with Christmas-colored buttercream and filling my cupcake tin with a variety of sprinkles. When the boys came home from school, we frosted the cookies (the usual pile of frosting on my youngest's cookies was at an all-time high that year) and listened to our favorite Christmas music together. The prep took hours, but the actual activity lasted maybe less than twenty minutes. The next year, which was an especially busy season for us, I brought home a container of Lofthouse cookies—store-bought soft, round cookies frosted perfectly with bright buttercream and topped with sprinkles. I thought maybe they'd be slightly disappointed, but thankfully, my boys were just as excited as if I had done all the cookie prep work from the year before. A solid win for this mom!

For this cake, I use cookies both on the outside and in a layer of eggless sugar cookie dough on the inside. I'm sure Santa would love to find a slice of this cake on a plate by the tree next to his usual tall glass of milk.

For the Funfetti Cake
- ¾ cup buttermilk (room temperature)
- ⅔ cup sour cream (room temperature)
- 4 egg whites (room temperature)
- ⅓ cup vegetable oil
- 1 tablespoon pure vanilla extract
- 1 tablespoon butter vanilla emulsion
- ½ teaspoon almond extract
- 1 box white cake mix
- ½ cup red and green coin or jimmy sprinkles

Eggless Sugar Cookie Dough Filling
- ½ cup (1 stick) unsalted butter, slightly softened
- 1 cup sugar
- 2 tablespoons milk
- 2 teaspoons pure vanilla extract
- ¼ teaspoon almond extract
- ¼ teaspoon salt
- 1 cup flour (heat-treated, if preferred; see Tip)

Vanilla Almond Buttercream
- 1 batch Vanilla Buttercream (page xvii; replace the vanilla extract with butter vanilla emulsion)
- ½ teaspoon almond extract
- Red and green gel coloring

For Decorating
- Mini Frosted Lofthouse Cookies (store-bought or homemade)
- Red and green Christmas sprinkles
- Piping bags
- 2 Wilton 1M piping tips

For the Funfetti Cake
Preheat the oven to 325°F, then prep three 6-inch round cake pans with a swipe of shortening and dusting of flour to prevent sticking.

In a large bowl, whisk together the buttermilk, sour cream, egg whites, oil, vanilla, butter vanilla emulsion, and almond extract until thoroughly combined. Sift in the cake mix and whisk until just combined. Do not overmix. Gently fold in the sprinkles. Split the batter evenly among the prepared pans.

Bake for 27 to 30 minutes, until the center is baked through. Let the cakes cool in the pan for a minute before flipping them out onto a wire rack to cool completely. Wrap and freeze the cakes before assembly.

For the Eggless Sugar Cookie Dough Filling

In the bowl of a stand mixer fitted with a paddle attachment, beat the butter and sugar together until it's light and fluffy. Add the milk, vanilla, almond extract, and salt and mix to combine. Add the flour and mix just to combine. Do not overmix. It should be the consistency of cookie dough—if not, add a touch more flour or a touch more milk until it's the consistency you'd like.

Split the dough in half. Line a 6-inch cake pan with plastic wrap. Press each portion of dough into the pan to make a disk. Wrap in plastic and chill to firm for about 20 minutes.

For the Vanilla Almond Buttercream

In the bowl of a stand mixer fitted with a paddle attachment, beat the buttercream and almond extract until evenly combined, then scrape down the sides with a spatula.

Reserve 2 cups of buttercream. Divide it evenly into two bowls; tint 1 cup red and 1 cup light green using the gel colorings.

To Assemble

Place a cardboard cake round on a cake turntable. Dot a little bit of untinted buttercream in the center of the round and spread it out with an angled icing spatula. Place the first chilled cake layer in the center. Add a thin layer of buttercream, then the cookie dough filling layer. Place the next cake layer on top, then repeat, making sure to line the layers up evenly. After adding the top cake layer, crumb coat the cake by spreading a thin layer of buttercream around the entire cake. Freeze for 2 minutes to set the buttercream.

Using a wooden spoon, beat out any air bubbles in the remaining buttercream. Finish frosting the cake as desired or follow the decorating instructions below.

To Decorate the Cake

Bake or purchase small (half-dollar size) frosted sugar cookies. Frost about 16 mini cookies with the red and green buttercreams and sprinkle with Christmas sprinkles. Set aside.

Transfer the rest of the red and green buttercream into two piping bags fitted with the Wilton 1M tips.

Spread a final layer of untinted buttercream around the entire cake, using a cake scraper for smooth sides and clean edges.

Add a touch of buttercream to the back of some of the mini sugar cookies (save 6 for the top) and press them onto the side of the frosted cake. Place a few Christmas sprinkles in the empty spaces between them.

Pipe small green and red swirls in a circle on top of the cake, and place a mini sugar cookie on top of each one.

TIPS: For the mini Lofthouse cookies, I used store-bought sugar cookies and then added my own frosting and sprinkles to match the cake. You can always make yours from scratch.

The sugar cookie dough is eggless, and I use heat-treated flour, so it's safe to eat raw—both as the cake filling and also as a few bites here and there while assembling the cake! You can order heat-treated flour online (I buy mine from DŌ cookie dough company) or make your own: just spread flour on a baking sheet and bake for 5 minutes in a 350°F oven. Let cool and store until needed.

Butter vanilla emulsion adds a really yummy cookie dough vanilla flavor. The butter vanilla emulsion is usually right next to the other emulsions at the craft or baking store.

If you can only find the sugar cookies frosted in colors you don't like, you can look for unfrosted cookies, or refrigerate them until chilled and then carefully slice off the frosting with a hot sharp knife.

CHOCOLATE PEPPERMINT MOLTEN LAVA CAKE

There's something so fun about a dessert that's both tasty and interactive. With a traditional lava cake, we all look for that exciting moment when you slice into it and gooey chocolate oozes out. I've always wanted to re-create that in a stacked cake but worried that the liquid nature of the filling would be too weak to support the layers. I also knew that by freezing and chilling my cake before assembly like I do, the filling might harden, thus losing the fun oozing-lava effect. But I found a solution! First, make the chocolate filling thin at room temperature; it will firm up when chilled for easy assembly and be fluid by showtime. (It should still ooze a little, but with a lovely fudgy texture.) Then, while stacking the cake, make sure to pipe a really strong, thick buttercream dam, and don't add too much filling in the middle. That way, the cake layers are sitting on the buttercream dam without touching the filling.

For Christmas, I added a bit of peppermint and dolled the cake right up with buttercream ruffles and peppermint candies all around.

For the Chocolate Peppermint Cake

- ¾ cup buttermilk (room temperature)
- ⅔ cup sour cream (room temperature)
- 3 large eggs plus 1 egg white (room temperature)
- ⅓ cup vegetable oil
- 1 tablespoon pure vanilla extract
- 1 teaspoon peppermint extract
- ¼ cup cocoa powder
- ¼ cup flour
- 1 box dark chocolate cake mix

For the Chocolate Molten Lava Filling

- 1½ cups heavy cream
- 1 cup semisweet chocolate chips

Chocolate Peppermint Buttercream

- 1 batch Vanilla Buttercream (page xvii)
- ⅔ cup cocoa powder
- 1 teaspoon peppermint extract

For Decorating

- Crushed candy canes (see Tip)
- Peppermint candies
- Piping bag
- Wilton 215 (petal) piping tip

For the Chocolate Peppermint Cake

Preheat the oven to 325°F, then prep three 6-inch round cake pans with a swipe of shortening and dusting of flour to prevent sticking.

In a large bowl, whisk together the buttermilk, sour cream, eggs, oil, vanilla, and peppermint extract until thoroughly combined. Sift in the cocoa powder, flour, and cake mix and whisk until just combined. Do not overmix. Split the batter evenly among the prepared pans.

Bake for 30 to 32 minutes, until the center is baked through. Let the cakes cool in the pan for a minute before flipping them out onto a wire rack to cool completely. Wrap and freeze the cakes before assembly.

For the Chocolate Molten Lava Filling

In a small microwave-safe bowl, stir together the heavy cream and chocolate chips. Heat in the microwave for 30 seconds and then stir until a sauce forms. It should be much thinner than a ganache filling or drip and should be a thick liquid at room temperature.

place the next cake layer on top, then repeat, making sure to line the layers up evenly. (Because this is a very oozy filling, you may want to insert a dowel through the cake layers to keep them in place.) After adding the top layer, crumb coat the cake by spreading a thin layer of buttercream around the entire cake. Freeze for 2 minutes to set the buttercream.

Using a wooden spoon, beat out any air bubbles in the remaining buttercream. Finish frosting the cake as desired or follow the decorating instructions below.

To Decorate the Cake

Spread a final layer of buttercream around the entire cake, using a cake scraper for smooth sides and clean edges.

Place the cake on a cookie sheet, then set the cookie sheet on a cake turntable. With one hand, gently press the crushed candy canes on the side of the cake along the bottom third, letting the excess fall onto the cookie sheet.

Transfer the remaining buttercream to a piping bag fitted with the Wilton 125 tip. For the swoop-curtain buttercream technique, hold the piping bag with the thick end of the tip against the side of the cake and pipe a crescent about 2 inches long, starting and ending at the top rim. Repeat the same motion to make a smaller swoop right on top of the first one. Repeat this technique around the rest of the cake.

Press the peppermint candies between the buttercream curtain swoops and crushed candy canes. Add a few peppermints and a sprinkle of crushed candy cane in a circle on the top of the cake.

For the Chocolate Peppermint Buttercream

In the bowl of a stand mixer fitted with a paddle attachment, beat together the buttercream, cocoa, and peppermint extract until evenly combined, then scrape down the sides with a spatula.

To Assemble

Place a cardboard cake round on a cake turntable. Dot a little bit of buttercream in the center of the round and spread it out with an angled icing spatula. Place the first chilled cake layer in the center. Add a thin layer of buttercream. Pipe a tall, thick dam around the outside rim of the frosted cake layer. Add about ½ cup chocolate filling in the center. Carefully

TIP: Instead of buying peppermints and removing all the wrappers from each one, you can buy crushed candy canes at most baking stores that are perfect to use as decoration. Unless you like unwrapping lots of things. In that case, carry on.

COCONUT ALMOND HOT CHOCOLATE CAKE *with Marshmallow Filling*

My husband and I have a tradition: around the beginning of every year, we schedule an afternoon tea at the Grand America Hotel in downtown Salt Lake City. The hallways are marble, the ceilings glitter with massive chandeliers, and there's usually a harpist playing. We always reserve a spot in velvet chairs by the large Victorian fireplace and are treated to a full tea service. Ryan and I spend the visit discussing our goals for the upcoming year: trips we'd like to take or things we'd like to do with our family, all while nibbling on tea sandwiches and a variety of pastries. We have especially come to love their coconut almond hot chocolate. It's my favorite and I order it every single time, so this cake was destined to happen. I'm happy to say it tastes just like my favorite moments of the year—sipping on hot cocoa in such a pretty place with someone I'm grateful to have built my life with.

Coconut Almond Hot Chocolate Cake

- ¾ cup buttermilk (room temperature)
- ⅔ cup sour cream (room temperature)
- 3 large eggs (room temperature)
- ½ cup hot chocolate mix
- ⅓ cup vegetable oil
- 1 tablespoon pure vanilla extract
- 1 tablespoon coconut emulsion
- 1 teaspoon almond extract
- 1 box dark chocolate cake mix

Marshmallow Filling

- 1½ cups, or 1 (7-ounce) container, marshmallow fluff
- ½ cup powdered sugar

Coconut Almond Hot Chocolate Buttercream

- 1½ cups (3 sticks) unsalted butter
- ⅔ cup hot chocolate mix
- ½ cup heavy cream (plus more if needed)
- 1 tablespoon pure vanilla extract
- 1 teaspoon coconut emulsion
- ½ teaspoon almond extract
- Pinch of salt
- 7 to 8 cups powdered sugar

For Decorating

- Small marshmallows, some cut in half
- White nonpareils
- Piping bags
- Wilton 6B, 18, and 32 piping tips
- Small coupler for the smaller piping tips

For the Coconut Almond Hot Chocolate Cake

Preheat the oven to 325°F, then prep three 6-inch round cake pans with a swipe of shortening and dusting of flour to prevent sticking.

In a large bowl, whisk together the buttermilk, sour cream, eggs, hot chocolate mix, oil, vanilla, coconut emulsion, and almond extract until thoroughly combined. Sift in the cake mix and whisk until just combined. Do not overmix. Split the batter evenly among the prepared pans.

Bake for 30 to 32 minutes, until the center is baked through. Let the cakes cool in the pan for a minute before flipping them out onto a wire rack to cool completely. Slice each cake round in half horizontally to create 6 layers. Wrap and freeze the cakes before assembly.

For the Marshmallow Filling

Stir together the marshmallow fluff and the powdered sugar; this keeps the filling from being too sticky when you slice the cake. Transfer to a piping bag and set aside.

To Assemble

Place a cardboard cake round on a cake turntable. Dot a little bit of buttercream in the center of the round and spread it out with an angled icing spatula. Place the first chilled cake layer in the center. Add a thin layer of buttercream. Pipe a buttercream dam around the outside rim of the frosted cake layer, and then pipe in a small amount of marshmallow filling. Place the next cake layer on top, then repeat with the rest of the cake layers, making sure to line the layers up evenly. After adding the top cake layer, crumb coat the cake by spreading a thin layer of buttercream around the entire cake. Freeze for 2 minutes to set the buttercream.

Using a wooden spoon, beat out any air bubbles in the remaining buttercream. Finish frosting the cake as desired or follow the decorating instructions below.

To Decorate the Cake

Spread a final layer of buttercream around the entire cake, using a cake scraper for smooth sides. Leave the top edge uneven for a more rustic look.

Add the remaining buttercream to two piping bags, one fitted with the Wilton 6B tip and one with the coupler (so you can switch between the two smaller piping tips). Pipe a few 6B stars around the sides of the cake at random. Press on the marshmallow halves, then switch between the smaller piping tips and add a few more smaller stars. Press on or throw on a few of the white nonpareils.

TIP: There's no real rhyme or reason to the fun sprinkle-and-buttercream decor on the side of this cake. Just start with the biggest elements and work your way down to the tiniest white nonpareils.

For the Coconut Almond Hot Chocolate Buttercream

In the bowl of a stand mixer fitted with a paddle attachment, beat the butter on medium speed until it's light and fluffy. Add the hot chocolate mix, heavy cream, vanilla, coconut emulsion, almond extract, and salt and beat again until combined, then scrape down the sides with a spatula. Continue to whip until there are no hot chocolate bits in the buttercream.

With the mixer on low speed, add the powdered sugar about ½ cup at a time. The buttercream will be thick. Add a little more heavy cream, 1 tablespoon at a time, to thin it out if needed, and then flip the mixer to high speed and beat until the buttercream is lighter in color and texture, about 2 minutes.

POMEGRANATE WHITE CHOCOLATE CAKE

When my grandmother passed, one of the things I kept of hers was a faux-fur coat. I imagine my grandma in her pearls, heels, bright lipstick, and fluffy white hair teased to perfection headed out for a night of dancing with my grandpa. I'd never really had a good reason to wear the coat, though. That is, until Ryan and I attended his law firm's Christmas party one year. It's a wonderful excuse to get dressed up and spend a grown-up night out. As I walked down the stairs to leave in my gold shimmery heels and black dress, I decided on a whim to grab Grandma June's fur coat—it needed a good night out at a Christmas party, just as Grandma would have loved. Ryan and I spent the evening drinking sparkling pomegranate juice, listening to a jazz combo, and feasting on an endless buffet of prime rib and every kind of pie I can imagine. I'd like to think Grandma would have loved to see it.

This cake is as elegant as that evening, and is made with classic white cake layers, pomegranate filling, and white chocolate buttercream. And although I love the ruby-red color of a pomegranate seed, we don't want any to bleed on our beautifully decorated cake, so I recommend placing the seeds on top of the cake right before your gathering.

Classic White Cake

- ¾ cup buttermilk (room temperature)
- ⅔ cup sour cream (room temperature)
- 4 large egg whites (room temperature)
- ½ cup vegetable oil
- 1 tablespoon pure vanilla extract
- 1 box white cake mix

Pomegranate Filling

- 1 cup fresh pomegranate seeds (see Tip)
- ½ cup sugar
- 2 tablespoons lemon juice
- 2 teaspoons cornstarch

White Chocolate Buttercream

- ½ cup white chocolate chips
- 3 tablespoons heavy cream
- 1 batch Vanilla Buttercream (page xvii)

For Decorating

- Decorative cake scraper
- Pomegranate seeds

For the Classic White Cake

Preheat the oven to 325°F, then prep three 6-inch round cake pans with a swipe of shortening and dusting of flour to prevent sticking.

In a large bowl, whisk together the buttermilk, sour cream, egg whites, oil, and vanilla until thoroughly combined. Sift in the cake mix and whisk until just combined. Do not overmix. Split the batter evenly among the prepared pans.

Bake for 27 to 30 minutes, until the center is baked through. Let the cakes cool in the pan for a minute before flipping them out onto a wire rack to cool completely. Wrap and freeze the cakes before assembly.

For the Pomegranate Filling

In a small saucepan over medium heat, stir together the pomegranate seeds, sugar, and lemon juice and cook, stirring, until thick and bubbly, about 5 minutes. Sift in the cornstarch and stir until thickened, about 2 minutes. Strain the seeds if desired. Place the filling in a bowl, cover, and refrigerate until thickened and cooled completely.

For the White Chocolate Buttercream

In a small microwave-safe bowl, heat the chocolate chips and heavy cream for 30 seconds and then stir until smooth. Let cool slightly.

In the bowl of a stand mixer fitted with a paddle attachment, beat the buttercream and the cooled white chocolate ganache until evenly combined, then scrape down the sides with a spatula.

To Assemble and Decorate

Place a cardboard cake round on a cake turntable. Dot a little bit of buttercream in the center of the round and spread it out with an angled icing spatula. Place the first chilled cake layer in the center. Add a layer of buttercream. Pipe a buttercream dam around the outside rim of the frosted cake layer, then add half the pomegranate filling in the center. Place the next cake layer on top, then repeat, making sure to line the layers up evenly. After adding the top cake layer, crumb coat the cake by spreading a thin layer of buttercream around the entire cake. Freeze for 2 minutes to set the buttercream.

Using a wooden spoon, beat out any air bubbles in the remaining buttercream. Spread an even layer of white buttercream around the entire cake, using a decorative cake scraper for smooth sides and clean edges.

Arrange a few pomegranate seeds around the bottom of the cake and in a crescent-moon shape on the top as garnish.

TIP: Pomegranates are a little tricky and messy if you've never worked with them before. The best way to remove the seeds is to slice the fruit in half with the stem on one side and the bottom on the other. Place it cut side down in a bowl, and tap the back with a wooden spoon. Most of the pomegranate seeds should pop right out, leaving behind the pesky little white pieces.

CHOCOLATE COCONUT CREAM PIE CAKE

I love making cakes inspired by pie flavors. Pies have wonderful combinations of creamy, crunchy, and sweet, and the flavors always translate really well to cake. For the creamy texture I love in chocolate coconut cream pie, I added soft chocolate pudding between the cake layers. To add even more coconut flavor, I frosted the entire cake in coconut buttercream, and for added texture, I wrapped the cake in a graham cracker crumble. The top of the cake looks just like a coconut cream pie with the chocolate drizzle, swirls of buttercream around the edges, and a crumble of chocolate pieces and toasted coconut. If you close your eyes while taking that first bite, you'll think you have just helped yourself to the real thing (maybe even better).

Coconut Cake with Graham Cracker Crust

- 9 graham crackers
- 5 tablespoons unsalted butter, melted
- ¾ cup buttermilk (room temperature)
- ⅔ cup sour cream (room temperature)
- 4 egg whites (room temperature)
- ⅓ cup vegetable oil
- 1 tablespoon pure vanilla extract
- 1 tablespoon coconut emulsion
- 1 box white cake mix

Chocolate Pudding Filling

- 1 (3.9-ounce) package instant chocolate pudding
- 2 cups milk

Coconut Buttercream

- 1 batch Vanilla Buttercream (page xvii)
- 1 tablespoon coconut emulsion

For Decorating

- 5 to 6 graham crackers, pulsed into crumbles in a food processor
- ½ cup chocolate chips
- ½ cup chocolate shavings or curls
- ½ cup toasted shredded coconut (see page 77)
- Piping bag
- Wilton 1M piping tip

For the Coconut Cake with Graham Cracker Crust

Preheat the oven to 325°F, then prep three 6-inch round cake pans with a swipe of shortening and dusting of flour to prevent sticking.

In a food processor, pulse together the graham crackers and melted butter until a fine crust forms. Split the crust evenly among the prepared pans and press to firm with the bottom of a glass or flat measuring cup (see Tip).

In a large bowl, whisk together the buttermilk, sour cream, egg whites, oil, vanilla, and coconut emulsion until thoroughly combined. Sift in the cake mix and whisk until just combined. Do not overmix. Split the batter evenly among the prepared pans.

Bake for 27 to 30 minutes, until the center is baked through. Let the cakes cool in the pan for a minute before flipping them out onto a wire rack to cool completely. Wrap and freeze the cakes before assembly.

For the Chocolate Pudding Filling

In a small bowl, whisk together the pudding mix and milk. Cover and place in the fridge to thicken.

For the Coconut Buttercream

In the bowl of a stand mixer fitted with a paddle attachment, beat the buttercream and coconut emulsion until evenly combined, then scrape down the sides with a spatula.

To Assemble

Place a cardboard cake round on a cake turntable. Dot a little bit of buttercream in the center of the round and spread it out with an angled icing spatula. Place the first chilled cake layer in the center (crust side up). Add a thin layer of buttercream. Pipe a buttercream dam around the outside rim of the frosted cake layer, then add about ½ cup of the chocolate pudding. Place the next cake layer on top, then repeat, making sure to line the layers up evenly. After adding the top cake layer, crumb coat the cake by spreading a thin layer of buttercream around the entire cake. Freeze for 2 minutes to set the buttercream.

Using a wooden spoon, beat out any air bubbles in the remaining buttercream. Finish frosting the cake as desired or follow the decorating instructions below.

To Decorate the Cake

Spread a final layer of buttercream around the entire cake, using a cake scraper for smooth sides and clean edges.

Press the graham cracker crumbs around the sides of the cake. In a small microwave-safe bowl, heat the chocolate chips until melted, for 30 second intervals, stirring in between. Drizzle the melted chocolate back and forth on top of the cake.

Add the remaining buttercream to a piping bag fitted with the Wilton 1M tip. Pipe swirl dollops around the top outside edge of the cake. Sprinkle with the chocolate shavings and toasted coconut.

TIP: When making your graham cracker crust, press the graham cracker crumble down firmly with either the bottom of a drinking glass or large measuring cup to make it very flat and even. This will ensure that the cake batter on top will bake evenly and the crust won't crumble as you flip the cake layers onto the wire rack to cool.

GINGERBREAD CAKE *with White Chocolate and Gingerbread Buttercream*

When we first moved into our neighborhood, it was a little before Christmas. We didn't know very many people, but I really wanted to reach out and get to know my new neighbors. I baked up a few batches of my favorite soft ginger cookies, dipped them in white chocolate, and added a few holly-berry sprinkles. One night, feeling a little nervous, I laced up my snow boots and delivered a few plates of cookies wrapped with ribbons to different homes. Ever since that evening, our neighbors and friends have told me how much they love those cookies and look forward to them each year.

This cake is inspired by those cookies, with gingerbread cake layers, white chocolate buttercream, and gingerbread buttercream stripes all around. I placed gingerbread men around the sides of the cake and piped gingerbread dollops in a crown on top.

Gingerbread Cake

- ⅔ cup buttermilk (room temperature)
- ⅔ cup sour cream (room temperature)
- ½ cup molasses (see Tip)
- 3 large eggs (room temperature)
- ¼ cup vegetable oil
- 1 tablespoon pure vanilla extract
- 1 teaspoon ground ginger
- ¼ teaspoon ground cloves
- 1 box spice cake mix

White Chocolate and Gingerbread Buttercreams

- ½ cup white chocolate chips
- 3 tablespoons heavy cream
- 1 batch Vanilla Buttercream (page xvii)
- 3 tablespoons molasses
- 1 teaspoon ground ginger
- Pinch of ground nutmeg
- 1 to 2 drops brown gel coloring

For Decorating

- Thick-stripe cake comb
- Tiny gingerbread-men sprinkles
- Piping bag
- Wilton 1A (circle) piping tip

For the Gingerbread Cake

Preheat the oven to 325°F, then prep three 6-inch round cake pans with a swipe of shortening and dusting of flour to prevent sticking.

In a large bowl, whisk together the buttermilk, sour cream, molasses, eggs, oil, vanilla, ginger, and cloves until thoroughly combined. Sift in the cake mix and whisk until just combined. Do not overmix. Split the batter evenly among the prepared pans.

Bake for 30 to 32 minutes, until the center is baked through. Let the cakes cool in the pan for a minute before flipping them out onto a wire rack to cool completely. Wrap and freeze the cakes before assembly.

For the White Chocolate and Gingerbread Buttercreams

In a small microwave-safe bowl, stir together the white chocolate chips and heavy cream. Microwave for 30 seconds and then stir until smooth. Let cool until close to room temperature.

In the bowl of a stand mixer fitted with a paddle attachment, beat the buttercream and the ganache mixture until evenly combined, and then scrape down the sides with a spatula.

Transfer 1½ cups of the buttercream to a separate bowl and stir in the molasses, ginger, cloves, nutmeg, and gel coloring. Add to a piping bag without a piping tip.

To Assemble

Place a cardboard cake round on a cake turntable. Dot a little bit of buttercream in the center of the round and spread it out with an angled icing spatula. Place the first chilled cake layer in the center. Add a layer of buttercream. Place the next cake layer on top, then repeat, making sure to line the layers up evenly. After adding the top cake layer, crumb coat the cake by spreading a thin layer of buttercream around the entire cake. Freeze for 2 minutes to set the buttercream.

Using a wooden spoon, beat out any air bubbles in the remaining buttercream. Finish frosting the cake as desired or follow the decorating instructions below.

To Decorate the Cake

Spread a final layer of buttercream around the entire cake, using a thick-stripe cake comb to create clean indents on the sides. The cleaner the indents, the cleaner the stripes will be later on. Freeze for 10 to 15 minutes. The buttercream should be very firm.

Pipe stripes of brown buttercream in the indents and immediately scrape with a flat cake scraper. Apply a little bit of pressure and scrape until the clean stripes start to show through.

Place the gingerbread-men sprinkles in the white stripes.

Transfer the remaining brown buttercream to a piping bag fitted with the Wilton 1A tip and pipe small dollops on the top of the cake around the edge.

TIP: Not all molasses is created equal. Some pack a lot more flavor than others. I like the full-flavor Brer Rabbit brand (look for the jar with the bunny on the front), which I find to be a lot sweeter than other brands. It works really well with the buttercream and cake layers without adding any bitterness. To help the molasses release easier from your measuring cup and make for faster cleanup, spray it with a little cooking spray first.

WHITE CHOCOLATE PEPPERMINT CAKE

Please tell me I'm not the only one who leaves Costco with things I didn't intend on adding to my cart? Around Christmastime one year, I spotted a bag of white chocolate peppermint pretzels. They were on sale, and I felt like it would be a crime if I left them behind. Unfortunately, they were incredibly delicious; I went through the bag very quickly and couldn't believe how amazing they were. When I went back to Costco, the pretzels were gone. Annoyed, I loaded up the rest of my groceries and headed for checkout. There in front of me was a woman who had filled up her entire cart with my new favorite snack. I was shocked at first but later impressed. She knew what she wanted and was hopefully planning for neighborhood or teacher gifts. Or maybe she was stocking up to enjoy those delicious pretzels year-round. Either way, the flavors remind me of my white chocolate peppermint cake, and that's something I could make in my kitchen anytime.

White Peppermint Cake

- ¾ cup buttermilk (room temperature)
- ⅔ cup sour cream (room temperature)
- 4 egg whites (room temperature)
- ⅓ cup vegetable oil
- 1 tablespoon pure vanilla extract
- 1 teaspoon peppermint extract
- 1 box white cake mix

White Chocolate Peppermint Buttercream

- ½ cup white chocolate chips
- 3 tablespoons heavy cream
- 1 batch Vanilla Buttercream (page xvii)
- ½ teaspoon peppermint extract
- 2 drops red gel coloring

White Chocolate Ganache Drip

- 1 cup bright-white chocolate candy melts
- ¼ cup heavy cream

For Decorating

- Red and white peppermint sprinkles
- White gumballs
- Thick-stripe cake comb

For the White Peppermint Cake

Preheat the oven to 325°F, then prep three 6-inch round cake pans with a swipe of shortening and dusting of flour to prevent sticking.

In a large bowl, whisk together the buttermilk, sour cream, egg whites, oil, vanilla, and peppermint extract until thoroughly combined.

Sift in the cake mix and whisk until just combined. Do not overmix. Split the batter evenly among the prepared pans.

Bake for 25 to 27 minutes, until the center is baked through. Let the cakes cool in the pan for a minute before flipping them out onto a wire rack to cool completely. Wrap and freeze the cakes before assembly.

For the White Chocolate Peppermint Buttercream

In a small microwave-safe bowl, stir together the white chocolate chips and heavy cream and then microwave for 30 seconds. Stir until smooth. Set aside to cool slightly.

In the bowl of a stand mixer fitted with a paddle attachment, beat the buttercream, white chocolate ganache, and peppermint extract until combined, then scrape down the sides with a spatula.

Transfer about 2 cups of the buttercream to a separate bowl and mix in the red gel coloring. Transfer the red buttercream to one piping bag and 2 cups of the white buttercream to another.

For the White Chocolate Ganache Drip

In a small microwave-safe bowl, stir together the chocolate melts and heavy cream and then microwave for about 30 seconds. Stir until

Place the next cake layer on top, then repeat, making sure to line the layers up evenly. After adding the top cake layer, crumb coat the cake by spreading a thin layer of white buttercream around the entire cake. Freeze for 2 minutes to set the buttercream.

Using a wooden spoon, beat out any air bubbles in the remaining buttercream. Finish frosting the cake as desired or follow the decorating instructions below.

To Decorate the Cake

Spread the white buttercream around the entire cake, using a stripe cake comb to create clean indents on the sides. The cleaner the indents, the cleaner the stripes will be later on. Freeze for 10 to 15 minutes to firm completely.

Pipe red stripes in the indents in the buttercream and then immediately scrape the sides of the cake with a flat cake scraper. Apply a little bit of pressure and scrape until the clean stripes start to show through.

Press the peppermint sprinkles on the side of the cake around the bottom. Freeze for 2 minutes to set.

Pipe on the ganache drip, squeezing a pool of ganache on the top edge and letting it cascade down the side of the cake. The more or less you squeeze, the deeper or shorter the drip will be. Let it sit for a few minutes to slightly firm up the drips, then add the gumballs and remaining peppermint sprinkles.

smooth, and then transfer to a drip bottle. Set aside.

To Assemble

Place a cardboard cake round on a cake turntable. Dot a little bit of buttercream in the center of the round and spread it out with an angled icing spatula. Place the first chilled cake layer in the center. Using the red and white buttercreams, pipe a target design to make the peppermint stripes between the layers (see Tip).

TIP: For the white-and-red stripes inside each cake slice, you'll need to pipe the buttercream in a target pattern. Pipe a small white circle in the center of the cake round. Pipe a red circle around the white circle, then repeat, alternating the white and red buttercreams until you reach the outside rim of the cake. This will make darling candy cane stripes when you cut into the cake.

GINGERBREAD CINNAMON ROLL CAKE
with Ginger Cookie Crust, Spiced Cream Cheese Buttercream, and Ginger Swirl Cookies

This cake takes two of my favorite comfort foods and combines them into one delicious cake. If you've ever baked up homemade cinnamon rolls or ginger cookies, you know how quickly your kitchen will smell like heaven. In my gingerbread cinnamon roll cake, each element I've added makes it extra tasty. The ginger cookie crust is made with crushed ginger cookies, and the cream cheese swirl in my gingerbread cake layers tastes just like the filling in cinnamon rolls. A touch of warm spices goes right into my cream cheese buttercream on the outside, and I gave the cake that familiar cinnamon-roll swirl on top with a dusting of cinnamon and a swirl of buttercream. On a whim, I was practicing that same swirl on a few of the ginger cookies nearby. I ended up loving it so much that I added them to the side of the cake for fun.

Gingerbread Cake

- 8 ounces ginger cookies (30 cookies)
- 6 tablespoons unsalted butter, melted
- 8 ounces (1 brick) cream cheese
- ¼ cup granulated sugar
- 1 tablespoon plus 1 teaspoon pure vanilla extract
- ⅔ cup buttermilk (room temperature)
- ⅔ cup sour cream (room temperature)
- 4 egg whites (room temperature)
- ⅓ cup vegetable oil
- ¼ cup molasses (see page 212)
- 1 teaspoon ground ginger
- ¼ teaspoon ground cloves
- 1 box spice cake mix

Spiced Cream Cheese Buttercream

- 1 cup (2 sticks) unsalted butter
- 8 ounces (1 brick) cream cheese
- ¼ cup heavy cream (plus more if needed)
- 1 tablespoon pure vanilla extract
- 1 teaspoon ground cinnamon
- ½ teaspoon ground ginger
- Pinch of ground cloves
- Pinch of salt
- 7 to 8 cups powdered sugar

Ginger Swirl Cookies

- Ginger cookies
- 1 cup reserved Spiced Cream Cheese Buttercream

For Decorating

- Ground cinnamon
- Piping bag
- Wilton 1A (circle) piping tip

For the Gingerbread Cake

Preheat the oven to 325°F, then prep three 6-inch round cake pans with a swipe of shortening and dusting of flour to prevent sticking.

In a food processor, blend together the ginger cookies and butter until a fine crust forms. Split the crust mixture evenly among the prepared pans and press to firm with the bottom of a glass or a flat measuring cup.

In a small bowl, use a hand mixer to beat together the cream cheese, sugar, and 1 teaspoon of the vanilla. Set aside.

In a large bowl, whisk together the buttermilk, sour cream, egg whites, oil, molasses, remaining 1 tablespoon vanilla, ginger, and cloves until thoroughly combined. Sift in the cake mix and whisk until just combined. Do not overmix. Split the batter evenly among the prepared pans. Dollop the cream cheese mixture on top of the gingerbread batter. With a knife, gently swirl the batter in a figure-eight pattern to create the marbled effect.

Bake for 35 to 37 minutes, until the center is baked through. Let the cakes cool in the pan for a minute before flipping them out onto a wire rack to cool completely. Wrap and freeze the cakes before assembly.

For the Spiced Cream Cheese Buttercream

In the bowl of a stand mixer fitted with a paddle attachment, beat the butter over medium speed until it's light and fluffy, then add the cream cheese and beat again until fully incorporated (see Tip). Add the heavy cream, vanilla, cinnamon, ginger, cloves, and salt and beat again until combined, then scrape down the sides with a spatula.

With the mixer on low speed, add the powdered sugar about ½ cup at a time. The buttercream will be thick. Add a little more heavy cream, 1 tablespoon at a time, to thin it out if needed, and then flip the mixer to high speed and beat until the buttercream is lighter in color and texture, about 2 minutes.

For the Ginger Swirl Cookies

Transfer about 1 cup of the prepared buttercream into a piping bag fitted with the Wilton 1A tip. Pipe a swirl, starting in the center of each cookie. Set aside to firm for about 10 minutes. To maintain the cookies' crispness, wait to place them on the cake until right before serving.

To Assemble and Decorate

Place a cardboard cake round on a cake turntable. Dot a little bit of buttercream in the center of the round and spread it out with an angled icing spatula. Place the first chilled cake layer in the center (crust side up). Add a layer of buttercream. Place the next cake layer on top, then repeat, making sure to line the layers up evenly. After adding the top cake layer, crumb coat the cake by spreading a thin layer of buttercream around the entire cake. Freeze for 2 minutes to set the buttercream.

Using a wooden spoon, beat out any air bubbles in the remaining buttercream. Spread a final layer of buttercream around the entire cake, using a cake scraper for smooth sides and clean edges.

Using a fine-mesh sieve, sprinkle cinnamon on the top of the cake. Blow or wave off the top to get rid of any loose cinnamon dust (this will allow the swirl piping to remain stuck to the top of the cake).

Add the remaining buttercream to the piping bag fitted with the Wilton 1A tip. Starting in the center of the top of the cake, slowly pipe a spiral until you reach the outside edge.

Right before serving, place the ginger swirl cookies on the side of the cake around the bottom, using a drop of buttercream to keep them in place.

TIP: Cream cheese is naturally much softer than butter, so you do not need to bring it to room temperature for the buttercream. However, you will need to make sure it has been whipped enough that it does not leave little white pockets in your buttercream. After you've whipped the butter and cream cheese together thoroughly, stop the mixer for a moment to check for little white bits. If you see them, just turn the mixer back on and keep mixing on high speed until they dissolve into the butter.

PEPPERMINT OREO SWIRL CAKE *with Dark Chocolate Ganache Drip*

When hosting a holiday gathering, one thing I love to serve is a hot chocolate bar. I lay out a long Christmas tablecloth, whip up a batch of hot chocolate, and put out little cookies, mix-ins, marshmallows, and different kinds of flavorings, so our guests can customize their own cup of hot cocoa. Hazelnut or peppermint are a couple of favorites, but there's nothing like a scoop of peppermint ice cream. It sounds crazy, but trust me: it will change your hot cocoa game completely. The ice cream melts beautifully into the rich chocolate. I dunked Oreos into this very concoction once, and the inspiration for this cake was born.

Peppermint Oreo Swirl Cake

- ¾ cup buttermilk (room temperature)
- ⅔ cup sour cream (room temperature)
- 4 egg whites (room temperature)
- ⅓ cup vegetable oil
- 2 tablespoons crushed candy canes
- 1 tablespoon vanilla bean paste
- 1 teaspoon pure vanilla extract
- ½ teaspoon peppermint extract
- 1 box white cake mix
- 6 Oreos, crushed (see Tip)
- 1 to 2 drops red gel coloring

Peppermint Oreo Buttercream

- 1 batch Vanilla Buttercream (page xvii)
- ½ teaspoon peppermint extract
- 1 to 2 drops red gel coloring
- ¼ cup crushed Oreos

Dark Chocolate Ganache Drip

- 1 cup dark chocolate candy melts
- ¼ cup heavy cream

For Decorating

- Crushed Oreos
- Crushed candy canes
- Peppermint candies

In a large bowl, whisk together the buttermilk, sour cream, egg whites, oil, crushed candy canes, vanilla bean paste, vanilla, and peppermint extract until thoroughly combined. Sift in the cake mix and whisk until just combined. Gently stir in the crushed Oreos. Do not overmix. Add the red gel coloring and swirl in the bowl (don't mix all the way—you want those deep-red swirl sections). Split the batter evenly among the prepared pans.

Bake for 27 to 30 minutes, until the center is baked through. Let the cakes cool in the pan for a minute before flipping them out onto a wire rack to cool completely. Wrap and freeze the cakes before assembly.

For the Peppermint Oreo Buttercream

In the bowl of a stand mixer fitted with a paddle attachment, beat the buttercream and peppermint extract until evenly combined, then scrape down the sides with a spatula.

Gently stir the red gel coloring in one section of the buttercream bowl (not all the way—you want a marbled watercolor look, so some of it needs to be left white), and then gently stir in the Oreo crumbles.

For the Dark Chocolate Ganache Drip

In a small microwave-safe bowl, stir together the candy melts and heavy cream. Microwave for 30 seconds and then stir until smooth. Transfer to a drip bottle and set aside.

For the Peppermint Oreo Swirl Cake

Preheat the oven to 325°F, then prep three 6-inch round cake pans with a swipe of shortening and dusting of flour to prevent sticking.

To Assemble

Place a cardboard cake round on a cake turntable. Dot a little bit of buttercream in the center of the round and spread it out with an angled icing spatula. Place the first chilled cake layer in the center. Add a layer of buttercream. Sprinkle on some crushed Oreos. Place the next cake layer on top, then repeat, making sure to line the layers up evenly. After adding the top

cake layer, crumb coat the cake by spreading a thin layer of buttercream around the entire cake. Freeze for 2 minutes to set the buttercream.

Using a wooden spoon, beat out any air bubbles in the remaining buttercream. Finish frosting the cake as desired or follow the decorating instructions below.

To Decorate the Cake

Spread the remaining buttercream around the entire cake, using a cake scraper for smooth sides and clean edges. Press some crumbled Oreos and crushed candy cane around the bottom edge of the cake. Freeze for 2 minutes to set the buttercream.

For the chocolate drip, squeeze a small amount of the ganache on the top edge of the cake, letting it pool on the edge and cascade down the sides. Repeat around the entire cake and on top. When the ganache is set, place a few peppermint candies and some crushed candy canes and crumbled Oreos on top.

> **TIP:** For my cookies-and-cream cakes, I usually pulse the Oreos into a fine powder and add it into my buttercream, creating a grayish color. For this cake, I knew I didn't want that. You only need to pulse your cookies a little bit. They should be a powder but with little bits here and there of white and black. Stir the Oreo bits into the cake batter and buttercream by hand or else you may end up still getting a bit of the gray color.

CHOCOLATE CRANBERRY CAKE *with White Chocolate Ganache Drip*

When you're writing a cookbook in the middle of summer and making cakes that are destined for the winter chapter, you tend to run into a few hiccups. For my chocolate cranberry cake here, I searched high and low for fresh cranberries. It was as if they had never existed, and I was worried about how I'd be able to pull off this delicious cake without actual cranberries. Thankfully, just when I was losing hope, my very thoughtful sister-in-law came to the rescue and spotted them in the freezer section. The temperatures out my window were triple digits that day, but the house smelled like Christmastime.

Chocolate Cranberry Cake

- ¾ cup buttermilk (room temperature)
- ⅔ cup sour cream (room temperature)
- 4 egg whites (room temperature)
- ⅓ cup vegetable oil
- ½ cup frozen cranberries
- 1 tablespoon pure vanilla extract
- ¼ cup cocoa powder
- ¼ cup flour
- 1 box devil's food cake mix

Cranberry Compote Filling

- 1 cup frozen (or fresh) cranberries, thawed
- ¼ cup plus 1 tablespoon sugar
- 3 tablespoons lemon juice
- 1 teaspoon pure vanilla extract
- 2 teaspoons cornstarch

Cranberry Buttercream

- 1 cup frozen (or fresh) cranberries
- 1 batch Vanilla Buttercream (page xvii)

White Chocolate Ganache Drip

- 1 cup white chocolate candy melts
- ¼ cup heavy cream

For Decorating

Fresh cranberries

For the Chocolate Cranberry Cake

Preheat the oven to 325°F, then prep three 6-inch round cake pans with a swipe of shortening and dusting of flour to prevent sticking.

In a large bowl, whisk together the buttermilk, sour cream, egg whites, oil, cranberries, and vanilla until thoroughly combined. Sift in the cocoa, flour, and cake mix. Whisk until just combined. Do not overmix. Split the batter evenly among the prepared pans.

Bake for 30 to 32 minutes, until the center is baked through. Let the cakes cool in the pan for a minute before flipping them out onto a wire rack to cool completely. Wrap and freeze the cakes before assembly.

For the Cranberry Compote Filling

In a small saucepan over medium heat, stir together the cranberries, sugar, lemon juice, and vanilla and cook, stirring, until slightly thickened, bubbling, and the cranberries have almost all "popped," about 5 minutes. Sift in the cornstarch and stir until thickened, about 1 minute. Transfer the cranberry filling to a glass dish, cover, and refrigerate until thickened and cooled completely.

For the Cranberry Buttercream

In a small saucepan, bring the cranberries and ½ cup of water to a boil. Reduce the heat to a simmer and cook until a thick reduction forms, 5 to 10 minutes. Let cool completely.

In the bowl of a stand mixer fitted with a paddle attachment, beat the buttercream and cranberry reduction until evenly combined, then scrape down the sides with a spatula.

For the White Chocolate Ganache Drip

In a microwave-safe bowl, stir together the candy melts and heavy cream. Microwave for about 30 seconds and then stir until smooth. Transfer to a drip bottle.

To Assemble

Place a cardboard cake round on a cake turntable. Dot a little bit of buttercream in the center of the round and spread it out with an angled icing spatula. Place the first chilled cake layer in the center. Add a thin layer of buttercream. Pipe a buttercream dam around the outside rim of the frosted cake layer, then add about ½ cup of the cranberry filling. Place the next cake layer on top, then repeat, making sure to line the layers up evenly. After adding the top cake layer, crumb coat the cake by spreading a thin layer of buttercream around the entire cake. Freeze for 2 minutes to set the buttercream.

Using a wooden spoon, beat out any air bubbles in the remaining buttercream. Finish frosting the cake as desired or follow the decorating instructions below.

To Decorate the Cake

Spread on a final layer of buttercream around the entire cake, using a cake scraper for smooth sides and clean edges. Freeze the cake for 2 minutes to set the buttercream.

Squeeze on the white chocolate drip, letting it pool on the top of the cake and cascade down the sides. Let set until firm, about 1 minute, then place the fresh cranberries in a crown around the top of the cake.

TIP: This cranberry filling is divine. I recommend doubling it and using it as an addition to your charcuterie board, as filling for your cranberry muffins, a spread for your breakfast toast, or as an excuse to make yet another chocolate cranberry cake.

CHRISTMAS FESTIVE WREATH CAKE

What You'll Need

- 1 cup white chocolate candy melts
- ¼ cup heavy cream
- 1 cake, stacked and frosted (see page xxv), chilled until firm
- 1 batch Small-Batch Vanilla Buttercream (page xvii) tinted deep emerald green (see Note)

- ½ cup red fondant, rolled into small spheres (or fresh cranberries)
- Silver dragées

- Drip bottle
- Angled icing spatula
- Cake turntable
- Piping bag
- Wilton 1M piping tip

1. In a small microwave-safe bowl, combine the candy melts and heavy cream. Stir, then microwave for 30 seconds. Stir again until smooth.

2. Transfer the white chocolate ganache to a drip bottle.

3. Pipe drips onto your chilled, frosted cake, letting the ganache pool a bit on the top edge of the cake and then cascade down the sides. The more you squeeze, the deeper the drip.

4. When all the drips have been piped around the sides of the cake, add a bit of ganache on top.

5. Using an angled icing spatula, immediately spread the ganache on top to meet the sides. Use the cake turntable to swirl the ganache in the middle.

6. Fit a piping bag with a Wilton 1M tip and fill it with the emerald-green buttercream. Start piping the wreath near the edge of the cake by squeezing and pulling the buttercream on a diagonal, then releasing to create a tapered tail.

8. Repeat this pattern, crossing each line in the opposite direction. Continue around the top of the cake.

NOTE: You may have enough buttercream left over after frosting the cake to make the wreath; if not, make the Small-Batch Vanilla Buttercream on page xvii.

As pretty as the dragées are on this cake, it's best to remove them before eating; they're meant just for decoration, not necessarily consumption.

7. Right next to the first buttercream line, pipe another diagonal line going the opposite direction and crossing over the first one.

CHRISTMAS
CUT-OUT TREE CAKE

What You'll Need

- 4 white cake rounds (see Note)
- 2 green cake rounds
- 1 thin brown cake round
- 1 batch Vanilla Buttercream (page xvii)
- Christmas tree and star sprinkles
- Cardboard cake round
- Cake turntables
- Angled icing spatula
- Cake scraper
- Piping bag
- Wilton 1M piping tip

1. Freeze the white cake rounds until they're solid and ready to carve.

2. Crumble the green and brown cakes into separate bowls, then add about ½ cup buttercream to each bowl to create a cake-pop consistency (think Play-Doh; it should hold its shape easily when squished).

3. In one of the white cake rounds, use a knife to carve a cylinder from the very center. This hole will be for the tree's trunk.

4. In two of the white cake rounds, carve an inverted cone shape. The smaller end of the cone should be an opening the same size as the hole for the tree's trunk shape. The wider end should come to within about 1 inch from the edge of the cake.

5. In the remaining cake round, carve a cone for the top of the tree; the point should reach the top of the cake and the wider end should come to within 1½ to 2 inches from the edge of the cake.

6. Press the brown cake mixture into the center of the cylinder cutout (for the trunk). Press the

green cake mixture into the cone cutouts in the other three cake rounds. Freeze the cake rounds.

7.   Place the first cake layer, with the brown "trunk," on a cardboard cake round in the center of a cake turntable.

8.   With the angled icing spatula, spread a thin layer of buttercream around the top of the cake, avoiding where the brown shows through.

9.   Place one of the open-cone cake rounds on top, with the wider end of the cone facing down. Add a layer of buttercream around the top of the cake, avoiding the space where the green is showing through. Repeat with the next open-cone layer.

10.   Place the last cake round, with the cone pointing up.

11.   Crumb coat the cake, smooth out the buttercream with a cake scraper, and freeze for 2 minutes to set the buttercream. To finish decorating the cake, over a cookie sheet, add a final coat of buttercream, press a layer of sprinkles onto the top and sides of the cake, and then pipe a few swirls on top using a piping bag fitted with a Wilton 1M tip. Add a few more sprinkles, including star sprinkles on top of the swirls.

NOTE: Make two batches of Classic White Cake batter (page 251). Split the batter into seven different 6-inch cake pans. Leave four of them white and use gel colors to tint two layers green and one brown. The white cake rounds should be full size, the green ones slightly thinner, and the brown the thinnest.

NEW YEAR'S EVE
BLACK-AND-WHITE COUNTDOWN CAKE

What You'll Need

- 1 cake, stacked and crumb coated (see page xxiv), remaining buttercream reserved
- Black gel coloring
- New Year's Eve–themed sprinkles
- 2 cups black candy melts
- ½ cup heavy cream
- Gold gumballs
- Cake turntable
- Thick stripe cake comb
- Flat cake scraper
- Cookie sheet
- Drip bottle
- Angled icing spatula
- Piping bag
- Wilton 1M piping tip

1. Place the cake on a cake turntable. Spread a final coat of buttercream around the entire cake. Holding the stripe cake comb vertically and at a 45-degree angle from the cake, carefully pull the cake comb around the outside of the cake to create stripe indents.

2. If stripe indents are not forming in some places, add more buttercream, then scrape again. You want clearly defined indentations: the cleaner and crisper the stripe indents are, the better your stripes will look later on. Leave the top edge unfinished. Freeze the cake for 10 minutes until the buttercream is solid.

3. With a sharp knife, slice off the top edge of the buttercream, holding the knife horizontally and turning the cake turntable.

4. Tint 1½ cups of the buttercream black using the gel coloring and transfer it to a piping bag with the tip snipped off. Pipe the black buttercream in the striped indents.

5. Working quickly, use a flat cake scraper to smooth out the stripes. It will look messy before it gets better! Apply a little bit of pressure and scrape until the clean stripes start to show through.

6. On the final turn, heat the cake scraper with hot water to make a clean finish.

7. To add the sprinkles, place the cake on the cookie sheet and then place the cookie sheet back onto the cake turntable. While the buttercream is still wet, place a handful of sprinkles along the bottom rim of the cake, letting the excess fall onto the cookie sheet. Freeze for 5 minutes to set, then use a knife to slice off any unfinished black edges on the top of the cake.

8. Make the ganache by mixing the black candy melts and heavy cream in a microwave-safe bowl. Microwave for 30 seconds and stir until smooth. If it's too thick, stir in a little more heavy cream. If it's too thin, stir in a few more candy melts. Transfer to a drip bottle. Pipe a pool of ganache on the top edge of the cake and carefully push the pool over the side. The more you squeeze, the deeper the drip. Repeat to make another drip about an inch away from the first one, then continue around the cake.

9. Pipe a pool of ganache on top of the cake. With an angled icing spatula, carefully pull the ganache to the edges (being careful not to disturb the edges of the drips). Swirl the ganache to the center by dragging the angled icing spatula from the edges to the center of the cake while turning the turntable.

10. Fit a piping bag with a Wilton 1M tip and fill it with the remaining white buttercream. Holding the piping bag perpendicular to the cake near the

edge, squeeze in one spot and carefully swirl the buttercream, twice or three times, around that single spot, and then stop squeezing while lifting up. Repeat to make swirls in a ring around the top of the cake.

11. Before the buttercream sets, add a few matching sprinkles.

12. Place a gumball on each of the piped swirls.

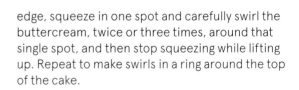

NEW YEAR'S EVE MIDNIGHT BUBBLY CAKE

What You'll Need

- 2 to 3 cups shimmery sanding sugar and gold sprinkle mix
- 1 cake, stacked and frosted (see page xxv); reserve ½ cup buttercream to finish decorating the cake
- Gold and white sixlets
- Cookie sheet
- 2 (6-inch) cardboard cake rounds
- 1 (8-inch) cardboard cake round
- Angled icing spatula
- Sparklers

1. Spread the shimmery sanding sugar and sprinkle mix on a cookie sheet, rocking the cookie sheet back and forth to spread the sugar in an even layer.

2. Gently remove the cake from the 8-inch cardboard cake round. Place the other 6-inch round on the top of the cake. Holding both ends of the cake on the cardboard, tip the cake sideways. Roll the cake in the sanding sugar.

3. Place the cake back onto the 8-inch cake board. Freeze for 5 minutes, then remove the top cake board by running a knife right between the cake and cake board.

4. Add more buttercream on top of the cake and spread it evenly with an angled icing spatula.

5. Add sanding sugar to the top of the cake.

6. Press the sanding sugar gently into the buttercream. Add a rim of gold sixlets along the bottom of the cake and a few gold and silver ones on top; use a little buttercream if needed to help

them stick. (Or apply them just before serving—they tend to roll away.) For fun New Year's flair, add a few sparklers on top!

NOTE: Stack and frost your cake on a 6-inch cardboard cake round taped to an 8-inch round; you'll need the cake to be on the 6-inch round in order to decorate it. Roll the cake in the sanding sugar before the buttercream sets so the sugar will stick.

VALENTINE'S DAY
SWEETHEART CELEBRATION CAKE

What You'll Need

- 1 cake, stacked and frosted (see page xxv)
- Valentine's Day–themed sprinkles
- 2 cups white candy melts
- ½ cup heavy cream
- Soft-pink gel coloring
- Drip bottle
- Gumballs

Fondant Roses

- ½ cup red fondant
- Rolling pin
- Wilton Easy Blooms Flower Cut-Out

Marbled Hearts

- White, pink, and red fondant
- ½ cup white candy melts
- Small heart cookie cutter
- White lollipop sticks

Chocolate Shards

- 2 cups white candy melts
- Valentine's Day–themed sprinkles
- Parchment paper
- Angled icing spatula

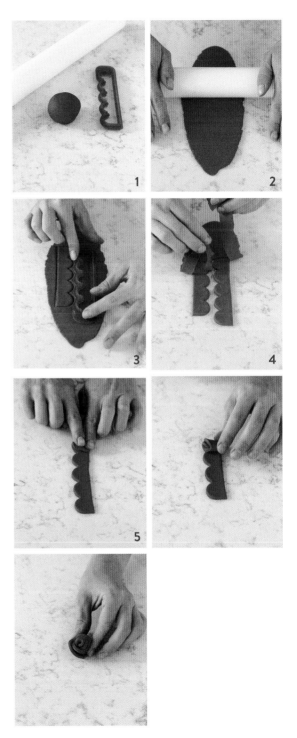

For the Fondant Roses

1. For the fondant roses, you'll need the red fondant, rolling pin, and the flower cutout tool.

2. Roll out the fondant to about ⅛-inch thickness.

3. Press the cut-out tool into the rolled-out fondant.

4. Peel away the excess fondant.

5. Starting at one end, roll the fondant in a straight line into a rose. Make 3 to 4, or as many as you'd like.

For the Marbled Hearts

6. For the marbled hearts, you'll need white, pink, and red fondant; the rolling pin; and a small heart cutter.

7. Roll the fondant into three long logs.

8. Twist the logs around and roll them together flat.

9. Roll the fondant into a ball.

10. Roll out the fondant flat again.

11. Press the heart cookie cutter into the fondant. Make about 5, or as many as you'd like. Let dry for about an hour until the hearts are firm.

12. In a microwave-safe bowl, microwave the candy melts until melted, about 30 seconds. Dip the end of a lollipop stick into the melted chocolate, then place it onto the back of a heart. Place it stick side down onto a surface to cool and set up completely.

For the Chocolate Shards

13. In a microwave-safe bowl, microwave the candy melts for about 30 seconds. Stir, then repeat one more time until they're thoroughly melted.

14. Pour the melted chocolate onto a sheet of parchment paper.

15. With an angled icing spatula, spread the chocolate to about ⅛-inch thickness.

16. Sprinkle the Valentine's Day sprinkles in different clusters before the chocolate hardens.

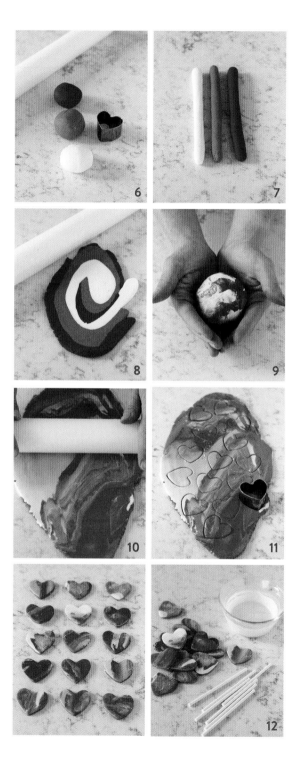

17. When the chocolate has hardened, use a hot, sharp knife (I heat mine with hot water) to make clean, long triangle slices.

To Assemble the Cake

18. Gently press the sprinkles around the bottom edge of the cake. Freeze the cake for 5 minutes to set the buttercream.

19. Make the ganache by mixing the white candy melts and heavy cream in a microwave-safe bowl. Microwave for 30 seconds and stir until smooth. If it's too thick, stir in a little more heavy cream. If it's too thin, stir in a few more candy melts. Microwave for another 30 seconds and stir, repeating until melted completely. Add one small drop of pink gel coloring and stir to tint the buttercream a soft pink. Transfer to a drip bottle. Pipe ganache drips around the top edge of the cake, then pipe a pool of ganache on top of the cake and spread it with an offset spatula. Freeze the cake until set.

20. Gently press in the chocolate shards, roses, marbled hearts, gumballs, and more sprinkles.

VALENTINE'S DAY SPRINKLE HEART CAKE

What You'll Need

- 1 cake, stacked and frosted (see page xxv); remaining buttercream reserved (you'll need about 2 cups)
- 2 cups Valentine's Day nonpareils sprinkles
- 2 (6-inch) cardboard cake rounds
- 1 (8-inch) cardboard cake round
- Parchment paper
- Cookie sheet
- Piping bag
- Wilton 6B piping tip

NOTE: Stack and frost your cake on a 6-inch cardboard cake round taped to an 8-inch round; you'll need the cake to be on the 6-inch round in order to decorate it. Roll the cake in the sprinkles before the buttercream sets so the sprinkles will stick.

1. Trace and cut out hearts from a sheet of parchment paper.

2. Place the parchment hearts in a random pattern on the sides of the cake. They should stick!

3. Pour the nonpareils into a cookie sheet and shake the sheet to spread them evenly.

4. Gently remove the cake from the 8-inch cardboard cake round. Place the other 6-inch round on the top of the cake (so you have 6-inch cardboard rounds on the top and bottom). Holding both ends of the cake on the cardboard, tip the cake sideways. Roll the cake into the nonpareils.

5. Shake the nonpareils to create an even layer again, then roll the cake again.

6. Make sure all the hearts are showing through and that the sprinkles come up to the edges.

7. Freeze for 5 minutes, then remove the top cake board by running a knife right between the cake and cake board. Carefully peel off the parchment hearts.

8. Add a thin layer of nonpareils on top and spread it with your hand.

9. With a piping bag fitted with a Wilton 6B tip, start the buttercream border by holding the piping bag perpendicular to the cake. Squeeze steadily, and slowly turn the piping tip to the side. Drag the tail while slowing the squeeze. It should taper off and make a tail. Start the next "shell" right on top of the tail and repeat around the entire cake.

Chapter 5

BIRTHDAY HITS *and* EVERYDAY CAKES

The most magical cakes of all are birthday cakes! In my family, we have a fun tradition: our sons choose *any* flavor combination they'd like for their birthday cake. Nothing is off-limits. They've loved choosing cakes inspired by their favorite candy, cookies, pies, and even ice cream flavors.

This joyful chapter is filled with cake flavors that don't necessarily revolve around a specific season. They can be made and enjoyed just about any day of the year. Whether it's a birthday, or any day (we don't always need an excuse to bake up a cake, right?), these delicious cakes are sure to become some of the most popular picks in your kitchen. year-round.

CLASSIC WHITE CAKE *with Vanilla Buttercream*

Everyone needs a surefire classic white cake recipe. If you don't have one yet, you're in luck; this one has worked for me—over and over again—for years. The layers are soft, tender, and decadent, with just enough of that "white cake" flavor. It's frosted with my favorite vanilla bean buttercream, which uses both vanilla bean paste *and* vanilla extract, creating an almost ice-cream-like flavor along with the classic American buttercream taste. If you only have one or the other, it's okay—no need to stress, it'll still come out just fine. But I do find using both yields the greatest flavor.

Classic White Cake

- ¾ cup buttermilk (room temperature)
- ⅔ cup sour cream (room temperature)
- 4 egg whites (room temperature)
- ⅓ cup vegetable oil
- 1 tablespoon pure vanilla extract
- 1 box white cake mix

Vanilla Bean Buttercream

- 1 batch Vanilla Buttercream (page xvii; use vanilla bean paste instead of extract)

For Decorating

- Sprinkles
- Piping bag
- Wilton 1M piping tip

For the Classic White Cake

Preheat the oven to 325°F, then prep three 6-inch round cake pans with a swipe of shortening and dusting of flour to prevent sticking.

In a large bowl, whisk together the buttermilk, sour cream, egg whites, oil, and vanilla until thoroughly combined. Sift in the cake mix and whisk until just combined. Do not overmix. Split the batter evenly among the prepared pans.

Bake for 27 to 30 minutes, until the center is baked through. Let the cakes cool in the pan for a minute before flipping them out onto a wire rack to cool completely. Wrap and freeze the cakes before assembly.

To Assemble

Place a cardboard cake round on a cake turntable. Dot a little bit of buttercream in the center of the round and spread it out with an angled icing spatula. Place the first cake layer in the center. Add a layer of buttercream. Place the next cake layer on top, then repeat, lining the layers up evenly. After adding the top cake layer, crumb coat the cake by spreading a thin layer of buttercream around the entire cake. Freeze for 2 minutes to set the buttercream.

Using a wooden spoon, beat out any air bubbles in the remaining buttercream. Finish frosting the cake as desired or follow the decorating instructions below.

To Decorate the Cake

Spread a final layer of white buttercream around the entire cake, using a cake scraper for smooth sides and clean edges. Place the cake on a cookie sheet and set the cookie sheet on the turntable. Press the sprinkles onto the side of the cake along the bottom.

Transfer the rest of the buttercream to a piping bag fitted with a Wilton 1M tip. Pipe a few swirls on top of the cake, then add a few sprinkles onto the swirls.

TIP: If you want your buttercream to have less of an ivory color, simply add in a tiny toothpick prick of violet gel coloring. Just like with color theory, the touch of purple mellows the yellow hue and leaves you with a white buttercream. You could also use white gel coloring to lighten the color.

YELLOW CAKE *with Cocoa Buttercream*

This classic flavor combo can be used for any celebration I can think of and is usually one of my most requested for friends and family. With moist yellow cake layers and a gorgeous chocolate buttercream, this cake will be on repeat for any party you have with your loved ones. (Don't forget the rainbow sprinkles!)

Classic Yellow Cake
- ⅔ cup buttermilk (room temperature)
- ⅔ cup sour cream (room temperature)
- 3 large eggs (room temperature)
- ⅓ cup vegetable oil
- 1 tablespoon pure vanilla extract
- 1 box yellow cake mix

Cocoa Buttercream
- 1½ cups (3 sticks) unsalted butter
- ⅔ cup cocoa powder
- ½ cup heavy cream (plus more if needed)
- 1 tablespoon pure vanilla extract
- Pinch of salt
- 7 to 8 cups powdered sugar

For Decorating
- Rainbow jimmies
- Piping bag
- Wilton 1M piping tip

For the Classic Yellow Cake

Preheat the oven to 325°F, then prep three 6-inch round cake pans with a swipe of shortening and dusting of flour to prevent sticking.

In a large bowl, whisk together the buttermilk, sour cream, eggs, oil, and vanilla until thoroughly combined. Sift in the cake mix and whisk until just combined. Do not overmix. Split the batter evenly among the prepared pans.

Bake for 27 to 30 minutes, until the center is baked through. Let the cakes cool in the pan for a minute before flipping them out onto a wire rack to cool completely. Wrap and freeze the cakes before assembly.

For the Cocoa Buttercream

In the bowl of a stand mixer fitted with a paddle attachment, beat the butter on medium speed until it's light and fluffy. Add the cocoa, heavy cream, vanilla, and salt and beat again until combined, then scrape down the sides with a spatula.

With the mixer on low speed, add the powdered sugar about ½ cup at a time. The buttercream will be thick. Add a little more heavy cream, 1 tablespoon at a time, to thin it out if needed, and then flip the mixer to high speed and beat until the buttercream is lighter in color and texture, about 2 minutes.

To Assemble

Place a cardboard cake round on a cake turntable. Dot a little bit of buttercream in the center of the round and spread it out with an angled icing spatula. Place the first cake layer in the center. Add a layer of buttercream. Place the next cake layer on top, then repeat, lining the layers up evenly. After adding the top cake layer, crumb coat the cake by spreading a thin layer of buttercream around the entire cake. Freeze for 2 minutes to set the buttercream.

Using a wooden spoon, beat out any air bubbles in the remaining buttercream. Finish frosting the cake as desired or follow the decorating instructions below.

To Decorate the Cake

Spread a final layer of buttercream around the entire cake, using a cake scraper for smooth sides and clean edges.

Place the cake on a cookie sheet and set the cookie sheet on the turntable. Press a handful of rainbow sprinkles along the bottom edge of the cake. Transfer the rest of the buttercream into a piping bag fitted with a Wilton 1M tip. Pipe a few swirl dollops on the top of the cake, then sprinkle on a few more rainbow jimmies.

DOUBLE FUNFETTI CAKE

Whether you call it funfetti or confetti cake, I know you've heard of this one. But have you heard of a *double* funfetti cake? I've added sprinkles not only to the cake batter but also to the buttercream. The bright colors from the rainbow jimmies make it perfect for any celebration, and a slice will surely brighten anyone's day. Add a few candles and customize it with your loved one's favorite color on the border, or place their favorite princess, character, or action figure on top to make it extra special.

Funfetti Cake
- ¾ cup buttermilk (room temperature)
- ⅔ cup sour cream (room temperature)
- 4 egg whites (room temperature)
- ⅓ cup vegetable oil
- 1 tablespoon pure vanilla extract
- 1 box white cake mix
- ½ cup rainbow jimmies

Funfetti Buttercream
- 1½ cups (3 sticks) unsalted butter
- ¼ cup heavy cream (plus more if needed)
- 1 tablespoon vanilla bean paste
- Pinch of salt
- 7 to 8 cups powdered sugar
- ⅔ cup rainbow jimmies

For Decorating
- Pink gel coloring
- Piping bag
- Wilton 6B piping tip

For the Funfetti Cake

Preheat the oven to 325°F, then prep three 6-inch round cake pans with a swipe of shortening and dusting of flour to prevent sticking.

In a large bowl, whisk together the buttermilk, sour cream, egg whites, oil, and vanilla until thoroughly combined. Sift in the cake mix and whisk until just combined. Do not overmix. Gently fold in the rainbow jimmies. Split the batter evenly among the prepared pans.

Bake for 27 to 30 minutes, until the center is baked through. Let the cakes cool in the pan for a minute before flipping them out onto a wire rack to cool completely. Wrap and freeze the cakes before assembly.

For the Funfetti Buttercream

In the bowl of a stand mixer fitted with a paddle attachment, beat the butter on medium speed until it's light and fluffy. Add in the heavy cream, vanilla bean paste, and salt and beat again until combined, then scrape down the sides with a spatula.

With the mixer on low speed, add the powdered sugar about ½ cup at a time. The buttercream will be thick. Add a little more heavy cream, 1 tablespoon at a time, to thin it out if needed, and then flip the mixer to high speed and beat until the buttercream is lighter in color and texture, about 2 minutes. Transfer about 2 cups of the buttercream to a separate bowl (to be tinted pink later), then toss the rainbow jimmies into the mixer bowl and mix on low until combined.

To Assemble

Place a cardboard cake round on a cake turntable. Dot a little bit of buttercream in the center of the round and spread it out with an angled icing spatula. Place the first chilled cake layer in the center. Add a layer of buttercream. Place the next cake layer on top, then repeat, making sure to line the layers up evenly. After adding the top cake layer, crumb coat the cake by spreading a thin layer of buttercream around the entire cake. Freeze for 2 minutes to set the buttercream.

Using a wooden spoon, beat out any air bubbles in the remaining buttercream. Finish frosting the cake as desired or follow the decorating instructions below.

To Decorate the Cake

Spread a final layer of buttercream around the entire cake, using a cake scraper for smooth sides and clean edges.

Tint the reserved buttercream pink with 1 drop of gel coloring. Transfer it to a piping bag fitted with a Wilton 6B tip. Pipe a shell border on the top and bottom rim of the cake.

TIP: The type of sprinkles you use matters. Jimmies are the longer rods. They hold their shape during baking and won't bleed. Coin sprinkles work just the same. I would steer clear of rainbow nonpareils (tiny spheres) in this particular cake. They tend to bleed into the cake and buttercream, making a greenish-purple hue instead of white with pockets of rainbow.

RED VELVET CAKE *with Almond Cream Cheese Buttercream*

This cake is one that I will always come back to. I've taken the classic red velvet cake up a few notches by adding in a touch of almond extract to my cream cheese buttercream. It seems like something so simple, but that hint of almond is what makes all the difference in flavor. To make the inside flavors part of the decoration, try adding on sliced almonds or a little crumble of red velvet cake on top.

Red Velvet Cake

- ¾ cup buttermilk (room temperature)
- ⅔ cup sour cream (room temperature)
- 3 large eggs (room temperature)
- ⅓ cup vegetable oil
- 1 tablespoon pure vanilla extract
- 1 box red velvet cake mix

Almond Cream Cheese Buttercream

- 1 cup (2 sticks) unsalted butter
- 8 ounces (1 brick) cream cheese
- ¼ cup heavy cream (plus more if needed)
- 1 tablespoon pure vanilla extract
- ½ teaspoon almond extract
- Pinch of salt
- 7 to 8 cups powdered sugar

For the Red Velvet Cake

Preheat the oven to 325°F, then prep three 6-inch round cake pans with a swipe of shortening and dusting of flour to prevent sticking.

In a large bowl, whisk together the buttermilk, sour cream, eggs, oil, and vanilla until thoroughly combined. Sift in the cake mix and whisk until just combined. Do not overmix. Split the batter evenly among the prepared pans.

Bake for 27 to 30 minutes, until the center is baked through. Let the cakes cool in the pan for a minute before flipping them out onto a wire rack to cool completely. Wrap and freeze the cakes before assembly.

For the Almond Cream Cheese Buttercream

In the bowl of a stand mixer fitted with a paddle attachment, beat the butter on medium speed until it's light and fluffy, then add the cream cheese and beat until fully incorporated. Add the heavy cream, vanilla, almond extract, and salt and beat again until combined, then scrape down the sides with a spatula.

With the mixer on low speed, add the powdered sugar about ½ cup at a time. The buttercream will be thick. Add a little more heavy cream, 1 tablespoon at a time, to thin it out if needed, and then flip the mixer to high speed and beat until the buttercream is lighter in color and texture, about 2 minutes.

To Assemble

Place a cardboard cake round on a cake turntable. Dot a little bit of buttercream in the center of the round and spread it out with an angled icing spatula. Place the first chilled cake layer in the center. Add a layer of buttercream. Place the next cake layer on top, then repeat, making sure to line the layers up evenly. After adding the top cake layer, crumb coat the cake by spreading a thin layer of buttercream around the entire cake. Freeze for 2 minutes to set the buttercream.

Using a wooden spoon, beat out any air bubbles in the remaining buttercream. Spread a final layer of buttercream around the entire cake, using a cake scraper for smooth sides and clean edges. Leave the top edge uneven for a more rustic look.

For the horizontal lines on the side of the cake, hold a straight icing spatula vertically against the bottom of the cake. Using a cake turntable, spin the cake around while slowly moving the straight icing spatula up. The swirls should inch higher with each turn of the turntable.

TIP: Almond extract has a very strong flavor, so a little bit goes a long way.

Catching all the red crumbs in the crumb coat will ensure your final buttercream layer is clean and spot-free.

CHOCOLATE CAKE *with Chocolate Cream Cheese Buttercream*

Do you remember that scene in *Matilda* when a child named Bruce was blamed for eating a missing slice of the principal's cake? His punishment was to eat an entire cake in front of the entire school, and every time I see that part, it doesn't actually seem like such a bad punishment! Rich chocolate layers slathered with chocolate buttercream are always a good idea . . . maybe not the whole cake at once, though. Despite that moment, I still can't think of that chocolate cake without my mouth watering. Every baker needs an amazing chocolate cake they can count on, and this one is it—although, maybe just one slice at a time.

Chocolate Cake
- ¾ cup buttermilk (room temperature)
- ⅔ cup sour cream (room temperature)
- 3 large eggs (room temperature)
- ⅓ cup vegetable oil
- ¼ cup mini chocolate chips
- 1 tablespoon pure vanilla extract
- ½ cup cocoa powder
- ¼ cup flour
- 1 box dark chocolate cake mix

Chocolate Cream Cheese Buttercream
- 1 cup (2 sticks) unsalted butter
- 8 ounces (1 brick) cream cheese
- ⅔ cup cocoa powder
- ½ cup heavy cream (plus more if needed)
- 1 tablespoon pure vanilla extract
- Pinch of salt
- 7 to 8 cups powdered sugar

For the Chocolate Cake
Preheat the oven to 325°F, then prep three 6-inch round cake pans with a swipe of shortening and dusting of flour to prevent sticking.

In a large bowl, whisk together the buttermilk, sour cream, eggs, oil, chocolate chips, and vanilla until thoroughly combined. Sift in the cocoa powder, flour, and cake mix and whisk until just combined. Do not overmix. Split the batter evenly among the prepared pans.

Bake for 30 to 32 minutes, until the center is baked through. Let the cakes cool in the pan for a minute before flipping them out onto a wire rack to cool completely. Slice each cake round in half horizontally to create 6 layers. Wrap and freeze the cakes before assembly.

For the Chocolate Cream Cheese Buttercream
In the bowl of a stand mixer fitted with a paddle attachment, beat the butter on medium speed until it's light and fluffy, then add the cream cheese and beat until fully incorporated. Add the cocoa, heavy cream, vanilla, and salt and beat again until combined, then scrape down the sides with a spatula.

With the mixer on low speed, add the powdered sugar about ½ cup at a time. The buttercream will be thick. Add a little more heavy cream, 1 tablespoon at a time, to thin it out if needed, and then flip the mixer to high speed and beat until the buttercream is lighter in color and texture, about 2 minutes.

To Assemble
Place a cardboard cake round on a cake turntable. Dot a little bit of buttercream in the center of the round and spread it out with an angled icing spatula. Place the first chilled cake layer in the center. Add a layer of buttercream. Place the next cake layer on top, then repeat, making sure to line the layers up evenly. After adding the top cake layer, crumb coat the cake by spreading a thin layer of buttercream around the entire cake. Freeze for 2 minutes to set the buttercream.

Using a wooden spoon, beat out any air bubbles in the remaining buttercream. Spread a final layer of buttercream around the entire cake, using the back of a spoon or end of a straight icing spatula in random swoops for a rustic look.

TIP: The beauty is in the imperfection. Even though I often opt for sleek lines and crisp edges, there is so much to love with the uneven rustic swirls on the side of this cake, made with the back of a spoon.

CHOCOLATE MALT CAKE

I love using malt powder in my desserts so much. I've used it two different ways in this special chocolate malt cake. First, you'll need chocolate malt powder (Ovaltine) for the cake layers and for part of the buttercream. Next, you'll need vanilla or plain malt powder for the rest of the buttercream. Both have a distinct taste but come together really well in appearance and flavor in this cake. The malt powder dissolves quickly, so no need to whip the buttercream longer on this one.

Chocolate Malt Cake

- ¾ cup buttermilk (room temperature)
- ⅔ cup sour cream (room temperature)
- ½ cup malted milk powder
- 3 large eggs plus 1 egg white (room temperature)
- ⅓ cup vegetable oil
- 1 tablespoon pure vanilla extract
- 1 box dark chocolate cake mix

Vanilla and Chocolate Malt Buttercreams

- 1½ cups (3 sticks) unsalted butter
- ½ cup plus 3 tablespoons heavy cream (plus more if needed)
- ½ cup malted milk powder
- 1 tablespoon pure vanilla extract
- Pinch of salt
- 7 to 8 cups powdered sugar
- ½ cup chocolate malt powder or cocoa powder

For Decorating

- Malt balls (Whoppers)
- Scalloped cake scraper

For the Chocolate Malt Cake

Preheat the oven to 325°F, then prep three 6-inch round cake pans with a swipe of shortening and dusting of flour to prevent sticking.

In a large bowl, whisk together the buttermilk, sour cream, malted milk powder, eggs, oil, and vanilla until thoroughly combined. Sift in the cake mix and whisk until just combined. Do not overmix. Split the batter evenly among the prepared pans.

Bake for 27 to 30 minutes, until the center is baked through. Let the cakes cool in the pan for a minute before flipping them out onto a wire rack to cool completely. Wrap and freeze the cakes before assembly.

For the Vanilla and Chocolate Malt Buttercreams

In the bowl of a stand mixer fitted with a paddle attachment, beat the butter on medium speed until it's light and fluffy. Add ½ cup of the heavy cream, the malted milk powder, vanilla, and salt and beat again until combined, then scrape down the sides with a spatula.

With the mixer on low speed, add the powdered sugar about ½ cup at a time. The buttercream will be thick. Add a touch more heavy cream to thin it out if needed, and then flip the mixer to high speed and beat until the buttercream is lighter in color and texture, about 2 minutes.

For the chocolate malt buttercream, transfer 2 cups of the buttercream to a separate bowl. Whisk in the chocolate malt powder and the remaining 3 tablespoons heavy cream. Transfer to a piping bag and set aside.

To Assemble

Place a cardboard cake round on a cake turntable. Dot a little bit of buttercream in the center of the round and spread it out with an angled icing spatula. Place the first chilled cake layer in the center. Add a thin layer of buttercream. Pipe a dam of vanilla malt buttercream around the outside rim of the frosted cake layer. Pipe the chocolate malt buttercream into the center. Place the next cake layer on top, then repeat, making sure to line the layers up evenly. After adding the top cake layer, crumb coat the cake by spreading a thin layer of vanilla malt buttercream around the top half and chocolate malt buttercream around the bottom half. Freeze for 2 minutes to set the buttercream.

Using a wooden spoon, beat out any air bubbles in the remaining buttercreams. Finish frosting the cake as desired or follow the decorating instructions below.

To Decorate the Cake

Spread a final layer of buttercream around the entire cake, using the vanilla malt buttercream on the top half and the chocolate malt buttercream on the bottom half. Use a scalloped cake scraper to make the bumpy pattern on the side of the cake (see Tip).

Gently press the malt balls over the entire top of the cake (see Tip).

TIP: Add a little dab of buttercream underneath the malt balls before placing them on the cake to keep them from rolling off at even the slightest bump.

When I'm using a cake scraper or comb on the side of a cake, I usually hold the blade angled about 45 degrees from the frosting to get the cleanest finish. For this particular scalloped cake design, however, you'll need to make the angle more like 75 degrees—that is, closer to perpendicular, although not pointing straight into the cake. This will ensure that the pointed sections of the cake comb evenly glide along the side of the cake.

TIP: Using cake combs can add more class and dimension to your cake decorating. The easiest way to get a clean swipe around the outside is to make sure your buttercream has no air bubbles (stir it with a wooden spoon until smooth before spreading it on your cake) and to add enough buttercream on the sides of your cake before scraping. The first time around won't be perfect, but if you keep scraping and holding the cake comb at a 45-degree angle while turning the turntable, you'll get there.

PEANUT BUTTER MARSHMALLOW CAKE
with Peanut Butter Buttercream and Marshmallow Filling (Fluffernutter)

Let's be honest, peanut butter and marshmallow fluff between two soft slices of bread—a Fluffernutter—sounds more like a dessert than a sandwich. But as you probably already guessed, it's a go-to sandwich flavor for kids and those who are still a kid at heart. When creating this cake, I wanted to amp up the peanut butter flavor even more, so I added in a peanut butter crust made from Nutter Butter cookies. I filled the cake with homemade marshmallow fluff and added peanut butter buttercream ruffles all around. You'll definitely need a tall glass of milk, just as with the famous Fluffernutter sandwich.

Peanut Butter Cake with Cookie Crust

- 16 Nutter Butter cookies (8 ounces)
- 3 tablespoons butter, melted
- Pinch of salt
- ¾ cup buttermilk (room temperature)
- ⅔ cup sour cream (room temperature)
- 2 large eggs plus 2 egg whites (room temperature)
- ⅓ cup vegetable oil
- ⅓ cup creamy peanut butter (I prefer Skippy)
- 1 tablespoon pure vanilla extract
- 1 box white cake mix

Marshmallow Filling

- 2 egg whites
- 1½ cups granulated sugar
- ½ cup cold water
- 1 teaspoon corn syrup
- 1 teaspoon pure vanilla extract
- 1 cup mini marshmallows

Peanut Butter Buttercream

- 1½ cups (3 sticks) unsalted butter
- ¼ cup heavy cream (plus more if needed)
- ½ cup creamy peanut butter
- 1 tablespoon pure vanilla extract
- Pinch of salt
- 7 to 8 cups powdered sugar

For Decorating

- Piping bag
- Wilton (petal) piping tip 124
- Crumbled Nutter Butter cookies

For the Peanut Butter Cake

Preheat the oven to 325°F, then prep three 6-inch round cake pans with a swipe of shortening and dusting of flour to prevent sticking.

In a food processor, pulse together the Nutter Butter cookies, melted butter, and salt until a crust forms. Split the crust mixture evenly among the prepared pans and press to firm with the bottom of a glass or flat measuring cup.

In a large bowl, whisk together the buttermilk, sour cream, eggs, oil, peanut butter, and vanilla until thoroughly combined. Sift in the cake mix and whisk until just combined. Do not overmix. Split the batter evenly among the prepared pans.

Bake for 27 to 30 minutes, until the center is baked through. Let the cakes cool in the pan for a minute before flipping them out onto a wire rack to cool completely. Wrap and freeze the cakes before assembly.

For the Marshmallow Filling

Over a double boiler (or metal stand mixer bowl over a small saucepan of boiling water), whisk together the egg whites, sugar, cold water, and corn syrup with an electric mixer until stiff peaks form. Remove from the heat. Add the mixer bowl to a stand mixer fitted with a whisk attachment. Add the vanilla and mini marshmallows and keep whisking until stiff peaks form. Let cool completely to thicken, then transfer to a piping bag.

For the Peanut Butter Buttercream

In the bowl of a stand mixer fitted with a paddle attachment, beat the butter on medium speed until it's light and fluffy. Add the heavy cream, peanut butter, vanilla, and salt and beat again until combined, then scrape down the sides with a spatula.

With the mixer on low speed, add the powdered sugar about ½ cup at a time. The buttercream will be thick. Add a little more heavy cream, 1 tablespoon at a time, to thin it out if needed, and then flip the mixer to high speed and beat until the buttercream is lighter in color and texture, about 2 minutes.

To Assemble

Place a cardboard cake round on a cake turntable. Dot a little bit of buttercream in the center of the round with an angled icing spatula. Place the first chilled cake layer in the center (crust side up). Add a thin layer of buttercream. Pipe a buttercream dam around the outside rim of the frosted cake layer, then add about ½ cup of the marshmallow filling. Place the next cake layer on top, then repeat, making sure to line the layers up evenly. After adding the top cake layer, crumb coat the cake by spreading a thin layer of buttercream around the entire cake. Freeze for 2 minutes to set the buttercream.

Using a wooden spoon, beat out any air bubbles in the remaining buttercream. Finish frosting the cake as desired or follow the decorating instructions below.

To Decorate the Cake

Spread a final layer of buttercream on top of the cake in an even layer.

Add the remaining buttercream to a piping bag fitted with a Wilton 124 tip. Holding the piping bag with the larger end of the piping tip against the cake, pipe a line of ruffles on the side of the cake starting at the top. Repeat to pipe another ruffle right underneath again and again until the

entire cake is covered. Top with a few crumbled Nutter Butter cookies around the outside top rim of the cake.

TIP: When making your buttercream ruffles, start from the top of the cake and work your way down. That way the top of the ruffle row doesn't get destroyed when piping the next one.

You can use store-bought marshmallow fluff in place of the homemade filling.

BETTER THAN "ANYTHING" CAKE

This cake has a couple aliases—a.k.a. "better than sex" or "BTS" cake (Sorry, Mom! I didn't name it!)—that stem from its over-the-top decadence. With rich chocolate cake layers soaked for hours in caramel, sweetened condensed milk, and chocolate sauce; a whipped cream topping studded with toffee bits; and even more caramel and chocolate drizzle on top, this cake is one that people keep coming back to when they want something extra tasty. It's typically made in a 9 × 13-inch pan, but I've decided to live on the edge by stacking it. As with my Black Forest Cake (page 141), you'll need to keep the cake cold and use whipped cream that has been stabilized. This cake is supposed to be pretty messy, so don't worry about clean edges and smooth sides. Just throw on the toffee bits, drizzle on the caramel and chocolate sauce, and it's all ready to be enjoyed.

➤➤

Chocolate Cake

- 1 cup buttermilk (room temperature)
- ½ cup sour cream (room temperature)
- 3 large eggs plus 1 egg white (room temperature)
- ⅓ cup vegetable oil
- ¼ cup dark cocoa powder
- ¼ cup mini chocolate chips
- 1 tablespoon pure vanilla extract
- ¼ cup flour
- 1 box dark chocolate cake mix

Cake Soak

- ½ cup Caramel Sauce Filling (page 153) (or store-bought caramel sauce)
- ½ cup sweetened condensed milk
- ½ cup chocolate sauce (homemade or store-bought)

For Decorating

- Stabilized Whipped Cream Frosting (page 141)
- Caramel sauce
- Chocolate sauce
- 4 cups toffee bits
- 10 to 12 Heath fun-size candy bars
- Piping bag
- Wilton 6B piping tip

For the Chocolate Cake

Preheat the oven to 325°F, then prep three 6-inch round cake pans with a swipe of shortening and dusting of flour to prevent sticking.

In a large bowl, whisk together the buttermilk, sour cream, eggs, oil, cocoa, chocolate chips, and vanilla until thoroughly combined. Sift in the flour and cake mix and whisk until just combined. Do not overmix. Split the batter evenly among the prepared pans.

Bake for 30 to 32 minutes, until the center is baked through. Let the cakes cool in the pan for a minute before flipping them out onto a wire rack.

Line the cake pans with plastic wrap and then carefully flip the still-warm cakes back into the pans. Poke holes all over the bottom of the cakes with a toothpick. For the soak, drizzle the caramel sauce, sweetened condensed milk, and chocolate sauce over the surface of the layers, letting them seep into the holes. Pull the plastic wrap over the top of the cakes, then let them soak overnight in the freezer.

To Assemble and Decorate

Place a cardboard cake round on a cake turntable. Dot a little bit of whipped cream in the center of the cake round and spread it with the angled icing spatula. Place the first chilled cake layer in the center. Add a layer of whipped cream. Drizzle on some caramel and chocolate sauce, and add some toffee bits. Working quickly, place the next cake layer on top, then repeat, making sure to line the layers up evenly. After adding the top cake layer, crumb coat the cake by spreading a thin layer of whipped cream around the entire cake. Freeze for 10 minutes to set. If your cakes are starting to slide a little, you may need to add a dowel or wrap the crumb coat in plastic wrap to keep it stabilized (see Tip).

Spread a final layer of whipped cream around the entire cake and press a layer of the toffee bits around the sides of the cake.

Add the remaining whipped cream to a piping bag fitted with the Wilton 6B tip, then pipe swirls around the outside top of the cake. Place the toffee candy on each swirl.

Drizzle caramel and chocolate sauce on top. When serving, add more caramel and chocolate drizzle off the sides.

TIP: If you're stacking a cake and notice it's leaning or the cake rounds are sliding around, push a wooden dowel into the center of the cake to stabilize it, then place it in the freezer and walk away for about 5 minutes. When you come back, both you and the cake will get along much better.

SUPERMAN CAKE

In the summer, my grandma June would often take my younger brother and me to a charming little shop called Gossner's. Dubbed "the little Switzerland of the Rockies," it has all kinds of cheeses, flavored milks, and other dairy specialties. They have a large window where we would watch cheese being made, and we'd often leave with large ice cream cones loaded with our favorite scoops. I would almost always get either cookies and cream or chocolate chip cookie dough, but my little brother would go for something called "superman ice cream." It was Play-Doh-looking ice cream with striking red, blue, and yellow hues. Each color was a different flavor, so you can imagine how every lick would bring a different combination of vanilla (yellow), cherry/strawberry (red), and bubble gum (blue). It made me smile when on a recent visit back to Utah, he sent our family a photo of a huge tub of superman ice cream. I guess some things never change.

Superman Ice Cream–Flavored Cake

- ¾ cup buttermilk (room temperature)
- ⅔ cup sour cream (room temperature)
- 4 egg whites (room temperature)
- ⅓ cup vegetable oil
- 1 tablespoon pure vanilla extract
- 1 box white cake mix
- 1 teaspoon vanilla bean paste
- ½ teaspoon bubble gum emulsion
- ½ teaspoon strawberry or cherry emulsion
- 1 drop yellow, blue, and red gel coloring

Superman Ice Cream–Flavored Buttercream

- 2 cups (4 sticks) unsalted butter
- ½ cup heavy cream (plus more if needed)
- 1 tablespoon pure vanilla extract
- Pinch of salt
- 9 cups powdered sugar
- ½ teaspoon bubble gum emulsion
- ½ teaspoon strawberry or cherry emulsion
- ½ teaspoon vanilla bean paste
- 1 drop yellow, blue, and red gel coloring

White Chocolate Ganache Drip

- 1 cup white chocolate candy melts
- ¼ cup heavy cream

For Decorating

- 3 sugar ice cream cones

For the Superman Ice Cream–Flavored Cake

Preheat the oven to 325°F, then prep three 6-inch round cake pans with a swipe of shortening and dusting of flour to prevent sticking.

In a large bowl, whisk together the buttermilk, sour cream, egg whites, oil, and vanilla until thoroughly combined. Sift in the cake mix and whisk until just combined. Do not overmix.

Split the cake batter evenly among three bowls. To the first bowl, add the vanilla bean paste and drop of yellow gel coloring. To the second, add the bubble gum emulsion and drop of blue gel coloring. To the third, add the strawberry emulsion and drop of red gel coloring. Stir gently.

Split the batter evenly among the prepared pans, alternating scoops of the three flavors to fill the pans. With a toothpick, gently swirl the batter in a figure-eight motion to create a marbled effect.

Bake for 27 to 30 minutes, until the center is baked through. Let the cakes cool in the pan for a minute before carefully flipping them out onto a wire rack to cool completely. Wrap and freeze the cakes before assembly.

For the Superman Ice Cream–Flavored Buttercream

In the bowl of a stand mixer fitted with a paddle attachment, beat the butter on medium speed until it's light and fluffy, about 2 minutes. Add

the heavy cream, vanilla, and salt and beat again until combined, then scrape down the sides with a spatula.

With the mixer on low speed, add the powdered sugar about ½ cup at a time. Add a little more heavy cream, 1 tablespoon at a time, if needed to thin it out, and then flip the mixer to high speed and beat until the buttercream is lighter in color and texture, about 2 minutes.

To each of two cups, transfer 1½ cups of buttercream (3 cups total). To one cup, add the bubble gum emulsion and blue gel coloring and stir. To the other, add the strawberry emulsion and red gel coloring and stir. Leave the rest of the buttercream white for now.

For the White Chocolate Ganache Drip

In a microwave-safe bowl, microwave the white chocolate candy melts and heavy cream for 30 seconds. Stir until smooth. Dip the large ends of the ice cream cones in the ganache, then pour the rest into a drip bottle. Place the cones on a sheet of parchment paper to set.

To Assemble and Decorate

Place a cardboard cake round on a cake turntable. Dot a little bit of the white buttercream in the center of the round and spread it out with an angled icing spatula. Place the first chilled cake layer in the center. Add a layer of buttercream. Place the next cake layer on top, then repeat, making sure to line the layers up evenly. After

adding the top cake layer, crumb coat the cake by spreading a thin layer of buttercream around the entire cake. Freeze for 2 minutes to set the buttercream.

Using a wooden spoon, beat out any air bubbles in the remaining buttercream. Tint the remaining white buttercream with the yellow gel coloring and add the vanilla bean paste. Spread a thin final layer of buttercream around the entire cake, alternating between the red, blue, and yellow buttercreams. Smooth it out with a cake scraper. Freeze for 5 minutes to firm.

Spread the remaining buttercream in three stripes in a 5 × 5-inch section in a food storage container. Freeze for 20 minutes, then use an ice cream scoop to create 3 or 4 "scoops" of buttercream to resemble ice cream. Place the scoops back on the cookie sheet and freeze to firm.

Add the drip to the cake, letting the drips cascade down the sides of the cake. Freeze for 2 minutes to set the ganache.

Place the "ice cream" scoops on top of the cake, then press the ganache-dipped cones onto the scoops.

TIP: This buttercream has three distinct colors, so when you're spreading them on the outside of the cake, don't smear them together too much or you'll end up with a cake that looks more like toffee or chocolate than superman ice cream.

COSMIC BROWNIE CAKE

Little Debbie Cosmic Brownies graced many a boxed lunch when I was growing up (and were probably also a hidden snack for parents with a bit of a sweet tooth). This cake is inspired by that childhood favorite, and to call it chocolate on chocolate would be an understatement—it's the brownie-like texture, thick-ganache layer, and of course, those signature rainbow-chip sprinkles that really make this something memorable.

Chocolate Cake
- ¾ cup buttermilk (room temperature)
- ⅔ cup sour cream (room temperature)
- ½ cup mini chocolate chips
- 3 large eggs plus 1 egg white (room temperature)
- ½ cup vegetable oil
- 1 tablespoon pure vanilla extract
- ½ cup dark cocoa
- ¼ cup flour
- 1 box dark chocolate cake mix

Chocolate Ganache
- 24 ounces Ghirardelli semisweet chocolate chips
- 1½ cups heavy cream

For Decorating
- 2 cups rainbow candy sprinkles
- 8 Little Debbie Cosmic Brownies

For the Chocolate Cake

Preheat the oven to 325°F, then prep three 6-inch round cake pans with a swipe of shortening and dusting of flour to prevent sticking.

In a large bowl, whisk together the buttermilk, sour cream, chocolate chips, eggs, oil, and vanilla until thoroughly combined. Sift in the cocoa, flour, and cake mix and whisk until just combined. Do not overmix. Split the batter evenly among the prepared pans.

Bake for 27 to 30 minutes, until the center is baked through. Let the cakes cool in the pan for a minute before carefully flipping them out onto a wire rack to cool completely. Wrap and freeze the cakes before assembly.

For the Chocolate Ganache

In a large glass bowl, stir together the chocolate chips and heavy cream. Microwave for 1 minute, then stir. Microwave for 30 seconds and stir again. Repeat until all the chips have melted and it's thick and smooth.

Let cool at room temperature until the ganache is thick enough to spread like frosting, 4 to 6 hours. You can put it in the refrigerator to speed up this step if you want.

To Assemble and Decorate

Place a cardboard cake round on a cake turntable. Dot a little bit of ganache in the center of the round and spread it out with an angled icing spatula. Place the first chilled cake layer in the center. Add a thick layer of ganache. Place the next cake layer on top, then repeat, lining the layers up evenly. After adding the top cake layer, crumb coat the cake by spreading the ganache in a thin layer around the entire cake. Freeze for 1 minute to set.

Working quickly so the ganache doesn't set before you add the sprinkles, add a final layer of ganache around the entire cake, using a cake scraper for smooth sides and clean edges.

Immediately press on or roll the rainbow candy sprinkles all around the cake. (See page 245 for the rolling technique.) Place the brownies around the top of the cake.

TIP: I found the rainbow chips at my local grocery store (Kroger). This cake has no buttercream—it's all chocolate ganache, just like on a Cosmic Brownie. When it comes to stacking and decorating the cake, the temperature of the ganache is key. It needs to spread like butter, and with a cold cake underneath, it can harden quickly. So work fast and get those rainbow chips right onto the sides.

CHOCOLATE CAKE *with Cookie Dough Filling and Cocoa Buttercream*

We're accustomed to eating cookie dough in a vanilla base when it comes to ice cream, but why not pair it with chocolate for something even better? I could see this cake as a perfect addition to any birthday party, with tall candles and bright-colored sprinkles on top. It's such a fun cake, and don't even try to keep those cookie dough balls away from me. You may want to double the cookie dough filling to have enough for snacking—or if you have eager little boys like I do who can't wait another second to taste test the dough one more time.

Chocolate Cake
- ¾ cup buttermilk (room temperature)
- ⅔ cup sour cream (room temperature)
- 3 large eggs (room temperature)
- ⅓ cup vegetable oil
- 1 tablespoon pure vanilla extract
- ¼ cup mini chocolate chips
- ½ cup cocoa powder
- ¼ cup flour
- 1 box dark chocolate cake mix

Eggless Cookie Dough
- 1 cup (2 sticks) unsalted butter, slightly softened
- 1 cup granulated sugar
- 1 cup packed brown sugar
- 2 cups flour (heat treated, if preferred; see page 198)
- ¼ cup milk
- 1 tablespoon pure vanilla extract
- ½ teaspoon salt
- ⅔ cup mini chocolate chips

Cocoa Buttercream
- 1½ cups (3 sticks) unsalted butter
- ⅔ cup cocoa powder
- ¼ cup heavy cream (plus more if needed)
- 1 tablespoon pure vanilla extract
- Pinch of salt
- 7½ cups powdered sugar

For Decorating
- Piping bag
- Wilton 6B piping tip

For the Chocolate Cake
Preheat the oven to 325°F, then prep three 6-inch round cake pans with a swipe of shortening and dusting of flour to prevent sticking.

In a large bowl, whisk together the buttermilk, sour cream, eggs, oil, vanilla, and mini chocolate chips until thoroughly combined. Sift in the cocoa powder, flour, and cake mix and whisk until just combined. Do not overmix. Split the batter evenly between the prepared pans.

Bake for 30 to 32 minutes, until the center is baked through. Let the cakes cool in the pan for a minute before flipping them out onto a wire rack to cool completely. Wrap and freeze the cakes before assembly.

For the Eggless Cookie Dough
In the bowl of a stand mixer fitted with a paddle attachment, beat together the butter, sugar, and brown sugar until light and fluffy. Add the flour, milk, vanilla, and salt and mix to combine. Add the chocolate chips and mix again. Split the cookie dough in half. Roll half into cookie dough balls to top the cake. For the other half, split the dough between two 6-inch cake pans lined with plastic wrap to form two flat cookie dough disks. Chill the cookie dough balls and disks before adding them to the cake.

For the Cocoa Buttercream
In the bowl of a stand mixer fitted with a paddle attachment, beat the butter on medium speed until it's light and fluffy. Add the cocoa powder, heavy cream, vanilla, and salt and beat again until combined, then scrape down the sides with a spatula.

With the mixer on low speed, add the powdered sugar about ½ cup at a time. The buttercream will be thick. Add a little more heavy cream, 1 tablespoon at a time, to thin it out if needed, and then flip the mixer to high speed and beat until the buttercream is lighter in color and texture, about 2 minutes.

To Assemble

Place a cardboard cake round on a cake turntable. Dot a little bit of buttercream in the center of the round and spread it out with an angled icing spatula. Place the first chilled cake layer in the center. Add a thin layer of buttercream. Press on the first cookie dough disk. Place the next cake layer on top, then repeat, making sure to line the layers up evenly. After adding the top cake layer, crumb coat the cake by spreading a thin layer of buttercream around the entire cake. Freeze for 2 minutes to set the buttercream.

Using a wooden spoon, beat out any air bubbles in the remaining buttercream. Finish frosting the cake as desired or follow the decorating instructions below.

To Decorate the Cake

Add a layer of buttercream on top of the cake, then transfer the remaining buttercream to a piping bag fitted with a Wilton 6B tip. Working in a horizontal line along the top rim, pipe a series of shells in one direction, working your way around the side of the cake. Repeat to pipe a second row right underneath. Continue all around and down the cake.

Place the cookie dough balls in a ring around the top rim of the cake.

TIP: You already have the perfect mold in your kitchen to make a clean cookie dough filling layer: your cake pans! Line two 6-inch cake pans with plastic wrap and press an even layer of cookie dough into the pans. Chill for about 10 minutes.

SAMOA COOKIE CAKE

When I was a little girl, my mom and I would go door-to-door selling Girl Scout Cookies in our neighborhood. I'd wear my brown sash with my patches and troop number on the front, and everyone always seemed so happy to see me. I think that was mostly because I would soon be delivering boxes of their favorite cookies. Samoas were my favorite (and still are!), and apparently most everyone else's, as I would drop off more purple boxes on delivery day than any others. This delicious cake has everything I love about those caramel coconut shortbread cookies, and I can confidently say it's in my top-five favorite cakes of all time.

Chocolate Cake with Shortbread Crust

- 20 shortbread cookies (11 ounces; such as Sandies)
- 5 tablespoons unsalted butter, melted
- Pinch of salt
- ¾ cup buttermilk (room temperature)
- ⅔ cup sour cream (room temperature)
- 3 large eggs (room temperature)
- ⅓ cup vegetable oil
- ½ cup mini chocolate chips
- 1 tablespoon pure vanilla extract
- 1 teaspoon caramel extract
- ½ cup dark cocoa powder
- ¼ cup flour
- 1 box dark chocolate cake mix

Caramel Sauce

- 1 cup granulated sugar
- 6 tablespoons salted butter
- ½ cup heavy cream
- ½ teaspoon salt

Toasted Coconut

- 14 ounces shredded coconut (either sweetened or unsweetened is fine)

Coconut Filling

- 1 cup Toasted Coconut
- ¼ cup Caramel Sauce
- ⅔ cup sweetened condensed milk

Chocolate Ganache Drip

- ½ cup chocolate melts
- ½ cup heavy cream

Salted Caramel Shortbread Buttercream

- 1½ cups (3 sticks) unsalted butter
- 8 shortbread cookies, pulsed to a fine powder
- ½ cup heavy cream (plus more if needed)
- 1 tablespoon pure vanilla extract
- 1 teaspoon caramel extract
- Pinch of salt
- 7 to 8 cups powdered sugar

For Decorating

- Samoa cookies (or Keebler Coconut Dream cookies)

For the Chocolate Cake with Shortbread Crust

Preheat the oven to 325°F, then prep three 6-inch round cake pans with a swipe of shortening and dusting of flour to prevent sticking.

In a food processor, pulse together the shortbread cookies, melted butter, and salt until a fine crust forms. Split the crust mixture evenly among the prepared pans and press to firm with the bottom of a glass or flat measuring cup.

In a large bowl, whisk together the buttermilk, sour cream, eggs, oil, mini chocolate chips, vanilla, and caramel extract until thoroughly combined. Sift in the cocoa, flour, and cake mix and whisk until just combined. Do not overmix. Split the batter evenly among the prepared pans.

Bake for 32 to 35 minutes, until the center is baked through. Let the cakes cool in the pan for a minute before flipping them out onto a wire rack to cool completely. Wrap and freeze the cakes before assembly. Increase the oven temperature to 350°F to make the toasted coconut.

For the Caramel Sauce

In a medium saucepan over medium heat, cook the sugar, stirring constantly with a wooden spoon, over medium heat until the sugar clumps melt and form an amber liquid, 2 to 5 minutes.

Add the butter, 1 tablespoon at a time, until melted. It will bubble a lot, so be careful and continue to stir. When all the butter has been added, let the mixture bubble for about a minute without stirring.

Slowly add the heavy cream and let boil for a minute without stirring; it will bubble up high in the pan, so make sure you use a pan that has enough space. Remove from the heat and add the salt. Let cool. Gently stir. Cover and refrigerate until making the filling and ready to use.

For the Toasted Coconut

Line a cookie sheet with parchment paper. Spread the coconut in a single layer on the prepared cookie sheet. Bake for 5 minutes, then stir. Bake for 1 minute, and stir again. Repeat until the desired level of toastiness is reached. Let cool completely.

For the Coconut Filling

In a small bowl, stir together 1 cup of the toasted coconut, ¼ cup of the caramel sauce, and the sweetened condensed milk. Set aside.

For the Chocolate Ganache Drip

In a microwave-safe bowl, stir together the chocolate melts and heavy cream, then microwave for about 30 seconds. Stir until smooth, then transfer to a drip bottle. Set aside.

For the Salted Caramel Shortbread Buttercream

In the bowl of a stand mixer fitted with a paddle attachment, beat the butter on medium speed until it's light and fluffy. Add the shortbread powder, remaining caramel, the heavy cream, vanilla, caramel extract, and salt and beat again until combined, then scrape down the sides with a spatula.

With the mixer on low speed, add the powdered sugar about ½ cup at a time. The buttercream will be thick. Add a little more heavy cream, 1 tablespoon at a time, to thin it out if

needed, and then flip the mixer to high speed and beat until the buttercream is lighter in color and texture, about 2 minutes.

To Assemble

Place a cardboard cake round on a cake turntable. Dot a little bit of buttercream in the center of the round and spread it out with an angled icing spatula. Place the first chilled cake layer in the center (crust side up). Add a thin layer of buttercream. Pipe a buttercream dam around the outside rim of the frosted cake layer, then add about ½ cup of the coconut filling. Drizzle on some of the chocolate ganache. Place the next cake layer on top, then repeat, making sure to line the layers up evenly. After adding the top cake layer, crumb coat the cake by spreading a thin layer of buttercream around the entire cake. Freeze for 2 minutes to set the buttercream.

Using a wooden spoon, beat out any air bubbles in the remaining buttercream. Finish frosting the cake as desired or follow the decorating instructions below.

To Decorate the Cake

Spread a final layer of buttercream around the entire cake, using a cake scraper for smooth sides and clean edges.

Cover the entire cake in the remaining toasted coconut. Press the sides gently with your hands or a cake scraper to create a flat, even layer. This will ensure that the drip will fall down the sides easier.

Add the drip to the cake, pooling a bit of it on the top edge and letting it cascade down the sides about an inch apart. Freeze for 5 minutes to set.

Place the Samoa cookies on top of the cake.

TIP: If you can't find Sandies cookies, you can use any other shortbread cookie for similar results. If the shortbread crust seems too crumbly right out of the food processor and you can't shape it in your hand, you may need to add another tablespoon or so of melted butter to bring it together.

TWIX CAKE

The flavors and textures in this cake come together in such an unforgettable way, tasting just like my favorite Twix candy bar. There's a shortbread crust baked right into chocolate cake layers, a caramel filling, caramel buttercream, a caramel drip, and chopped-up Twix bars on top. When you're done, it should look like slicing right into a giant Twix.

Chocolate Cake with Shortbread Crust

- 20 shortbread cookies (11 ounces; such as Sandies)
- 5 tablespoons unsalted butter, melted
- Pinch of salt
- ¾ cup buttermilk (room temperature)
- ⅔ cup sour cream (room temperature)
- 3 large eggs (room temperature)
- ⅓ cup vegetable oil
- ½ cup mini chocolate chips
- 1 tablespoon pure vanilla extract
- 1 teaspoon caramel extract
- ½ cup dark cocoa powder
- ¼ cup flour
- 1 box dark chocolate cake mix
- Caramel Sauce (page 281)

Salted Caramel Shortbread Buttercream

- 1½ cups (3 sticks) unsalted butter
- 8 shortbread cookies, pulsed to a fine powder
- ½ cup heavy cream
- 1 tablespoon pure vanilla extract
- 1 teaspoon caramel extract
- Pinch of salt
- 7 to 8 cups powdered sugar

For Decorating

- 8 Twix candy bars, chopped
- Piping bag
- Wilton 1M piping tip
- 3 to 4 shortbread cookies

For the Chocolate Cake with Shortbread Crust

Preheat the oven to 325°F, then prep three 6-inch round cake pans with a swipe of shortening and dusting of flour to prevent sticking.

In a food processor, pulse together the shortbread cookies, melted butter, and salt until a fine crust forms. Split the crust mixture evenly among the prepared pans and press to firm with the bottom of a glass or flat measuring cup.

In a large bowl, whisk together the buttermilk, sour cream, eggs, oil, mini chocolate chips, vanilla, and caramel extract until thoroughly combined. Sift in the cocoa, flour, and cake mix and whisk until just combined. Do not overmix. Split the batter evenly among the prepared pans.

Bake for 32 to 35 minutes, until the center is baked through. Let the cakes cool in the pan for a minute before flipping them out onto a wire rack to cool completely. Wrap and freeze the cakes before assembly.

For the Salted Caramel Shortbread Buttercream

In the bowl of a stand mixer fitted with a paddle attachment, beat the butter on medium speed until it's light and fluffy. Add the shortbread powder, heavy cream, vanilla, caramel extract, and salt and beat again until combined, then scrape down the sides with a spatula.

With the mixer on low speed, add the powdered sugar about ½ cup at a time. The buttercream will be thick. Add a little more heavy cream, 1 tablespoon at a time, to thin it out if needed, and then flip the mixer to high speed and beat until the buttercream is lighter in color and texture, about 2 minutes.

To Assemble

Place a cardboard cake round on a cake turntable. Dot a little bit of buttercream in the center of the round and spread it out with an angled icing spatula. Place the first chilled cake layer in the center (crust side up). Add a thin layer of buttercream. Pipe a buttercream dam around the outside rim of the frosted cake layer, then add about ½ cup of the caramel filling. Place the next cake layer on top, then repeat, making sure to line the layers up evenly. After adding the top cake layer, crumb coat the cake by spreading a thin layer of buttercream around the entire cake. Freeze for 2 minutes to set the buttercream. This is a naked cake, so this will be the final layer of buttercream. Finish frosting the cake as desired or follow the decorating instructions below.

To Decorate the Cake

Add the caramel sauce to a drip bottle and squeeze onto the cake, pooling a bit of it on the top edge and letting it cascade down the sides about an inch apart. Freeze for 5 minutes to set.

Add the rest of the buttercream to a piping bag fitted with a Wilton 1M tip. Pipe a shell pattern around the top rim of the cake, pulling the "tail" of the shell toward the center. Place a pile of chopped Twix in the center. Slice the shortbread cookies in half, and place the cookies (flat side down) around the bottom rim of the cake.

TIP: The consistency of a caramel drip may be a little tricky to master, often feeling either too thick or too thin. For a more reliable consistency, you can add a few white chocolate chips to thicken up the caramel without changing the color too much. Or you can always use Wilton brand's Salted Caramel Candy Melts. They behave like chocolate, all while tasting like salted caramel.

THIN MINT CAKE

If you don't have a designated Girl Scout you order Thin Mints from, here's a secret: you can find basically the same cookies at the store. They're called Grasshoppers, and they taste almost exactly like my beloved Thin Mints. They'll work perfectly for this cake, too. You're going to need a few boxes to make this cake come to life, because we use Thin Mints not only in the crust of the cake but in the gorgeous buttercream. And let's not forget about the top of the cake. The cookies look like they're defying gravity (I'm already getting major Elphaba from *Wicked* vibes from this cake anyway); the trick is to place them on the cake when the drip is just about to set.

Chocolate Mint Cake with Mint Cookie Crust

- 40 Thin Mint or Grasshopper cookies (10 ounces)
- 4 tablespoons butter, melted
- ⅔ cup buttermilk (room temperature)
- ⅔ cup sour cream (room temperature)
- 3 large eggs (room temperature)
- ⅓ cup vegetable oil
- 1 tablespoon pure vanilla extract
- ½ teaspoon mint extract
- ¼ cup cocoa powder
- 1 box dark chocolate cake mix

Chocolate Ganache Filling and Drip

- 1 cup chocolate melts
- ¼ cup heavy cream

Mint Cookie Buttercream

- 1 batch Vanilla Buttercream (page xvii)
- 10 Thin Mint or Grasshopper cookies, pulsed to a powder in a food processor
- 1 teaspoon mint extract
- 1 to 2 drops green gel coloring (see Tip)

For Decorating

- 12 Thin Mint or Grasshopper cookies

For the Chocolate Mint Cake with Mint Cookie Crust

Preheat the oven to 325°F, then prep three 6-inch round cake pans with a swipe of shortening and dusting of flour to prevent sticking.

In a food processor, pulse together the Thin Mints and melted butter until a fine crust forms.

Split the crust mixture evenly among the three prepared pans and press to firm with the bottom of a glass or flat measuring cup.

In a large bowl, whisk together the buttermilk, sour cream, eggs, oil, vanilla, and mint extract until thoroughly combined. Sift in the cocoa powder and cake mix and whisk until just combined. Do not overmix. Split the batter evenly among the pans.

Bake for 33 to 35 minutes, until the center is baked through. Let the cakes cool in the pan for a minute before flipping them out onto a wire rack to cool completely. Wrap and freeze the cakes before assembly.

For the Chocolate Ganache Filling and Drip

In a microwave-safe bowl, stir together the chocolate melts and heavy cream and then heat for 30 seconds. Stir until smooth, and then transfer to a drip bottle. Set aside.

For the Mint Cookie Buttercream

In the bowl of a stand mixer fitted with a paddle attachment, beat together the buttercream, Thin Mint powder, and mint extract until evenly combined, then scrape down the sides with a spatula. Mix in the gel coloring.

To Assemble

Place a cardboard cake round on a cake turntable. Dot a little bit of buttercream in the center of the round and spread it out with

an angled icing spatula. Place the first chilled cake layer in the center. Add a thin layer of buttercream. Pipe a buttercream dam around the outside rim of the frosted cake layer, and then add about ¼ cup of the chocolate ganache. Place the next cake layer on top, then repeat, making sure to line the layers up evenly. After adding the top cake layer, crumb coat the cake by spreading a thin layer of buttercream around the entire cake. Freeze for 2 minutes to set the buttercream.

Using a wooden spoon, beat out any air bubbles in the remaining buttercream. Finish frosting the cake as desired or follow the decorating instructions below.

To Decorate the Cake

Spread a final layer of buttercream around the entire cake, using a cake scraper for smooth sides and clean edges. Freeze for 2 minutes.

Add the chocolate drip to the cake, letting it pool a bit on the top edge and cascade down the sides about an inch apart. Freeze for 5 minutes to set.

Press the Thin Mints on top and around the bottom sides of the cake.

TIP: Your buttercream will become a shade darker after a day. If you'd like a lighter mint green, add maybe a single drop and imagine what it would look like a touch darker. I wanted it to be deep and rich, so I opted for two or three drops here.

MONSTER COOKIE CAKE

This cake has everything we all love about monster cookies—creamy peanut butter, soft oatmeal, mini chocolate chips, and mini M&M's—all wrapped up into a gorgeous cake that will have you thinking about your next slice the second you finish licking your plate. It's a bright and cheery cake, made even more fun by the scoops of cookie dough on top that look like ice cream. You could even double the cookie dough and add it between the cake layers. (See the Chocolate Cake with Cookie Dough Filling recipe, page 279, for the technique.)

Monster Cookie Cake

- ½ cup old-fashioned oats
- ¾ cup buttermilk (room temperature)
- ½ cup sour cream (room temperature)
- 3 large eggs (room temperature)
- ⅓ cup vegetable oil
- ¼ cup creamy peanut butter (I prefer Skippy)
- ¼ cup mini chocolate chips
- 1 tablespoon pure vanilla extract
- 1 butter golden or white cake mix
- ⅓ cup mini M&M's

Eggless Monster Cookie Dough

- ½ cup (1 stick) butter, slightly softened
- ½ cup granulated sugar
- ½ cup packed brown sugar
- 2 tablespoons milk
- 2 tablespoons pure vanilla extract
- ¼ teaspoon salt

- 1 cup flour (heat treated, if preferred; see page 198)
- ½ cup mini chocolate chips
- ½ cup mini M&M's
- 3 tablespoons quick oats

Chocolate Ganache Drip

- 1 cup chocolate melts
- ¼ cup heavy cream

Peanut Butter Buttercream

- 1½ cups (3 sticks) unsalted butter
- ⅔ cup creamy peanut butter
- ¼ cup heavy cream (plus more if needed)
- 1 tablespoon pure vanilla extract
- Pinch of salt
- 7 to 8 cups powdered sugar

For Decorating

- Mini chocolate chips
- Mini M&M's
- Cookie dough scoop

For the Monster Cookie Cake

Preheat the oven to 325°F, then prep three 6-inch round cake pans with a swipe of shortening and dusting of flour to prevent sticking.

In a small saucepan over medium heat, stir together the oats and 1½ cups of water. Bring the mixture to a boil and cook until the oats are tender and the liquid has been absorbed, 5 to 10 minutes. Transfer the oatmeal to a small glass bowl, cover, and refrigerate until cooled completely.

In a large bowl, whisk together the cooked oatmeal, buttermilk, sour cream, eggs, oil, peanut butter, mini chocolate chips, and vanilla until thoroughly combined. Sift in the cake mix and whisk until just combined. Gently stir in the mini M&M's. Do not overmix. Split the batter evenly among the prepared pans.

Bake for 32 to 35 minutes, until the center is baked through. Let the cakes cool in the pan for a minute before flipping them out onto a wire rack to cool completely. Wrap and freeze the cakes before assembly.

For the Eggless Monster Cookie Dough

In the bowl of a stand mixer fitted with a paddle attachment, cream together the butter, sugar, and brown sugar. Scrape down the sides with a spatula and add the milk, vanilla, and salt, and mix until combined. Add the flour, mini chocolate chips, mini M&M's, and oats, then mix on medium speed until thoroughly combined. Use a cookie scoop to portion out scoops of dough onto a

cookie sheet. Cover with plastic wrap and set aside.

For the Chocolate Ganache Drip

In a microwave-safe bowl, stir together the chocolate melts and heavy cream and heat for 30 seconds. Stir until smooth, and then transfer to a drip bottle. Set aside.

For the Peanut Butter Buttercream

In the bowl of a stand mixer fitted with a paddle attachment, beat the butter on medium speed until it's light and fluffy. Add the peanut butter, heavy cream, vanilla, and salt and beat again until combined, then scrape down the sides with a spatula.

With the mixer on low speed, add the powdered sugar about ½ cup at a time. The buttercream will be thick. Add a little more heavy cream, 1 tablespoon at a time, to thin it out if needed, and then flip the mixer to high speed and beat until the buttercream is lighter in color and texture, about 2 minutes.

To Assemble

Place a cardboard cake round on a cake turntable. Dot a little bit of buttercream in the center of the round and spread it out with an angled icing spatula. Place the first chilled cake layer in the center. Add a layer of buttercream. Place the next cake layer on top, then repeat, making sure to line the layers up evenly. After adding the top cake layer, crumb coat the cake by spreading a thin layer of buttercream around the entire cake. Freeze for 2 minutes to set the buttercream.

Using a wooden spoon, beat out any air bubbles in the remaining buttercream. Finish frosting the cake as desired or follow the decorating instructions below.

To Decorate the Cake

Spread a final layer of buttercream around the entire cake, using a cake scraper for smooth sides and clean edges.

Place the mini chocolate chips and mini M&M's along the bottom of the cake. Freeze for 2 minutes.

Add the chocolate drip to the cake, letting it pool a bit on the top edge and cascade down the sides about an inch apart. Freeze for 5 minutes to set.

Place the cookie dough scoops on top of the cake.

TIP: When I toss any add-ins into my cake batter, I try to find the tiniest version possible. Mini chocolate chips and mini M&M's are the perfect size for inside and outside the cake, and don't overpower the shape or flavor.

HOSTESS CUPCAKE CAKE

This cake brings a smile to my face because it looks just like a giant Hostess cupcake. I brought all those familiar flavors—the chocolate cake, whipped cream, and ganache—right into our cake, even down to the signature looped swirl across the top of the cake.

Chocolate Cake

- ¾ cup buttermilk (room temperature)
- ⅔ cup sour cream (room temperature)
- 3 large eggs (room temperature)
- ⅓ cup vegetable oil
- ¼ cup mini chocolate chips
- 1 tablespoon pure vanilla extract
- ½ cup cocoa powder
- 1 box dark chocolate cake mix

Stabilized Whipped Cream Filling

- 2 cups heavy whipping cream
- 2 teaspoons unflavored powdered gelatin
- 2 cups powdered sugar

- 1 teaspoon pure vanilla extract

Chocolate Ganache

- 2 cups good-quality chocolate chips or chopped chocolate
- 2 cups heavy cream

Mini-Batch Vanilla Buttercream

- 4 tablespoons unsalted butter
- 1 teaspoon heavy cream (plus more if needed)
- ½ teaspoon pure vanilla extract
- Pinch of salt
- 2 cups powdered sugar

For Decorating

- Piping bag
- Wilton 10 piping tip

For the Chocolate Cake

Preheat the oven to 325°F, then prep three 6-inch round cake pans with a swipe of shortening and dusting of flour to prevent sticking.

In a large bowl, whisk together the buttermilk, sour cream, eggs, oil, mini chocolate chips, and vanilla until thoroughly combined. Sift in the cocoa powder and cake mix and whisk until just combined. Do not overmix. Split the batter evenly among the prepared pans.

Bake for 30 to 32 minutes, until the center is baked through. Let the cakes cool in the pan for a minute before flipping them out onto a wire rack to cool completely. Wrap and freeze the cakes before assembly.

For the Stabilized Whipped Cream Filling

Place the metal bowl and whisk attachment of a stand mixer in the freezer to chill for about 10 minutes. Attach them to the stand mixer and beat the heavy cream and gelatin together on low speed, medium speed, then high speed, each for about a minute until stiff peaks form. Add the powdered sugar and vanilla. Whisk again to thicken. Place in a piping bag and set aside.

For the Chocolate Ganache

In a medium microwave-safe bowl, stir together the chocolate chips and heavy cream and microwave for 1 minute. Stir, then heat again for 30 seconds. Stir again and repeat until smooth. Let cool to room temperature, then whip the ganache in the stand mixer with the paddle attachment until it reaches a buttercream-like texture.

For the Mini-Batch Vanilla Buttercream

In a medium bowl with a hand-mixer, beat the butter until it's light and fluffy. Add the heavy cream, vanilla, and salt and beat again until combined, then scrape down the sides with a spatula.

Add the powdered sugar and mix again. Add in a little more heavy cream, 1 teaspoon at a time, to thin it out if needed. Set aside.

To Assemble and Decorate

Place a cardboard cake round on a cake turntable. Dot a little bit of ganache in the center of the round and spread it out with an angled icing spatula. Place the first chilled cake layer in the center. Add a thin layer of buttercream. Pipe a ganache dam around the outside rim of the frosted cake layer, then add about ½ cup of the whipped cream filling. Place the next cake layer on top, then repeat, making sure to line the layers up evenly. After adding the top cake layer, crumb coat the cake by spreading a thin layer of buttercream around the entire cake. Freeze for 2 minutes to set the ganache.

Working quickly so the ganache doesn't firm up too fast against the cold cake, spread a final layer of ganache around the entire cake, using a cake scraper for smooth sides and clean edges. Freeze for 2 minutes.

For the swirl on top, place the buttercream into a piping bag fitted with the Wilton 10 tip. Pipe on a few loops from one end of the top of the cake to the other.

> **TIP:** For an even cake slice, make sure to pipe the buttercream dam the same thickness and add an equal amount of filling between each cake layer. Get eye level when stacking your cakes to make sure everything is lined up perfectly, and you will have straight slices as a result.

RAINBOW-STRIPED LUCKY CHARMS CAKE

I love turning cereal flavors into cake flavors. This one was a delight to create with both the cereal pieces and brightly colored marshmallows. The best way to get a true cereal flavor infused into the cake and buttercream is by soaking the cereal pieces in the liquids you'll be using. In this case, I soaked the non-marshmallow pieces in my buttermilk and heavy cream until all the flavor had been released. I tossed a few marshmallows in the cake batter, and it ended up making such a cool funfetti effect. Stripes on the outside of the cake highlight the cereal colors. The slightly tan and speckled look in the lighter buttercream stripes is from pulsing the cereal pieces into a powder and tossing it right into the buttercream. With a few more marshmallows pressed on to decorate and rainbow buttercream swirls, this cake is as bright and cheery as the cereal itself.

Lucky Charms Cake

- 1 cup buttermilk (room temperature)
- ½ cup crushed Lucky Charms cereal (marshmallow pieces removed; see Tip)
- ⅔ cup sour cream (room temperature)
- 4 egg whites (room temperature)
- ⅓ cup vegetable oil
- 1 tablespoon pure vanilla extract
- 1 box white cake mix
- ½ cup crushed Lucky Charms marshmallows

Lucky Charms Buttercream

- ¼ cup heavy cream (plus more if needed)

- ½ cup Lucky Charms cereal (marshmallows removed), plus ½ cup cereal (marshmallows removed) pulsed into a fine powder
- 1½ cups (3 sticks) unsalted butter
- 1 teaspoon pure vanilla extract
  Pinch of salt
- 7 to 8 cups powdered sugar
  Pink, yellow, green, blue, and purple gel coloring

For Decorating

Lucky Charms marshmallows
Stripe cake comb
Piping bag
Wilton 1M piping tip

For the Lucky Charms Cake

Preheat the oven to 325°F, then prep three 6-inch round cake pans with a swipe of shortening and dusting of flour to prevent sticking.

In a small bowl, stir together the buttermilk and crushed cereal. Let soak until the cereal flavor seeps into the buttermilk, about 20 minutes.

In a large bowl, whisk together the cereal milk, sour cream, egg whites, oil, and vanilla until thoroughly combined. Sift in the cake mix and whisk until just combined. Do not overmix. Gently fold in the marshmallows. Split the cake batter evenly among the prepared pans.

Bake for 25 to 27 minutes, until the center is baked through. Let the cakes cool in the pan for a minute before flipping them out onto a wire rack to cool completely. Wrap and freeze the cakes before assembly.

For the Lucky Charms Buttercream

Just like for the cake batter, stir together the heavy cream and crushed cereal (not the powdered cereal—you'll need that a little later), and let soak for at least 15 minutes.

In the bowl of a stand mixer fitted with a paddle attachment, beat the butter on medium speed until it's light and fluffy. Add the cereal milk, vanilla, salt, and powdered cereal and beat again until combined, then scrape down the sides with a spatula.

With the mixer on low speed, add the powdered sugar about ½ cup at a time. The buttercream will be thick. Add a little more heavy cream, 1 tablespoon at a time, to thin it out if needed, and then flip the mixer on high speed and beat until the buttercream is lighter in color and texture, about 2 minutes.

To Assemble

Place a cardboard cake round on a cake turntable. Dot a little bit of buttercream in the center of the round and spread it out with an angled icing spatula. Place the first chilled cake layer in the center. Add a layer of buttercream. Place the next cake layer on top, then repeat, making sure to line the layers up evenly. After adding on the top cake layer, crumb coat the cake by spreading a thin layer of buttercream around the entire cake. Freeze for 2 minutes to set the buttercream.

Using a wooden spoon, beat out any air bubbles in the remaining buttercream. Finish frosting the cake as desired or follow the decorating instructions below.

To Decorate the Cake

Add a final layer of buttercream on the top and sides of the cake, using a stripe cake comb to make clean indents on the side of the cake. The crisper the indents, the cleaner the stripes will be later on. Freeze for at least 10 minutes so that the buttercream is very firm.

Split the buttercream into five different bowls and tint each bowl a different color: pink, yellow, green, blue, and a little bit of purple. Place the colors in individual piping bags.

Pipe the pink, yellow, green, and blue in the indents in the buttercream and then immediately scrape the sides of the cake with a flat cake scraper. Apply a little bit of pressure and scrape until the clean stripes start to show through. Place marshmallows in various places.

Add the remaining colored buttercream to a piping bag fitted with a Wilton 1M tip. Pipe rainbow swirls around the top of your cake.

TIP: When you soak the cereal, don't include the marshmallow pieces because they shed their color very easily and you could very well end up with a green goop. Likewise, gently fold the marshmallow pieces into the cake batter before baking. You want to see the individual colors peeking through the cake layers.

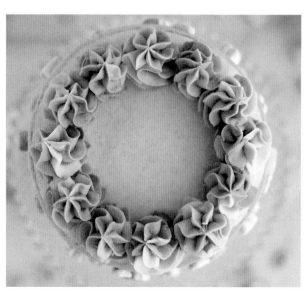

CHOCOLATE PEANUT BUTTER CAKE

This cake is by far my most popular. I've had repeat requests for it from friends and family, and it's a number one favorite with my readers across the globe. It's one of my favorite cakes of all time, too, so I don't blame them. Stripes of thick whipped peanut butter and cocoa buttercreams envelop this chocolate cake. I always add mini chocolate chips along the bottom and on top for texture, and it doesn't seem complete without a few Reese's peanut butter cups to crown this one as the king of cakes.

Chocolate Cake

- ¾ cup buttermilk (room temperature)
- ⅔ cup sour cream (room temperature)
- 3 large eggs (room temperature)
- ⅓ cup vegetable oil
- ¼ cup mini chocolate chips
- 1 tablespoon pure vanilla extract
- ½ cup cocoa powder
- 1 box dark chocolate cake mix

Peanut Butter Buttercream

- 1 batch Vanilla Buttercream (page xvii)
- ⅔ cup creamy peanut butter (I prefer Skippy)
- ½ cup cocoa powder

For Decorating

- Reese's peanut butter cups
- Mini chocolate chips
- Stripe cake comb
- Piping bag
- Wilton 1M piping tip

For the Chocolate Cake

Preheat the oven to 325°F, then prep three 6-inch round cake pans with a swipe of shortening and dusting of flour to prevent sticking.

In a large bowl, whisk together the buttermilk, sour cream, eggs, oil, mini chocolate chips, and vanilla until thoroughly combined. Sift in the cocoa powder and cake mix and whisk until just combined. Do not overmix. Split the batter evenly among the prepared pans.

Bake for 30 to 32 minutes, until the center is baked through. Let the cakes cool in the pan for a minute before flipping them out onto a wire rack to cool completely. Wrap and freeze the cakes before assembly.

For the Peanut Butter Buttercream

In the bowl of a stand mixer fitted with a paddle attachment, beat the buttercream and peanut butter until evenly combined, then scrape down the sides with a spatula.

Transfer 2 cups of the buttercream to a separate bowl and stir in the cocoa powder until combined. Transfer to a piping bag without a piping tip. Set aside.

To Assemble

Place a cardboard cake round on a cake turntable. Dot a little bit of buttercream in the center of the round and spread it out with an angled icing spatula. Place the first chilled cake layer in the center. Add a layer of buttercream. Place the next cake layer on top, then repeat, making sure to line the layers up evenly. After adding the top cake layer, crumb coat the cake by spreading a thin layer of buttercream around the entire cake. Freeze for 2 minutes to set the buttercream.

Using a wooden spoon, beat out any air bubbles in the remaining buttercream. Finish frosting the cake as desired or follow the decorating instructions below.

To Decorate the Cake

Spread a final layer of buttercream around the entire cake, using a stripe cake comb to make clean indents on the side of the cake. The crisper the indents, the cleaner the stripes will be later on. Freeze for at least 10 minutes so that the buttercream is very firm.

When the stripe indents are firm to the touch, pipe the cocoa buttercream in the indents and then immediately scrape the sides of the cake with a flat cake scraper. Apply a little bit of pressure and scrape until the clean stripes start to show through.

Add the remaining peanut butter and cocoa buttercreams to a piping bag fitted with a Wilton 1M tip. Pipe a buttercream swirl on top of the cake along the outside rim, then place a Reese's

peanut butter cup right next to it. Repeat around the top of the cake. Sprinkle some mini chocolate chips in the center. Add small chocolate chips along the bottom rim of the cake.

TIP: You won't need to make two separate buttercreams for these gorgeous stripes. You'll just reserve a little of the peanut butter buttercream and whip it up with some cocoa powder. You only need enough cocoa buttercream to fill in the indents between the stripes.

RED VELVET OREO CAKE

I can't decide if this cake is more perfect for Valentine's Day or Halloween with its black-and-white exterior and deep red velvet inside. For me, it's perfect for any day you want to celebrate with a cake that will knock your socks off. In addition to making a cookies-and-cream buttercream, I tossed a few Oreo crumbles right into the cake batter (the more cookies I can squeeze into this cake, the better). It looks like Oreo funfetti, and the little pockets of cookie in the soft cake layers make for something truly special that you wouldn't exactly expect. With a tall glass of milk nearby, you'll wonder why you ever settled for just cookies and milk, when you can now enjoy cookies-and-cream red velvet cake instead.

Red Velvet Oreo Cake
- ¾ cup buttermilk (room temperature)
- ⅔ cup sour cream (room temperature)
- 3 large eggs (room temperature)
- ⅓ cup vegetable oil
- 1 tablespoon pure vanilla extract
- 1 box red velvet cake mix
- 8 crushed Oreo cookies (about ½ cup)

Speckled Oreo Cream Cheese Buttercream
- 1 cup (2 sticks) unsalted butter
- 8 ounces (1 brick) cream cheese
- ⅛ cup heavy cream
- 1 tablespoon pure vanilla extract
- Pinch of salt
- 7 to 8 cups powdered sugar
- ¼ cup small Oreo crumbles

Dark Chocolate Drip
- 1 cup black (or dark) chocolate melts (see Tip)
- ¼ cup heavy cream

For Decorating
- 15 Oreo cookies (mini and regular)

For the Red Velvet Oreo Cake
Preheat the oven to 325°F, then prep three 6-inch round cake pans with a swipe of shortening and dusting of flour to prevent sticking.

In a large bowl, whisk together the buttermilk, sour cream, eggs, oil, and vanilla until thoroughly combined. Sift in the cake mix and whisk until just combined. Do not overmix. Fold in the crushed Oreos. Split the batter evenly among the prepared pans.

Bake for 27 to 30 minutes, until the center is baked through. Let the cakes cool in the pan for a minute before flipping them out onto a wire rack to cool completely. Wrap and freeze the cakes before assembly.

For the Speckled Oreo Cream Cheese Buttercream
In the bowl of a stand mixer fitted with a paddle attachment, beat the butter until it's light and fluffy, then add the cream cheese and beat until fully incorporated. Add the heavy cream, vanilla, and salt and beat again until combined, then scrape down the sides with a spatula.

With the mixer on low speed, add the powdered sugar about ½ cup at a time. The buttercream will be thick. Add a little more heavy cream, 1 tablespoon at a time, to thin it out if needed, and then flip the mixer to high speed and beat until the buttercream is lighter in color and texture, about 2 minutes. Gently stir in the Oreo crumbles by hand.

For the Dark Chocolate Drip
In a microwave-safe bowl, stir together the chocolate melts and heavy cream and heat for 30 seconds. Stir until smooth, then transfer to a drip bottle. Set aside.

To Assemble
Place a cardboard cake round on a cake turntable. Dot a little bit of buttercream in the center of the round and spread it out with an

angled icing spatula. Place the first chilled cake layer in the center. Add a layer of buttercream. Place the next cake layer on top, then repeat, making sure to line the layers up evenly. After adding the top cake layer, crumb coat the cake by spreading a thin layer of buttercream around the entire cake. Freeze for 2 minutes to set.

Using a wooden spoon, beat out any air bubbles in the remaining buttercream. Finish frosting the cake as desired or follow the decorating instructions below.

To Decorate the Cake

Spread a final layer of buttercream around the entire cake, using a cake scraper for smooth sides and clean edges. Press mini Oreos around the bottom of the cake. Freeze for 2 minutes to set the buttercream.

Add the chocolate drip to the cake, letting it pool a bit on the top edge and cascade down the sides about an inch apart. Freeze for 5 minutes to set.

Press the full-size Oreo cookies on top, then add a bit of Oreo crumble.

TIP: A typical chocolate drip is either brown or dark brown, but I wanted this one to match the Oreos. I used black chocolate candy melts for the ganache, but you could easily add a drop of black gel coloring to brown ganache to get the same color.

CHOCOLATE SODA CAKE

One thing I loved so much about visiting my grandparents' house when I was growing up was being allowed to pick out a cold root beer, cream soda, Sprite, or orange soda from the mini fridge in their garage. We didn't always have soda around at my house, so this was such a fun treat. I still remember sitting by the firepit and sipping on my own can of soda after a long day helping them in the yard.

Here, I wanted to create a fun soda cake that used actual soda in the buttercream and cake layers. I failed miserably the first few attempts. I even tried making the soda into a reduction and adding it in that way. Finally I tried using soda syrup (found online, but you can grab it at any liquor store or any place that sells mix-ins for drinks) and it worked perfectly! The cola flavor came right through and it tasted just like the real thing.

Chocolate Soda Cake

- ½ cup buttermilk (room temperature)
- ⅔ cup sour cream (room temperature)
- 3 large eggs plus 1 egg white (room temperature)
- ⅓ cup vegetable oil
- 1 tablespoon pure vanilla extract
- ⅓ cup sugarcane cola syrup
- ¼ cup flour
- 1 box devil's food cake mix

Soda Buttercream

- 1½ cups (3 sticks) unsalted butter
- ¼ cup heavy cream (plus more if needed)
- ¼ cup cocoa powder
- ¼ cup sugarcane cola syrup
- 1 tablespoon pure vanilla extract
- Pinch of salt
- 7 to 8 cups powdered sugar

Small-Batch Vanilla Bean Buttercream

- ½ cup (1 stick) unsalted butter
- 2 tablespoons heavy cream (plus more if needed)
- 1 teaspoon vanilla bean paste
- Pinch of salt
- 4 cups powdered sugar

For Decorating

- 8 maraschino cherries with stems
- Zig-zag cake scraper
- Piping bag
- Wilton 1M piping tip

For the Chocolate Soda Cake

Preheat the oven to 325°F, then prep three 6-inch round cake pans with a swipe of shortening and dusting of flour to prevent sticking.

In a large bowl, whisk together the buttermilk, sour cream, eggs, oil, vanilla, and cola syrup until thoroughly combined. Sift in the flour and cake mix and whisk until just combined. Do not overmix. Split the batter evenly among the prepared pans.

Bake for 27 to 30 minutes, until the center is baked through. Let the cakes cool in the pan for a minute before flipping them out onto a wire rack to cool completely. Wrap and freeze the cakes before assembly.

For the Soda Buttercream

In the bowl of a stand mixer fitted with a paddle attachment, beat the butter on medium speed until it's light and fluffy. Add the heavy cream, cocoa powder, cola syrup, vanilla, and salt and beat again until combined, then scrape down the sides with a spatula.

With the mixer on low speed, add the powdered sugar about ½ cup at a time. The buttercream will be thick. Add a little more heavy cream, 1 tablespoon at a time, to thin it out if needed, and then flip the mixer to high speed and beat until the buttercream is lighter in color and texture, about 2 minutes.

For the Small-Batch Vanilla Bean Buttercream

In the bowl of a stand mixer fitted with a paddle attachment, beat the butter on medium speed until it's light and fluffy. Add the heavy cream, vanilla bean paste, and salt and beat again until combined, then scrape down the sides with a spatula.

With the mixer on low speed, add the powdered sugar about ½ cup at a time. The buttercream will be thick. Add a little more heavy cream, 1 tablespoon at a time, to thin it out if needed, and then flip the mixer to high speed and beat until the buttercream is lighter in color and texture, about 2 minutes.

To Assemble

Place a cardboard cake round on a cake turntable. Dot a little bit of cola buttercream in the center of the round and spread it out with an angled icing spatula. Place the first chilled cake layer in the center. Add a layer of buttercream. Place the next cake layer on top, then repeat, making sure to line the layers up evenly. After adding the top cake layer, crumb coat the cake by spreading a thin layer of buttercream around the entire cake. Freeze for 2 minutes to set the buttercream.

Using a wooden spoon, beat out any air bubbles in the remaining buttercream. Finish frosting the cake as desired or follow the decorating instructions below.

To Decorate the Cake

Spread the remaining cola buttercream around the entire cake, then use a zig-zag-patterned cake scraper on the side of the cake, moving it up and down while turning the cake turntable.

Transfer the vanilla buttercream to a piping bag fitted with a Wilton 1M tip. Pipe 8 buttercream swirls around the top of the cake and add a cherry on top of each swirl.

TIP: Don't be afraid to move your cake comb around while spinning your turntable. While you might usually hold it straight, moving it up and down makes for such a fun wave pattern. It almost looks like an optical illusion if you stare at it long enough.

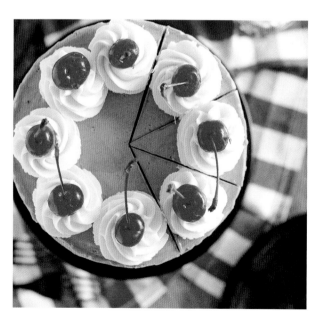

CIRCUS ANIMAL COOKIE CAKE *with Almond White Chocolate Buttercream*

Circus Animal cookies are such a delight. This cake, with a strong almond and white chocolate flavor throughout and pink-and-white exterior, tastes and looks like them. The rainbow nonpareils are a must. And good news: they are everywhere in the grocery store. They will probably be everywhere in your kitchen, too, if you don't put a cookie sheet under the cake when you're adding them on.

Almond Swirl Cake

- 1 cup buttermilk (room temperature)
- ⅔ cup sour cream (room temperature)
- 4 egg whites (room temperature)
- ½ cup vegetable oil
- 2 teaspoons clear vanilla extract
- 1 teaspoon almond extract
- 1 box white cake mix
  Pink gel coloring

White Chocolate Buttercream

- ½ cup white chocolate chips
- ½ cup heavy cream
- 1½ cups (3 sticks) unsalted butter
- 1 teaspoon clear vanilla extract
- 1 teaspoon almond extract
  Pinch of salt
- 7 to 8 cups powdered sugar
  Pink gel coloring

For Decorating

- 10 to 12 frosted Circus Animal cookies
  Rainbow nonpareils
  Stripe cake comb
  Piping bag
  Wilton 6B piping tip

For the Almond Swirl Cake

Preheat the oven to 325°F, then prep three 6-inch round cake pans with a swipe of shortening and dusting of flour to prevent sticking.

In a large bowl, whisk together the buttermilk, sour cream, egg whites, oil, vanilla, and almond extract until thoroughly combined. Sift in the cake mix and whisk until just combined. Do not overmix. Divide the batter evenly into two bowls, then tint half the batter pink with one or two drops of the gel coloring. Alternating between the pink and white cake batters, split the batter evenly among the prepared pans. With a toothpick, swirl the batter in a figure-eight pattern to create a marbled effect.

Bake for 27 to 30 minutes, until the center is baked through. Let the cakes cool in the pan for a minute before flipping them out onto a wire rack to cool completely. Wrap and freeze the cakes before assembly.

For the White Chocolate Buttercream

In a microwave-safe bowl, stir together the white chocolate and ¼ cup of the heavy cream. Heat for 30 seconds and then stir until smooth. Let cool slightly.

In the bowl of a stand mixer fitted with a paddle attachment, beat the butter on medium speed until light and fluffy. Add the white chocolate ganache, remaining ¼ cup cream, the vanilla, almond extract, and salt and beat until combined, then scrape down the sides with a spatula.

With the mixer on low speed, add the powdered sugar about ½ cup at a time. The buttercream will be thick. Add a little more heavy cream, 1 tablespoon at a time, to thin it out if needed, and then flip the mixer to high speed and beat until the buttercream is lighter in color and texture, about 2 minutes. Transfer half of the buttercream to a separate bowl and tint it with the gel coloring.

To Assemble

Place a cardboard cake round on a cake turntable. Dot a little bit of buttercream in

the center of the round and spread it out with an angled icing spatula. Place the first chilled cake layer in the center. Add a layer of pink buttercream. Place the next cake layer on top, then repeat, making sure to line the layers up evenly. After adding the top cake layer, crumb coat the cake by spreading a thin layer of buttercream around the entire cake. Freeze for 2 minutes to set.

Using a wooden spoon, beat out any air bubbles in the remaining buttercreams. Finish frosting the cake as desired or follow the decorating instructions below.

To Decorate the Cake

Spread a final layer of white buttercream around the entire cake, using a stripe cake comb to make clean indents on the side of the cake. The crisper the indents, the cleaner the stripe will be later on. Freeze for at least 10 minutes so that the buttercream is very firm.

Transfer the pink buttercream to a piping bag, cut off the top, and pipe it into the stripe indents. Immediately scrape the sides of the cake with a flat cake scraper. Apply a little bit of pressure and scrape until the clean stripes start to show through.

Place the cake on a cookie sheet, and place the cookie sheet on a turntable. Press the frosted animal cookies and nonpareils around the sides of the cake.

Transfer the remaining pink buttercream to a piping bag fitted with a Wilton 6B tip. Pipe a shell border along the top rim of the cake. Sprinkle the top of the cake with more nonpareils.

ÉCLAIR CAKE *with Graham Cracker Crust, Whipped Chocolate Ganache, and Custard Filling*

While living in Provo, Utah, I had a neighbor invite us over to teach us how to make éclairs and cream puffs. The classic pastry has always been a bit of a mystery to me. He took his time, carefully showing us each step while he made the pâte à choux, filled the hollowed-out shells with cream, and topped a few of them with chocolate. They truly were a labor of love and tasted incredible. I tried to use some of those familiar elements in this show-stopping éclair cake. The custard inside really steals the show when paired with soft vanilla bean cake layers and chocolate ganache. I added a graham cracker crust for texture and topped the cake off with as many éclairs as I could fit.

Vanilla Cake with Graham Cracker Crust

- 9 graham crackers
- 6 tablespoons unsalted butter, melted
- ¾ cup buttermilk (room temperature)
- ⅔ cup sour cream (room temperature)
- 4 egg whites (room temperature)
- ⅓ cup vegetable oil
- 1 tablespoon pure vanilla extract
- 1 box white or vanilla cake mix

Vanilla Custard Filling

- 1 cup whole milk
- ½ cup sugar
- 1½ tablespoons cornstarch
- 2 egg yolks, whisked
- 1 teaspoon vanilla bean paste

Whipped Chocolate Ganache

- 2 cups semisweet chocolate chips
- ½ cup heavy cream

For Decorating

- Homemade or store-bought mini éclairs
- Piping bag
- Wilton 1A piping tip

For the Vanilla Cake with Graham Cracker Crust

Preheat the oven to 325°F, then prep three 6-inch round cake pans with a swipe of shortening and dusting of flour to prevent sticking.

In a food processor, pulse together the graham crackers and melted butter until a crust forms. Split the mixture evenly among the prepared pans and press to firm with the bottom of a glass or flat measuring cup.

In a large bowl, whisk together the buttermilk, sour cream, egg whites, oil, and vanilla until thoroughly combined. Sift in the cake mix and whisk until just combined. Do not overmix. Split the batter evenly among the prepared pans.

Bake for 30 to 32 minutes, until the center is baked through. Let the cakes cool in the pan for a minute before flipping them out onto a wire rack to cool completely. Wrap and freeze the cakes before assembly.

For the Vanilla Custard Filling

In a small saucepan over medium heat, whisk together the milk, sugar, and cornstarch and cook, whisking constantly, until thickened, 3 to 5 minutes. While continuously whisking, add in the egg yolks very slowly (a little at a time) so they don't scramble. Remove from the heat, then whisk in the vanilla bean paste. Transfer to a glass dish, cover, and refrigerate until thickened and cooled completely.

For the Whipped Chocolate Ganache

In a medium glass bowl, stir together the chocolate chips and heavy cream. Microwave for 1 minute, then stir until there are no lumps and it's thick and creamy. Set aside to cool for about 30 minutes, then whip with a whisk to fluff it up until it's spreadable.

To Assemble and Decorate

Place a cardboard cake round on a cake turntable. Dot a little bit of the whipped ganache in the center of the round and spread it out with an angled icing spatula. Place the first chilled cake layer in the center (crust side up). Add a layer of ganache. Pipe a dam around the outside rim of the cake and then add about ½ cup of the custard filling. Place the next cake layer on top, then repeat, making sure to line the layers up evenly. After adding the top cake layer, pipe a little bit of ganache between the layers on the outside, leaving the outside with an unfinished (or naked) look.

Pipe a layer of ganache on top, then add the rest of the ganache to a piping bag fitted with a Wilton 1A tip. Pipe a few dollops around the top and place a sliced éclair on top of each. Fill the middle in with sliced éclairs.

TIP: You're already making a cake. If you don't make homemade éclairs to go on top, no one is going to side-eye your efforts. Just grab a box from the freezer section. The cake itself will taste so incredibly delicious, no one will suspect you didn't make them from scratch.

You could also use store-bought vanilla pudding mix in place of the homemade custard filling.

FUNFETTI COTTON CANDY CAKE *with*
Striped Cotton Candy Buttercream

I created a cotton candy cake long ago that continues to be a favorite for my readers' children on their birthdays. But here it has been newly improved by adding a funfetti element to the cake layers and actual cotton candy in the two-toned stripes on the side of the cake. The cotton candy extract gives the cake a bit of flavor, but using the real thing takes this cake up just a few more notches.

Funfetti Cotton Candy Cake

- ¾ cup buttermilk (room temperature)
- ⅔ cup sour cream (room temperature)
- 4 egg whites (room temperature)
- ⅓ cup vegetable oil
- 1 tablespoon pure vanilla extract
- 2 teaspoons cotton candy extract
- 1 box white cake mix
- ¼ cup light blue and pink sprinkles

Striped Cotton Candy Buttercream

- 1½ cups (3 sticks) unsalted butter
- ¼ cup heavy cream (plus more if needed)
- 1 tablespoon pure vanilla extract
- 1 teaspoon cotton candy extract
- Pinch of salt
- 7 to 8 cups powdered sugar
- 1 cup pink cotton candy
- 1 cup blue cotton candy
- Light pink gel coloring
- Light blue gel coloring

For Decorating

- Stripe cake comb
- Piping bag
- Wilton 6B piping tip

For the Funfetti Cotton Candy Cake

Preheat the oven to 325°F, then prep three 6-inch round cake pans with a swipe of shortening and dusting of flour to prevent sticking.

In a large bowl, whisk together the buttermilk, sour cream, egg whites, oil, vanilla, and cotton candy extract until thoroughly combined. Sift in the cake mix and whisk until just combined. Do not overmix. Gently stir in the sprinkles. Split the batter evenly among the prepared pans.

Bake for 27 to 30 minutes, until the center is baked through. Let the cakes cool in the pan for a minute before flipping them out onto a wire rack to cool completely. Wrap and freeze the cakes before assembly.

For the Striped Cotton Candy Buttercream

In the bowl of a stand mixer fitted with a paddle attachment, beat the butter on medium speed until it's light and fluffy. Add the heavy cream, vanilla, cotton candy extract, and salt and beat again until combined, then scrape down the sides with a spatula.

With the mixer on low speed, add the powdered sugar about ½ cup at a time. The buttercream will be thick. Add a little more heavy cream, 1 tablespoon at a time, to thin it out if needed, and then flip the mixer to high speed and beat until the buttercream is lighter in color and texture, about 2 minutes.

To each of two small bowls, transfer 1 cup of buttercream (2 cups total). To one bowl, stir in the pink cotton candy and 1 drop of light pink gel coloring. To the other, stir in the blue cotton candy and 1 drop of light blue gel coloring. Transfer each color to a piping bag and set aside. Leave the rest of the buttercream white.

To Assemble

Place a cardboard cake round on a cake turntable. Dot a little bit of pink and blue

entire cake. Freeze for 2 minutes to set the buttercream.

Using a wooden spoon, beat out any air bubbles in the remaining white buttercream. Finish frosting the cake as desired or follow the decorating instructions below.

To Decorate the Cake

Spread a final layer of white buttercream around the entire cake, using a stripe cake comb to create clean indents on the side of the cake. The crisper the indents, the cleaner the stripes will be later on. Freeze for at least 10 minutes so that the buttercream is very firm.

Pipe the pink and blue buttercream in the striped indents, and then immediately scrape the sides of the cake with a flat cake scraper. Apply a little bit of pressure and scrape until the clean stripes start to show through.

Add the remaining buttercream (white, pink, and blue) to a piping bag fitted with a Wilton 6B tip. Pipe star dollops around the entire top of the cake.

TIP: There's no rhyme or reason to the marbled buttercream stripes. Once your white buttercream stripe indents have frozen solid, pipe in a little blue and pink buttercream here and there between the stripes and then immediately scrape away the excess. There may be a little purple created in the process, but it all adds to the whimsical flow of this already dreamy cake.

buttercream in the center of the round and spread it out with an angled icing spatula. Place the first chilled cake layer in the center. Add a layer of pink and blue buttercream. Place the next cake layer on top, then repeat, making sure to line the layers up evenly. After adding the top cake layer, crumb coat the cake by spreading a thin layer of white buttercream around the

ACKNOWLEDGMENTS

Writing another cookbook has been a surreal process for me. Cake has taken me far beyond where I could have ever dreamed it would. I thank God every day I get to share something that can be a reason for people to gather with their loved ones and celebrate with a cake on the table! Cake has brought together a global community of bakers who have always supported me, and each other, in this journey. Thank you, friends, for giving me that gift, baking along with me, and sharing your passion with your loved ones, too.

I couldn't have created this cookbook without my husband, Ryan, and our blondie boys, Jake and Liam. You've seen how life sometimes comes crashing in waves, and you've stood beside me every minute. Your support means the world to me always, and I love you.

My family has always been a support for me in my cake world, and I'd like to thank them for asking for my extra cake slices, getting excited about my new flavors, and being there through the ups and downs life has thrown at us. Dad would have gotten a real kick out of some of these cake flavors. Your shortest sister (and daughter) loves you so very much.

We all need a cheerleader who will believe in us even when we don't believe in ourselves. I'm truly grateful for my literary agent, Irene Goodman, for fiercely being in my corner, never giving up on me, and for providing straightforward, positive, and uplifting words of encouragement throughout this journey. You made all the difference for me in finding my stride, and I can't thank you enough.

I'd also like to give my most heartfelt thanks to my publishing team at HarperCollins. Stephanie and Jacqueline (and everyone!), I couldn't have done any of this without you. I couldn't have put my recipes and heart into better hands. I couldn't have had a better team working on every page. And I couldn't be happier with what we created. I'm truly grateful we could make this cake book together.

INDEX

Note: Page references in *italics* indicate full-page photographs.